PENGUIN BOOKS

THE PENGUIN HISTORY OF THE CHURCH

Volume Seven

Owen Chadwick was born in 1916 and from 1947 taught history at Cambridge University, where from 1968 to 1983 he was the Regius Professor of Modern History. He has worked on the history of Christian ideas and life. His books include *John Cassian, The Victorian Church, From Bossuet to Newman, The Secularization of the European Mind, Newman, The Popes and European Revolution, The Making of the Benedictine Ideal, Hensley Henson, The Spirit of the Oxford Movement, Britain and the Vatican during the Second World War* and *Michael Ramsey: A Life*. Owen Chadwick is also the author of *The Reformation*, the third volume in the Penguin History of the Church series.

OWEN CHADWICK

THE CHRISTIAN CHURCH
IN THE COLD WAR

PENGUIN BOOKS

PENGUIN BOOKS

Published by the Penguin Group
Penguin Books Ltd, 27 Wrights Lane, London W8 5TZ, England
Penguin Books USA Inc., 375 Hudson Street, New York, New York 10014, USA
Penguin Books Australia Ltd, Ringwood, Victoria, Australia
Penguin Books Canada Ltd, 10 Alcorn Avenue, Toronto, Ontario, Canada M4V 3B2
Penguin Books (NZ) Ltd, 182–190 Wairau Road, Auckland 10, New Zealand

Penguin Books Ltd, Registered Offices: Harmondsworth, Middlesex, England

First published by Allen Lane The Penguin Press 1992
Published with minor revisions and some new material in Penguin Books 1993
1 3 5 7 9 10 8 6 4 2

· Sections of Part One were basd upon the Sir D. Owen Evans Lectures (1989)
at the University College of Wales, Aberystwyth

Printed in England by Clays Ltd, St Ives plc

Thanks to the
Rockefeller Foundation of Bellagio
for help with work in Italy
and to Michael Bourdeaux
for kind advice

Contents

Part One   EASTERN EUROPE

1. The Beginnings of the Cold War   3

The Russian Conquests.   Reconstruction.
The Morality of Tyrannicide.   The Federal Republic of Germany.
Christianity and the Holocaust.   Pope Pius XII and Communism.

2. The Attack upon Christianity in Eastern Europe   19

The Secular Rites.   Monks and Nuns.
The State Control of the Churches.   The Christian Cooperators.

3. Violence   46

Albania.   The 'Destruction' of the Uniats.

4. Show Trials   60

Tiso in Slovakia.   Stepinac in Yugoslavia.   Mindszenty in Hungary.

5. The Effects of the Marxist Attack   73

Acts of Aggression.   Opinion Polls.
Christianity and the History of the Nations.
Division in the East European Churches.
Orthodox Church Leaders in Eastern Europe.
Catholic Church Leaders in Eastern Europe.

Part Two   WESTERN EUROPE

6. The West and Marxism   111

The Second Vatican Council and the Cold War.
Religious Liberty.   The Council and Communism.

7. The Way of Worship 123

The Language of the Liturgy.   New Forms of Prayer.

8. Charisma 135

The Charismatics.   Pilgrimages.   Saints.

9. The Ministry 147

Married Priests?   The Ordination of Women.
Retirement for Age.

10. Monks and Nuns 161

The Historic Orders.   Mount Athos.
Other Greek Monasteries and Nunneries.
Protestant Monks and Nuns.   Taizé.

11. Ethics 173

Divorce.   Contraception.   Abortion.   Torture.

12. Church and State in Western Europe 181

Constitutions.   Taxes.   The Head of the State.
Movements to Separate Church and State.   Spain.
Greece.   Germany.   Switzerland.

13. Perestroika 193

The Election of Pope John Paul I in 1978.
The Election of Pope John Paul II in 1978.   Gorbachev.

Suggestions for Further Reading 219

Index 227

PART ONE

===

EASTERN EUROPE

1

The Beginnings of the Cold War

The Allies who beat Hitler divided Europe between them and then quarrelled, chiefly because they were afraid of each other, but also because Communists who were Russia's allies behaved outrageously in Greece, with a murderous civil war, and then seized power in Poland and Czechoslovakia and all the countries where Russia was now dominant. Western Europe so feared the tyranny of Stalin that it started building lines of defence. At times the quarrel came near to threats of war, hence the name Cold War.

Hitler begot among his opponents, at least among his Western opponents, a sensation that morality among nations was all-important to humanity. Stalin headed a Communist empire and Communism was officially atheist. Therefore first the iniquity of the Nazis and then the irreligion of the Soviet system, which threatened the West, helped to generate religious strength in Europe and America. The revival did not last long, but for a time more people thought about their moral and religious obligations, more young people (especially if they were educated) went to church, and governments were willing to encourage religious education, as with the Education Act in the Britain of 1944.

Those who looked back upon the nightmare age that was just past saw religious men and women among the leaders of those who stood out in resistance to nationalism, tyranny and racialism. Pastor Martin Niemöller, who served for eight years in concentration camps, and whom the nations valued as the hero of German resistance to Hitler's philosophy, said that the world saw the Protestant Churches of Germany aided by American Protestants to be the only hope for the future of Germany. In the United States the large Lutheran community was conscious of the need to save and rebuild the Lutheran Churches of Germany, the source of their own being. The victory over Japan was celebrated in all the Western countries with Christian services in which statesmen and military commanders joined. General MacArthur said that Christian principles gave moral force to the defeat of Japan and were the key to Allied policies. President Truman, head of America where there was supposed to be total separation between Church and State, issued a proclamation setting aside 13 May 1945 as a national day of prayer. He said that Christianity and democracy were based upon the same principles. General Chiang Kai-shek said for China that Christianity was the answer to the problems of the world. It was noticed that even half the Nazis charged with war crimes showed an interest in religion, but then they were close to eternity. The Nazi governor of Poland, Hans Frank, claimed at his trial, with a superb improbability, to have done everything that he could to help the Churches during the war. All the Churches had an interest in the drafting of the United Nations Charter and the new formulation of the idea of human rights. The West found it marvellous to see the crucifix returning into Austrian schools.

But in the Russian zones the bishops were excluded at first from their pastoral care. Many Western churchmen wanted freedom for religion to be built into the peace treaties and had no idea that there never would be a peace treaty. Europe was divided by a frontier which at first was only a frontier of ideology and then grew higher in fits and crises until the building of the Berlin Wall in 1961. To the east of this Iron Curtain all the states of Europe except Greece and Turkey were under governments that were officially materialist and had the duty of promoting atheism and a materialist philosophy. To the west, all the states, except the two surviving dictatorships in Spain and Portugal, had a democratic polity and most of their people, including or especially the people of Spain and Portugal, still thought that they were Christian states. Never before in its long history had Europe been divided in quite this political way over religion.

THE RUSSIAN CONQUESTS

The Russians acquired by the war a territory larger than Spain and Portugal. Some of the pieces acquired were small, like former Japanese islands in the northern Pacific; but some of the annexations had a numerous people, and their acquisition complicated the task of Russian government by bringing into the empire so many more non-Russians, many of them educated and caring about their Churches: 10 million people from eastern Poland, partly Orthodox and partly Catholic; 6 million in the Baltic states, about half Catholic and half Protestant; nearly 6 million people in Bessarabia and Moldavia and Bukovina, dominantly Orthodox but with some Catholics; nearly 1 million in the Carpathians (Orthodox and Uniat); and nearly 0.5 million in East Prussia, from which many of the Germans were expelled with suffering but where some remained as Lutherans. There were also 2 million German prisoners of war who were held for years in Russia as a labour force to replace the millions of Russian dead. Prisoners of war had little chance of religion but not no chance: army chaplains or pastors who were prisoners were able to serve some of them. In total this was a very big addition to Russia's peoples, and to its responsibilities, and to its potential Christian force. In a Marxist frame, it could only be held together by a despotism.

The violent transformation of central Europe was terrible for the peoples and the Churches. Millions were thrown out of eastern Poland and were settled in what for centuries was eastern Germany but now became western Poland, and millions of Germans were thrown out of their homes in Silesia and East Prussia in conditions of cruelty. This meant that large areas of eastern central Europe, formerly Protestant in majority, became Catholic in population for the first time since the Reformation. In both cases – uprooted Poles in what was once eastern Germany, uprooted Germans moving into the new Germanies – the Churches had to cope with the well-known experience that the loss of a home sometimes means the loss of religion, so close is faith to the hearth; but they gained from the other well-known experience, that many emigrants cling to their religion as a link with their former homes.

RECONSTRUCTION

In the countries of Europe which had been occupied by the Nazis, some bishops were accused of cooperating with the Nazis. In the West there was pressure that they be removed from their sees; in the east they were usually brought before courts, in trials intended to make churchmen look scandalous, and sentenced to dramatic terms of imprisonment. The Vatican found itself under pressure from the postwar French government to remove some forty bishops from their sees; but by negotiation, and by the good sense of General de Gaulle, and because churchmen had played a big part in French resistance, the number of bishops removed from their sees came down to five. In West Germany, the Lutheran Bishop Marahrens of Hanover, who had behaved weakly but not worse than weakly under the Nazis and now imagined that he could still continue eminent in the German Church, found himself under intense pressure and disappeared from office. In the East, things were far worse.

Some of the survivors were heroes: Martin Niemöller above all, but also several other pastors or priests who suffered under the Nazi tyranny. Such people were now demanded for the leading positions in their Churches. Otto Dibelius, whom the Nazis ejected from his Lutheran see of Berlin–Brandenburg in 1933 and arrested several times, was now made the Bishop of Berlin–Brandenburg again. Hanns Lilje had acted bravely as a leading member of the Confessing Church against the Nazis and escaped execution by a hair's breadth; he became the Lutheran Bishop of Hanover in succession to Marahrens. Bishop Wurm of Württemberg, one of the leaders of the Confessing Church under the Nazis, now became the president of the new Federated Evangelical Church of West Germany. The Bishop of Oslo, Eivind Berggrav, defied the Nazi quislings in Norway and was now a hero in the Protestant west of Europe and America. Most of the stalwart resisters failed to survive. Those who for various reasons did survive now became the leaders of the European Churches.

The quality for which people looked when choosing a Church leader was his record under the reign of terror. But the quality that copes with terror is not always the quality most needed in the government of a Church. Many of those mentioned above had the qualities of a leader – Dibelius, Wurm, Lilje, Berggrav. But there were others whose quality lay in their toughness and their conscience rather than in their wisdom. Some people were made bishops and some people became professors at universities more for their record than because they were quite suitable for the job that now had to be done. The most notable of these was Martin Niemöller himself. He was now a world personality: he had to be given high office in the Church. He became the Foreign Secretary of the Federated German Church and the bishop of one of the German dioceses (though he would not use the word bishop), and later one of the presidents of the World Council of Churches. He was a truly big man but he was not blessed with an interest in administration and he had no conception of being a representative figure. Somehow he always remained a lonely man even in his own Church, until in 1970 this hero of the past had a lecture broken up by German students. Berggrav in Norway was another big man, but his greatest virtues did not include prudence.

Dibelius had a record of courage under Hitler, and had protected a half-Jewish secretary until the end. But he was also a tough Prussian aristocrat of the political right and an autocrat by temperament. He thought sociology was a form of atheism and that all modern evil started with the French Revolution. This did not make him the best person to cope with a diocese which lay partly in the Russian zone of Germany. He was so outspoken against the Communist attack on the Churches in East Germany that he was stopped from travelling in those areas of his diocese. He went on and on because a successor could not be agreed; he finally resigned at the age of eighty-six in 1966. He gave stability and strength to the western German Church but he was a confronter of Communism and the Socialist left, so that his long reign in Berlin made him also part of the Western forces in the Cold War. That complicated a little the lives of the Churches.

THE MORALITY OF TYRANNICIDE

Could a Christian plot to murder a tyrant? Ever since the debates on tyrannicide in the later sixteenth century, and the execution of King Charles I of England, the moral tradition of Christian Europe had held that this was not only wrong but very wicked. In England the celebration of Guy Fawkes's Day was an annual reassertion of its wickedness. The death of Louis XVI of France by the guillotine, the attempt to murder the French emperor Louis Napoleon, the association of the murder of tsars with the bombs of 'anarchists', and the killing of Tsar Nicholas II and his family by Bolsheviks only confirmed the traditional moral doctrine derived from St Paul's Epistle to the Romans: that the powers that be are ordained by God even if they are tyrants (as was Nero in the time of St Paul) and that a Christian must render to Caesar the things that are Caesar's. If the ruler orders what is immoral, he or she or it must be disobeyed, but by a passive resistance. To kill a tyrant is immoral; to plot revolution is impossible for a Christian.

The Nazi occupation of Europe altered all this. In Norway, Bishop Berggrav would not accept that a tyrannical government was one of the powers that be which are ordained by God. Several of the German leaders of the conspiracy against Hitler in July 1944 were Christian men. Stauffenberg, the officer who planted the bomb under Hitler's table and by the merest mischance failed to kill him, was a Catholic. Dietrich Bonhoeffer, the Lutheran pastor who was related to several of the Protestant leaders in the conspiracy, was not part of it only because he was arrested some time before the event and was in prison at the time; but he wholly approved of the idea of tyrannicide and paid for his minimal role in it with his life; afterwards he was considered as a martyr and a hero by the Churches. In the occupied territories, French priests gave every sort of moral support to guerrilla leaders in the Maquis. This was much easier to justify in Christian morality, because everyone agreed that an illegal occupier of another's country had not the claims upon loyalty which even a bad government which was more or less legal could demand.

But in strict Christian ethic, was Bonhoeffer right? Once you allow the murder of a king to be justified morally, who is to decide whether a king is a tyrant? Would you open the door to any crackpot who determined that a President Lincoln or a President Kennedy must be removed for the good of the world? However much they hated Hitler, some strict Lutheran theologians still concluded, after the event when all was known, that tyrannicide was not a moral course. The people did not go with them. Throughout West Germany could be found streets named or rechristened as Stauffenberg Street or Bonhoeffer Avenue.

In 1952 there was a famous law suit. Major Remer was the soldier of the Berlin garrison who suppressed the conspiracy against Hitler of July 1944 and so ensured that the plot failed. In 1951 he was prosecuted for slander when he accused some of the conspirators of being traitors and said that their disloyalty was a stain on the shield of honour of the German corps of officers. The case drew in the moralists on both sides, and not all the Christian thinkers stood on the side against General Remer. Two of the most eminent professors from Göttingen University came into court to testify that a Christian had a duty to resist tyranny not only by passive disobedience. In court Remer was almost lost sight of in a far wider argument on the moral duty of loyalty to the State, the binding nature of oaths of loyalty and the duty (if a duty it was) to try to overthrow an immoral regime. He was sentenced to three months' imprisonment and disappeared from history.

During the 1930s at Hemer, in West Germany, a village memorial to the fallen in the First World War gained two swastikas and an inscription about their immortal heroism which was a quotation from Hitler's book *Mein Kampf*. After another World War the citizens added the names of the fallen of 1939–45 and obliterated the name of the author of the text. But they left the text and the swastika. It was 1984 before anyone minded the monument. And yet – just outside was the site of Stalag VIA, the largest of the camps for prisoners of war, where nearly all the prisoners were Russians. During the last months of war 60,000 prisoners died, many from undernourishment. In 1984 someone at last realized that the deaths which the village remembered with gratitude were part of a vaster earthshaking twilight of the gods.

THE FEDERAL REPUBLIC OF GERMANY

For the first time since the Holy Roman Empire was ended by Napoleon's threats, there appeared outside Austria a German state in which Catholics slightly outnumbered Protestants. Wittenberg and the heart of the Protestant Reformation lay in what was now the German Democratic Republic – East Germany. The old Catholic areas of Germany, apart from Austria, were Bavaria and the Rhineland: and these were at the heart of the new Federal Republic of Germany – West Germany. The first Chancellor of the Federal Republic, Konrad Adenauer, was a Catholic who had lain concealed in a monastery through the Nazi years.[1] His tough personality symbolized a Christian, pro-West, anti-Communist, anti-Russian stance – defend liberty and the right to worship by arming the West against the Eastern threat – and so for a time he helped to make the Cold War colder. He had no faith whatever that the rival social systems of East and West Europe could coexist peacefully and he saw any appeasement of the East as treachery. Bonn, the capital of West Germany, lay at the centre of the Catholic Rhineland.

The main opposition party – the Social Democratic Party (SPD) – was further to the left in politics and was the party for which a majority of Protestants voted. These often satirized Adenauer as though Cardinal Frings of Cologne was his second-in-command. (In 1965 the Catholic bishops at last ceased to recommend that their people should vote CDU.) Immediately after the war the SPD was more to the left than it later became and some Catholics thought of it as red. As the SPD moderated

1. Born 1876 at Cologne of a simple Catholic home; in 1917 Mayor of Cologne: a member of the Centre Party, that is the Catholic Party. The Nazis imprisoned him twice which was a qualification for postwar service. In 1945–6 he was the chief founder of a new party, the Christian Democratic Union (CDU), to promote Christian principles in politics. It had a continuity with the old Centre Party which the Nazis destroyed but was intended to include Protestants. The party won a workable result in the first election (1949) and Adenauer was therefore Chancellor of West Germany; he remained so until 1963.

its more radical tones it began to attract Catholic voters, but not many.

The Churches were part of the quarrel between East Germany and West. Unlike these states, they were not at first divided by a frontier. After Germany was divided into two, they were able to continue to organize meetings. These meetings became the political symbol of an ultimate German unity despite the partition. The great annual assembly from 1949 onwards was the *Kirchentag*, which both Easterners and Westerners were able to attend. The last such meeting which could be an event for both Easterners and Westerners was held at Leipzig in 1954, when it was attended by half a million people. Its intention was religious. Its effect was dramatically, by then stridently, political. The final rally of this Church occasion was a vast demonstration against Communism. It could not go on. It helped to make the East German need for the Berlin Wall.

The immediate past was pain. Most had not known what frightfulness their people committed and were conscious that most of those who had been aware of frightfulness had not had the courage to intervene. On 19 October 1945 a group of Protestant clergy headed by Martin Niemöller[2] published a confession of guilt, the so-called Stuttgart Declaration. It was resented by many Germans, who saw that there was a lot of other guilt in a World War. It was accused of being politically motivated, since the Germans could get Western aid for their starving people only if they told the West that they repudiated Nazism utterly. It was also said that corporate penitence is meaningless: the only true penitence is the sorrow of an individual. But the political motive, though there was a hint of it in the documents, was not the real reason for the Stuttgart Declaration. There was a genuine agony of penitence; and if other people also had guilt, that was their concern. The Catholic German bishops met at Fulda and published a declaration accepting penitence along the same lines.

The worst part was the self-doubt – was it really possible that we Germans, a people at the centre of European culture, could have done such things? And if we had not done such things in our

2. Famous names of the Church struggle against Hitler: Wurm, Lilje, Heinemann (later president of the Federal Republic), Niemöller, Asmussen, Meiser, Dibelius, etc. – eleven in all.

own persons, how could we have accepted, and how could some
of us have rejoiced in, a government that was capable of doing
such things? It had to be accepted that a Christian civilization
was a frailer construction than anyone had realized.

CHRISTIANITY AND THE HOLOCAUST

The behaviour of the Churches during the Nazi reign of terror
gave ammunition to those who hated Churches. And even apart
from those who hated Churches, the Jews had undergone an
experience which was the most traumatic in the history of persecution. Some Jews were vocal in their criticism of the Christians
for their failure to stand up to the tyrant who murdered Jewish
people.

Was there something in Christianity which made it anti-
Semitic? That is, were the Christians in any part responsible,
however remotely and indirectly, for the horrors that had happened? Christian moralists in Germany started the serious study
of anti-Semitism and of the effect upon a people of such sayings
as 'It was the Jewish people who crucified Jesus.' There was a
disagreement. The radical critics held that there was indeed a
connection between near-contemporary murder and the anti-
Semitism of folk memory. Whereas others held that there was no
continuity between the mob pogroms against the Jewish people in
the Middle Ages and the new social anti-Semitism of a modern
industrial age.

In 1963 the West German Churches suffered under their most
severe onslaught of this sort. Rolf Hochhuth, a journalist and
playwright, put on the play *Der Stellvertreter* (the title was translated
as *The Deputy*, or *The Representative*). This play portrayed Pope Pius
XII, the Pope during the Second World War, as just that sort of
Christian clergyman that the Jewish critics of Christianity under
the Nazis said that he was: a man who refused to do anything to
save the Jews, though he could have done something even under
his own nose in Rome. He failed thus, the play alleged, partly to
preserve the Catholic Church and its institutions and partly to

save the investments of the Vatican. This last charge was absurd; and the main charge was also offensive, in that it was not true that Pius XII did nothing to save Jews. The true historical question was whether he had done all that he could and should. And this individual case was part of a far bigger question: whether under the reign of terror everyone, Catholic or Protestant, did what he or she could and should.

The controversy was unpleasant in West Germany, but it had a side-benefit in clearing the air about a question which troubled the German soul in its attitudes to its immediate past. What had happened, and whether it could have been stopped, and whose was the responsibility, and what was the structure of the Nazi State – all these were brought out into the open, to the benefit of history and with a feeling of relief that at last the past could be faced.

In the old Germany, Catholics and Protestants were far apart, like Catholics and Protestants in Ireland. The folk memories of the Thirty Years War still worked subconsciously. The pressures of the Nazi Party and the sharing of persecution and concentration camps changed attitudes which in any case would have been changed, more slowly, by the social processes of the modern age. There was now far more common endeavour and common worship. The chief sign of this better atmosphere was the growing number of mixed marriages between Catholics and Protestants.

A symbol of the change was the reputation of Martin Luther. In 1938 almost all Catholic Germany held Luther to be a villain. By 1960 this had changed: it was freely confessed by Catholics that the primary causes of the Protestant Reformation were faults in the late-medieval Catholic Church. Scholars of both sides worked together on Luther, until in 1987 the day came when Pope John Paul II went to West Germany and publicly said that the protest of the Reformation had helped the spiritual renewal of the Catholic Church. Some Lutherans were so encouraged by these developments that they asked Rome to cancel the excommunication of Martin Luther, but the Vatican thought that this would be meaningless and inappropriate.

POPE PIUS XII AND COMMUNISM

When the Russians overran eastern Europe in 1945, the situation of Catholics was not a calamity. Poland, Lithuania and Slovakia were largely Catholic countries. Hungary and Yugoslavia had big Catholic populations; Romania had a Catholic minority; Bulgaria and Albania had small Catholic minorities.

As long ago as 1864 a Pope had declared that socialism and Communism were as bad as Bible Societies. This was the beginning of a hundred years of antipathy. In that century socialism and Communism (for they soon came to be distinguished) grew more and more powerful, until in the end they overshadowed the world. Yet Popes still went on saying that no Catholic can be a Communist.

The Catholic Church believed in certain freedoms, and one of those freedoms was the right to private property. The Church could never accept orthodox Marxist doctrine that the nature of a society is a class war. Still less could it accept the doctrine that religion is bad for people and for society and ought to be abolished. Therefore no Catholic could be a Communist.

It need not have become so rigid. The encyclical *Rerum Novarum* of Pope Leo XIII (1891) was hostile to socialism but encouraged a Catholic social thought, under which umbrella radical Catholics developed ideas akin to socialism. There thus came to be the possibility of a Catholic mind far more open towards socialism. If all that Leo XIII said was true, might there be an alliance between social Catholics and unCatholic socialists? Their aims were distinct, but in practice they were not dissimilar.

The traditional Church refusal to say that one form of constitution is better than another also offered a hope for reconciliation. The Church works with whatever sort of government a people obeys. It would not condemn Communism solely because a Communist state had a one-party system of government.

By 1948 great numbers of Catholics were forced to live under Communist rule. Prudence demanded that the Pope did not say once again that no Catholic can be a Communist. For if he said so, he made all Catholics in the Communist states look disloyal to their state.

What complicated the Pope's life was Italian politics. Italy became a democratic republic in 1946. The Italian Communist Party was a candidate for power, with a numerous backing in the constituencies. It was the strongest Communist Party in Western Europe. Italy was tense. The Communist leader Togliatti attacked the Pope as the agent of the imperialists. In Emilia in the chaotic north during the last months of war and after, where armed bands professed allegiance to Communism and hatred of the Church, fifty-two priests were murdered between 1944 and 1946. It was not surprising that the Pope was obsessed by the Communist peril.

For eighty years, since the making of a united Italy, the Pope depended upon the complaisance of an Italian government which tolerated the existence of the Vatican and its international role. No one in the Vatican could contemplate a future under an Italian government which thought religion deplorable, or an atheistical government sitting in the old palace of the Popes on the Quirinal.

In this predicament, every Catholic must be used to keep the Communists from power. Again it must be said loudly that no Catholic can be a Communist. This must be asserted for Italian reasons – or more than Italian reasons, for the international Church rested upon the security of an Italian base. Cardinal Schuster of Milan instructed his clergy to refuse absolution to Communists. The lay leader of Catholic Action in Italy, Luigi Gedda, went to unscrupulous lengths in his zeal to save Italy from a Communist victory in a general election. The Communists failed to gain a majority, and from that moment until now Italy has had a Christian-Democrat majority friendly to Popes. The scare made the Pope's resolution firm.

The decision which most affected Eastern Europe was a ruling of the Holy Office which Pope Pius XII confirmed (2 July 1949). The ruling ran thus:

It has been asked whether
(a) it is lawful to subscribe as members of a Communist party? No.
(b) it is lawful to publish or write articles etc. advocating Communism? No.

(c) it is lawful for priests to administer sacraments to those
who do (a) or (b)? No.

This ruling did not say that no Catholic can be a Communist. It
said only that no Catholic could pay subscriptions to a Communist
party or advocate Communism publicly. Despite this caution, it
was understood in Eastern Europe to be a reassertion of the
doctrine that no Catholic can be a Communist and a (further)
proof that the Vatican was an enemy of all the Communist states.
But by that time the Communist states needed no such proof.
They were determined to do what they could to discourage religion
and in time, with better education and better science and the lapse
of years so that old people died and the young did not acquire the
habit of religion, they might eradicate it from society. They wished
to do this even if the Pope had said nothing. That he said things
against them only gave them matter for the propaganda war
against religion inside their states. This decision of the Holy Office
had grave consequences in Eastern Europe.

Pius XII, the Pope during the Second World War, was also the
last Pope to have been formed and brought up in the age when
the Pope was 'the prisoner in the Vatican'. Ever since the Italians
robbed the Pope of his historic state to make a united Italy, the
Popes had moved from being the political force in Europe which
once they were to being men of an other-worldly reputation. Now
they were not so much a force in the world as a sanctuary of the
spirit separated from the world; as though the head of the Church
turned himself into someone more like a monk. Pius XII carried
this feeling to its ultimate point. He was prayerful. He was felt
even by those close to him to be caring and yet remote. He
was not only a spiritual near-hermit by reason of his religious
aspiration: by nature he was also something of a lone man who
preferred to work by himself.

During the later part of his reign, after the ending of the Second
World War, he continued to separate the Church from the world
because in these hurried industrial times purity could be found
only in quiet. In 1950 he disturbed a lot of Christians by making
it essential for Catholics to believe in the doctrine of the Assumption – the belief that the body of the Blessed Virgin was carried to
heaven and she did not die. Four years later, when it was said to

be a Marian year, another encyclical declared the Blessed Virgin to have a royal dignity. He was devoted to the pilgrimage to Fatima in Portugal, where little children in 1917 saw visions of the Blessed Virgin who gave them rather anti-Communist messages. In intellectual matters he warned Catholics against reconciling themselves with the intellectual trends of the modern age (*Humani Generis*, 1950) and he made a saint of Pope Pius X, the Pope who denounced in the most unmeasured language any accommodation between the Catholic faith and the intellectual trends of his contemporaries in divinity.

Despite his profound other-worldliness, Pius XII was a political Pope because Popes cannot be apolitical. He was a Pope of the political right, like so many of his predecessors since the Italians started to unify Italy, but more so because of the fear of Communism.

The time from 1948 to 1991 was a good time for the papacy politically. Until 1870 it was troubled by ruling a lot of Italy while being incompetent to rule it well. From 1870 to 1922 it was troubled by having to live in Italy under a succession of hostile liberal governments. From 1922 to 1943 it had to live with a Fascist dictator and from 1943 to 1944 with a German dictator, and from 1944 to 1948 with the violence of postwar Italy. But from 1948 it had a friendly and democratic government in Italy which gave freedom to the Church and yet supported it. It was the best time for Popes since the French Revolution.

In the West, Pius XII's hostility to Communism led to friendly and favourable agreements with the two Iberian dictators, Salazar in Portugal (1940) and Franco in Spain (1953). His experiences with Mussolini and Hitler led him to think it important to protect the see of Rome against Italian governments by making the Vatican more international. When he became Pope, more than half the cardinals were Italians. That was traditional: Italian is the language of the Curia. When he died, the Italians were one-third of the cardinals. This was a historic change in the constitution of the Holy See.

But in the Pope's last years, after he was about seventy-eight, illness and old age added to his natural solitariness and to the life of the spirit in another world to make government almost impossible. While the world demanded more and more of the

Catholic Church, its head lived in a narrow circle, hardly able to take a decision for himself. Since some decisions had to be taken they were inevitably taken by junior persons and some of them were bad. Catholic bishops who dealt with Rome found this a difficult time. And these few short years, when so much needed doing and Rome could do so little, added to the demand for a successor who would come out at the world. While there was a Cold War, and a vast change in the world through the decolonizing process, and there were revolutionary ideas in the Church, the Pope sat still before the altar.

2

The Attack upon Christianity
in Eastern Europe

It was the duty of Marxist governments to get rid of religion. In their eyes religion was backward-looking, provided erroneous views of the world, divided society by unnecessary internal barriers, drew young people into unproductive work, discouraged the real improvement of society by turning minds to a dream world, was an expression of bourgeois attitudes and acted as a brake upon justice for the proletariat. Ideally it should vanish from the minds of humanity. In addition, since none of the main religions reconciled their adherents to doctrines of class war or the dictatorship of the proletariat, insecure Communist governments saw the religious bodies as possible sources of dissent or disloyalty and believed that in a wise constitution the State should keep a tight hold on whatever the Churches did.

How this doctrine was interpreted varied according to the circumstances of the country, and the history of the country, and the attitudes of the Communist dictators, and the behaviour of the chief bishops and pastors. At the brutal end, the State destroyed religion, by murder if necessary.

Orthodox Marxism held it right to hinder religion but not by violence which made martyrs. Therefore it was wrong to ban religious acts provided that they were private. In addition, some eastern European states nominally subscribed to a vague doctrine of human rights, which included freedom to practise a religion. If people were foolish enough to be religious in private, they must be permitted to be so. This meant that prayers inside churches, synagogues or mosques must be sanctioned. It also meant that the churches or mosques must be allowed to have clergymen and therefore some new clergymen as the old ones died and therefore some training for future clergy. But the normal attitude, in the first years after the Second World War, permitted no practice of religion outside churches or mosques (for example, no processions in the streets, no preaching on soapboxes, no religious education in schools, no religion to be broadcast on radio or television, no religious books to be sold in bookshops but only at the back of the church).

Also, although governments had to allow churches and mosques and some clergy, nothing was laid down about how many churches or mosques could be open and how many clergy could be trained. Since it was obvious to them that it was antisocial that churches should be open or that young men should be encouraged to join a profession which was thought to be akin to being an astrologer or a conjurer, all the states during the first years closed churches when they had an excuse – such as a need for a new arterial road, a need for a new school, not enough people to keep up the building, inability of the congregation to find a priest, etc. And although governments allowed seminaries, they allowed many fewer seminaries, they interviewed candidates and discouraged them, and in only one country, Poland, did they allow enough young people to be trained to meet the losses through death or ill health. The average age of priests or pastors increased in Western Europe. It increased still more in most of Eastern Europe. Clergy and even bishops – especially bishops, for a reason that we shall see – were begged to continue though they were long past work.

Again, since governments had to permit religious practice but regarded religious practice as antisocial, they felt they had every right to discourage people from engaging in it. They could not expect old people to refrain from a habit which they had formed many years ago. Therefore they had to direct their endeavours towards the young.

How this discouragement was carried out varied from state to state. In the nastier forms there was an endeavour to discredit the Churches – by propaganda trials, for example, of persons accused of cooperating with Nazis, or of treasonable behaviour towards a people's society, or of shifting currency about in an underhand manner. Such trials could be blown up on the media where the Churches had no right to reply. But after a time the charge of treasonable behaviour to a people's society was found to rebound. When the government was itself unpopular, Church leaders who were accused of resisting it won respect or even popularity, which was not the intention. Before long that type of trial ceased to be a

show trial and became only a way of keeping troublesome clergy
in order.

The normal form of discouragement of religion was through
education. Governments must ensure that the doctrine that they
believed – *all religion is superstition or invented to oppress the people* –
was propagated by the State. They had a right and a duty to show
the people, especially the coming generation, the ills which religion
brings. Much the most important part of this education was in
school. Religious education was not quite universally banned from
schools. No schools were left as denominational, except a very
small number in Hungary.

To justify the banning of religious education from State schools
was easy – France and some other democracies had done the same,
on the plea of separation of Church and State. Most of the Eastern
states thought it unjust to ban voluntary religious education; that
is, to stop children being taught the catechism at someone's home,
or the pastor's house, or the church, or even the premises of the
State school out of school hours.[1] But this voluntary religious
education was discouraged by the State officers. They explained
to children who attended Sunday school that this could be a
disadvantage in their future careers. They explained to parents
that by sending their children to Sunday school they risked damage
to their children's chances of higher education or of a worthwhile
job when adult.

This varied much according to the state and the denomination.
After the first Stalinist years, such pressure happened little in most
of Yugoslavia, or in Romania or Hungary. The pressure against
parents was powerful in Czechoslovakia[2] and the Baltic states and
Russia. Poland had more religious education than anywhere else
in Europe; and yet the pressure upon parents who sent their
offspring and upon priests who taught them was uncomfortable.

1. (a) No RE under eighteen or at all, voluntary or not: USSR, Albania,
Bulgaria, for a time. (b) RE in schools outside class hours: Czechoslovakia,
Hungary, East Germany – but pressure against, especially in Czechoslovakia.
(c) Catechism on church premises: Poland, Romania, Yugoslavia – pressure
against it at first, but persistently only in Poland.
2. In Czechoslavakia we have statistics: children registered for RE in 1964, 4
per cent in all the country; in 1967 (nearing the Prague Spring), Bohemia 13 per
cent, Slovakia 38 per cent; in 1970 after the destruction of the Prague Spring,
Bohemia 22 per cent, Slovakia 52 per cent; and thereafter a rapid fall.

Except in Poland, these methods kept *open* voluntary religious education restricted to a minority of the possible children.

If the children were not to get religion, their teachers must not be religious, for religion could be caught when it was not taught. Departments of education had no trouble in keeping the openly pious out of higher education and secondary education, as they kept them out of the civil service. Thereby they lost some good teachers, but in their eyes no one could be a good teacher if he or she practised a religion. Among the vast numbers of teachers in elementary schools they could not be so rigid in their choice of staff. The most that they could do was to exclude men and women whose piety was too conspicuous.

In every school the teachers were under an obligation to provide a course in scientific materialism. This meant showing the pupils that a theory of God was not needed to explain the world, so they had to learn enough science to understand the causes of thunder and lightning, the truth of evolution – how humanity is descended from the apes (as it was put in the cruder textbooks) – and how modern science has made the idea of miracle impossible. It also meant showing the children that the effects of religion are bad, so they had to learn of the trials of witches, or the tortures of the Inquisition, or the support of Churches for the oppressive classes.

This positive part was harder to achieve than the banning of religion from schools. In 1973, for example, the Czech government issued sensible guidelines: teachers must combat (1) an 'idealist' view of the world, that is, a denial of materialist philosophy; (2) the idea that religion is needed for moral citizenship; (3) the idea that emotional life has something lacking without a religious side; (4) the idea that institutions which encourage religion can be useful to society. Teachers were also to show that some rites are superstitious, and how at bottom a religious ideology is an ideology of social reaction.

It sounded all right, but it was not practical. Textbooks on materialism were hard to find and when found they were bad. The Czechs had to use translations of Russian books, and despised them as so crude that educated Czechs could not bear them. The number of militant atheists in the teaching profession was not high, for the reason that atheism was not an ideology calculated to produce militants; and teachers who cared about the children knew that a child needed to keep its confidence in its parents as well as in its teachers and so they shrank from evoking a contradiction between home and school. The result was that even in many Russian schools, where in theory the antireligious pressure was most persistent, religion was not mentioned. Teachers justified this by an attitude of common sense. If religion is unimportant, why make it important by attacking it? The government thought this attitude wrong. They believed it a mistake to keep religion out of school, because it was necessary to society that irreligion should be in school. But it was the teachers, and not the government, who had to care for the children.

To foster irreligion among adults required lecturers, museums, institutes for the study of religion and atheist clubs.

Museums to prove the evil of religion contained examples of superstition, miracle-working objects, reports of witchcraft or inquisitors, instruments of branding, thumbscrews, whips, Christ as the oppressor. Most of these museums were poor affairs, but then most museums had dreary little displays. The most famous was the former cathedral of the Virgin of Kazan at Leningrad, because it had housed the miraculous icon of the Virgin found at Kazan in 1579 and brought first to Moscow in 1612 and then to Petrograd (Leningrad) by Tsar Peter the Great. It was a neo-classical building on fifty-six great Finnish granite columns and, as a memorial to the Russian victory over Napoleon, was hung with trophies of battle like French eagles, and held the tomb of Marshal Kutuzov on the place where he said his prayers before he set out to harry the French emperor out of Russia. It was not the first such museum after the Bolshevik Revolution, for it was not opened until 1932, but its director, a friend of Lenin, was an authentic historian and amassed a good library and a fine collection of icons. It took its work seriously, with a staff of travelling lecturers who went into schools and clubs and factories, and with a touring exhibition on legends of the Bible. But it attracted more by being a first-class museum than by being an anti-God museum. This was proved statistically. In 1979 it was shut for two years; when it was reopened the whips and thumbscrews had disappeared and it was a good museum on the history of religion, with a decided but more subtle slant against religion. In 1956 it had 257,000 visitors. For the new display in 1983 it had 700,000 visitors.

Outside Russia and Albania the states hardly bothered with these museums. In Poland it was said that they would not dare to open such a museum because the people might turn violent.

In Gorky there was a preposterous piece of education, done in earnest: the primary-school children assembled their own anti-God museum, gave guided tours to parents and lent interesting pieces to the local factories.

The travelling lecturers found it as hard to get an audience as travelling preachers in Western countries. Their standard of performance was low. Not many people wanted the job. In some countries the lecturers did not exist. But at universities there was always a department of Marxist-Leninist philosophy, and this might have with it an institute for the study of religion. Some of the academics in the faculties of philosophy had standards of scholarship. But where they had such standards they pursued knowledge for its own sake and not to promote atheism. They were no more irreligious than schools of logical-positivist philosophy in the West, which were often irreligious.

Atheist clubs were successful in Bulgaria. Probably they were more successful as clubs than as atheist clubs, but every town of any size had one and some of the leading citizens belonged. In Russia a meeting of the Komsomol (Communist youth movement) could serve the function of an atheist club. But in most of the Eastern states such clubs had hardly more social importance than clubs of rationalists in the West.

Most states had a subsidized atheist journal, to which the subscribers were few and of which the readers were fewer. But from 1959 Russia had a journal *Nauka i Religiya* (Science and Religion) which printed over 300,000 copies and was well up in Western atheism and its arguments and knew about Western critical scholarship of the Bible.

THE SECULAR RITES

The people of Europe needed rites for the great moments of life – birth, adulthood, marriage, death. From time immemorial they had celebrated these events by Christian rites, so that a religious ceremony was entangled with a human need. At first the Stalinist regimes imagined that all such rites and ceremonies were human weakness and superstition: that for marriage one need do no more than open a registry office with a desk, and for a funeral no more than provide a friend to orate in a crematorium. They put it about that it was more patriotic, or more educated, or more socially responsible not to get married in church, and they banned church weddings unless the ceremony came *after* the registry office.

But, as time passed, the regimes realized, not without dismay, that these rites of religion had more persistence among the people than any other religious practices. Babies were baptized, and boys and girls were confirmed, and brides liked churches, and nearly everyone wanted a pastor at their funeral. Therefore the question arose of providing atheist rites for the other great moments of life as was already done with weddings, and, since so many brides preferred churches, the question arose whether the non-religious wedding should be made jollier. If they wanted to discourage confirmation, they must supply an alternative form of dedication. If they wanted to discourage weddings in church, they needed to warm up their registry offices. If they wanted fewer funerals conducted by a priest, they needed to think how reverence was to be satisfied by a State rite while religion was not encouraged – and this last was the hardest of all. Most of these State attempts at ersatz rites were failures – sometimes ridiculous failures – for the human race knows that ceremonies have to have been invented a long time ago if they are not to feel absurd.

The ritual-planners found their work awkward. They wanted to move away from the past, but the people would accept no ritual which did not remind them of past ways of marking occasions. Somehow a rite needed to express the folk memory of centuries, and this ideal of folk memory did not appeal to Bolshevik reformers.

But by the sixties they accepted as given that a rite needed to be linked to the cultural heritage if it was to command a people's affections. The State trained 'ritualists' – 'ritual service workers' – in how to conduct such rites.

Of the four great moments, the two which mattered were adulthood and marriage. No one could influence a baby towards religion by baptizing it, and no one could influence towards religion someone who was dead. And babyhood had less importance in that throughout the European Churches, Western as well as Eastern, infant baptism seemed to Christians of the later twentieth century to be less urgent than formerly and quite Christian families neglected that sacrament. But there were Communist rites of dedicating a new baby when it was registered, and there is evidence of moderate success for such a rite in the Ukraine and Leningrad. There they invented a naming ceremony and, by a statistic of 1977, more than half of all babies went through this ceremony – a high number by standards elsewhere. But this did not mean that nearly half were baptized. In 1977 in Estonia – a more religious country by tradition than some of the Soviet Union – just under 4 per cent of all babies were baptized (the area was, however, one where the Baptist Churches did well, so infant baptisms were not all the baptisms). At the atheist naming ceremony there was music by choir or instruments; the child was given a medal with a picture of a tree, or a tractor, or a power line, or Lenin; and there were godparents, though they were called 'honorary parents'. In some areas the makers of ritual reluctantly accepted the term 'christening' to describe the rite, because the people would call it nothing else.

The people wanted such occasions, and if their church was strange to them, or closed, they wanted to go to the Palace of Babies or the Wedding Palace. Normally only the first wedding could be celebrated in these palaces. The Russian bride was still in white, the bridegroom in black. There was the giving and receiving of a ring. Actually it was a religious rite without any of the theological words.

Marriage rites were difficult to replace. Families and couples were not solely wishing for glamour when they opted for a church and a pastor. They felt marriage to be a turning-point which ought to be consecrated before eternity. In many countries the church wedding (after the State wedding) remained quite common (in Lithuania a quarter of all weddings); though civil servants and heads of industry and professors and teachers dared not go to church. In other countries it grew rare; in the Soviet Union perhaps as many as 3 per cent of all weddings in 1976 – which was quite a lot in so vast a country.

In 1959 Russia opened in Leningrad its first Palace of Weddings, in an old chateau on the Neva. This recognized the need for colour and ritual at a wedding. At the entrance a flame burned, lit from the fire at the war cemetery which commemorated the fallen – here was the link with the sense of the sacred, for many in Russia felt something sacred about men and women who died to save the country from the Nazis.

The link with the war dead was also used at atheist funerals. A lot of people went to bury their dead with gratitude for the past, but still with the hope that someone would say a word of eternity. As a result atheist funerals were nearest to religious rites. The ritualists could not stop the people throwing earth on the coffin so they later adopted this into their own rite. They had no reason to object to the words 'eternal rest'. By the end of the 1970s the Ukraine had twenty-two Houses of Mourning. For the numbers of people who died, that was a handful.

Slowly, then, most of the Marxist regimes accepted the need for public rituals. To be domiciled fully among a people, such rituals needed use over generations. In the time-span of this book they failed to gather enthusiasts. If the people were going to have a ceremony they preferred the old one that they had known, which sounded an unmuffled trumpet of eternity.

But in two countries the makers of ritual succeeded with rites of adulthood. This happened in countries where the prevailing religion was Lutheran, for among the Lutherans confirmation was a key in the devotional and social tradition.

On the Baltic the decline of religion was very plain in Estonia and Latvia, not least because of numerous Russian immigrants. The old confirmation was turned into a smiling family festival, with thousands of young people and friendly junketing. This was then married to ceremonies on graduating from school, which were already used in the Russian tradition. Texts from Karl Marx or Lenin were read, but probably they were boring. The Balts were content with a family festival which, like a Western secularized Christmas, had a continuity with the past and where the sentiment was more important to them than any rite.

The State held spring festivals and New Year festivals which were conscious rivals to Christmas and Easter, with processions and games and sometimes a prize-giving to good workers. Like some of the Christians in East or West, the makers of ritual could not resist the temptation to make it 'meaningful', with harangues about hard work, or peace, or the beauty of a collectivist society.

In Poland such rites had no chance and the government hardly bothered. In Czechoslovakia the government worked hard and vainly at the rites. But in East Germany the rite of *Jugendweihe* was the most successful of all. The reason for this success was naked power.

'Youth-consecration' was intended to take the place of confirmation. In the ritual the candidate swore allegiance to socialism and the East German state in a form which was difficult for the conscientious Christian boy or girl to accept honestly, though the government presented it as merely a State affair which no Christian child need have any scruples about. Otto Dibelius, the Lutheran Bishop of Berlin (on the Western side), sent a message to his diocese (in much of which he was not allowed to travel) that this ceremony was impossible for a Christian. Other bishops, both Catholic and Protestant, shared his opinion. This youth-consecration was in theory a voluntary act but in fact it gained a social compulsion, because without it the young people had difficulty getting into higher education. The Communist Party insisted to teachers and parents that the ceremony was in the interests of the children. Placards in many shop windows urged children to undergo the ceremony. The opinion of the bishops could not stand up against the interests of education. By 1960 most children took *Jugendweihe*; by 1983 nearly all children of the right age. It remains to be seen what will happen to so widely accepted a rite after the fall of the Communist regime.

MONKS AND NUNS

Not all the states made monks and nuns illegal, but the system made it hard to be a nun and harder to be a monk. Convents depended partly on endowments – but there were none now that did not belong to the State. If the monk was driven out of education, how could he eat? If he cultivated an allotment, that belonged to the State. The nuns were driven out of hospitals as well as schools and there was no endowment to allow them to be contemplatives – how could they eat? In addition many of the states dissolved all the monasteries as part of the seizure of their endowments, and some of them banned any community of people from living together for any common purpose. The Czechoslovak government said that it was not illegal to be a monk or a nun but it was illegal to wear habits or to live in religious communities or to accept novices – so after all it was illegal, whatever it pretended.

None of this was true of the Orthodox countries – Russia, Romania, Bulgaria and Yugoslavia. Since an Orthodox bishop has to be a monk, to allow the religion at all was to allow monks. Nevertheless in all these states, especially in Russia, the pressure against monks did not make it easy to find bishops.

In Poland, monks and nuns were always plentiful, though they became fewer because they were driven out of schools and therefore did not have the same jobs to do. After the early Stalinist onslaughts, Yugoslavia was well supplied with such religious. The Franciscans had worked for centuries in the Catholic areas of Yugoslavia and by 1975 there were again more than 1,000 Franciscans as pastors or teachers; the number of Catholic monks and friars that year was 2,817. In 1966 the Serbian Orthodox had only 242 monks, but many more nuns, and some of the historic male houses were taken over by nuns. East Germany had no restriction on religious orders and by 1979 there were nearly as many monks and nuns as in the Catholic provinces of Yugoslavia.

In Romania the monasteries slowly declined while the nunneries grew. From 1948 onwards Patriarch Justinian conducted a good reform of the religious houses. The government then saw that they began to be too popular and limited the numbers and prevented young people from joining. But at the end of 1975 there were still about 2,200 monks and nuns, with the largest houses all female.

When Hungary dissolved all the religious orders, it allowed three monasteries and three nunneries to run schools. That meant about 250 religious, and each was allowed two novices a year to help with the teaching. Otherwise, of the 11,538 monks and nuns of 1950, there survived as religious about 100 living in an old people's house and some 460 males running parishes.

But the trouble for the State was that nuns had rendered services which it could not replace – in the care of the old and the dying, or of the abnormal children. The State meant to use secular nurses for these but failed to find the people. Therefore modestly, and with the sisters getting older, and with only surreptitious young recruits, the nuns continued some of their historic work. By 1975 Czechoslovakia had not a single monk, unless he was underground, but still had 8,000 nuns engaged in hospices and hospitals, and some of them wore garments quite like a nun's habit.

In the middle of the 1980s Hungary let the Church found a new order of nuns – the Community of the Protectress of Hungary. It could receive novices, and the Vatican allowed nuns of dissolved houses to join. The State needed the nuns but the old religious orders were still illegal, so there had to be a new order. The State Church Office had to certify to the government that the new order was not identical with any of the old.

Russia, with a large Orthodox Church, had to allow monasteries and nunneries. But the government thought them homes of superstition and an anachronism in a socialist society. It struggled to close them or to limit their influence.

At the time of the Bolshevik Revolution there were about 100,000 monks and nuns. In the Civil War they suffered agonies and many houses were destroyed. But after the Second World War Russia acquired more of the Ukraine, and some of eastern Poland, and Bessarabia, and the Baltic States, and with these came some 104 houses with about 5,000 monks and nuns. Hence almost all the Russian monasteries lay in western Russia. The exception was Zagorsk, east of Moscow, the headquarters of the patriarchate. In the mid-1950s there were still 90 religious houses. In 1980 there were 16 to 18 houses, with about 1,500 religious. The average age was high but there were young monks too. The State forced the patriarch to forbid monasteries to tonsure monks under the age of thirty.

The State closed the religious houses by high taxes, by taking lands in the public interest, by occupying part of buildings said to be too large for the monks and putting in tenants who did not go with a quiet life, like a barracks or a bar for drunken policemen, and by trying to stop pilgrimages to their shrines. Where the monastery survived, it often had fewer monks. In the Ukraine, Pochaev monastery, which was famous in all Russia, had 146 monks in 1961 and 35 monks twenty-two years later. Zagorsk was the success. It was a tourist goal, was famous outside Russia, and trained many of the clergy. During recent years it seems to have had about 90 to 100 monks. The Monastery of the Dormition at Odessa was helped to survive because it trained clergy, but also because it became the summer resort of the patriarch. There was another big house near Pskov, 'The Monastery of the Caves', which survived because it was in what was once Lutheran Estonia. It worked a big farm and received many pilgrims. The State failed to force its monks to get rid of a good abbot with an independent mind, but when he died it forced them under a brutal abbot whom they detested. Yet each of these houses had its special holy man or starets whom the people would seek out for counsel or absolution. In the people's eyes the starets was much more important than the abbot: he was the old and holy Russia. And a part of the ideal of self-denial was the refusal to complain but to bear quietly whatever happened.

Nunneries were usually bigger. They kept going by making vestments, or bread for the sacrament, or by painting of icons, but the nuns might also work on some nearby collective farm. The nuns were not all old. Sometimes the State forced them to share a building with a monastery. One of the largest nunneries, the Convent of the Protecting Veil of Our Lady, on a hill above Kiev, sheltered Jews and wounded Red Army soldiers during the war and so won a claim to the people's gratitude.

THE STATE CONTROL OF THE CHURCHES

Each Communist state had a ministry for Church affairs, with one of various names.[3] In some states this was not new: Russia had one under the tsars, Prussia under the Hohenzollern, Germany under Hitler. The old ministers were Christians who were supposed to do their best for the Church, though as the State rather than the Church saw 'the best'. The new ministers were atheists whose job was to see that Churches did not become political and did not counter Communism or demand too many of the resources of the State in people or buildings.

In a society where the State owned all the property, these ministries were a necessity. An office had to license a group of people to use a building, or sanction the materials and the use of labour to repair the building, or organize the payment of the clergy (where the State paid clergy from former Church endowments). Therefore the State had an easy control over the Church. If a bishop was fractious, he got no leave to build a new church and no means of mending an old church; if he was very fractious he was removed from office. Except in East Germany and later in Poland, all the states insisted on some control over the choice of persons for bishoprics and pastorates. This was normally interpreted so as to prevent the appointment of anyone likely to be a critic of the Communist Party; sometimes it was interpreted so as to prevent the appointment of anyone of character to a leading place.

The choosing of bishops worked easily in the Orthodox states (Romania, Bulgaria, Russia, Serbia) where the Churches were accustomed to a measure of State approval. In Serbia (after the early Stalinist years) it worked happily enough: a synod of electing bishops engaged in quiet negotiation with a representative of the

3. USSR, Council for Religious Affairs; Poland, Ministry for Religious Affairs; East Germany, Secretariat of State for Church Affairs; Czechoslovakia, State Office for Church Affairs; Hungary, State Church Office; Romania, Department of Cults; Bulgaria, a sub-department of the Foreign Office (!). *Religion in Communist Lands*, 13, 1 (1985), 54ff.

government but the layman could not simply tell them whom they must elect. The Romanian dictator invented a unique system for electing bishops, in which the Communist MPs and Party officials of the diocese were on the board of electors with the Church representatives. This system produced some really good bishops and some others who were sycophants of the dictator. Several of the Russian bishops, chosen where the hand of the State lay heavy upon the synod, were surprisingly good; others were yes-men and little more. What made it difficult to find bishops in Orthodoxy was the rule that they must be monks, at a time when the states rigidly controlled the number of monasteries. This had two side-effects: old bishops going on long after they should have retired, and bishops chosen as laymen of the minimum age (thirty or just over) who became successively monk, deacon, priest and bishop within the space of three weeks, thereby widening the pool of potential bishops to every unmarried or widowed member of the Church but making the rule about the monkhood of bishops absurd.

In the Protestant communities the system did not work badly. The East German government respected the Lutheran constitution. If a diocese elected a 'bad' bishop (meaning, strong against the State) it would suffer. In Estonia and Latvia there was frequent deadlock − the Church refusing to have the person the State wanted, the State refusing to have the person the Church electors wanted − but such deadlocks meant that the State could not force the Church to take anyone it would not vote for, though after many months or years Church electors sometimes felt it the lesser evil to vote for the person whom they did not want, to end so damaging an interregnum. The Hungarian Lutherans divided on whether to accept the election of a bishop who was chosen after the valid bishop was thrown out of office by Stalinist villainy. But the new bishop was chosen by churchmen as well as by State approval. With the Protestants, the ministeries for Church affairs had the problem that Lutheran and Reformed Churches more easily got on without bishops than did the Orthodox or the Roman Catholics: if they could not get the person they wanted, they were known to prefer to have no one at all. At more than one 'election' of a Protestant State-appointed bishop in Slovakia, the faithful demonstrated noisily against the newcomer.

In the Roman Catholic states (Slovenia, Croatia, Slovakia, Poland, Lithuania and two-thirds of Hungary) the choice of bishops was a source of endless friction. For the last hundred years the Vatican had claimed the right to approve every appointment of a bishop and this was now in canon law. But Rome allowed concordats under which the State had kept the right to veto its nominations, or in some cases the State had kept the right to nominate and the Vatican had the veto. The Communist states abolished unilaterally all these concordats but insisted on keeping the right to approve bishops. Then there was trouble. The Vatican refused to appoint bishops whom it knew to be anti-Vatican, but some States would have no other bishops. The trouble for the Vatican was that whenever there was disagreement, which was the normal situation, the State did not care if the see stayed empty whereas the Vatican minded.

But it was not easy for the State. It had to find a man who would be against the Vatican and friendly to Communism and not awkward and yet who was big enough and moral enough to command the respect of the clergy. This meant that it chose either from no possibles or from a very small number of possibles. Hence in several states there were long vacancies in sees, an unwillingness of bishops to retire lest there be an election, clergy begging bishops not to retire even though they were ill, and an ageing of bishops in their office until they were past their work.

The system was worst for the Catholic Church in Lithuania and Slovakia and at first in Hungary. In 1940 there were twelve Lithuanian bishops. Thirty years later there were two, because they had survived (aged seventy-five and seventy-six). In Czechoslovakia, more than once there were no effective bishops at all; all the dioceses were run, or half-run, or not run, by clerical administrators approved by the State. These had to be chosen by chapters. On one occasion when the State thrust in an administrator without election by a chapter it did not work well for the State. But if a chapter did not choose the person whom the State wanted, the State pushed new canons into the chapter to secure the election.

The system was best for the Catholic Church in Poland and in the states of northern Yugoslavia, Croatia and Slovenia. It was not good in the Stalinist phase, but from the 1960s compromise started to work with the Vatican. In Poland the Church achieved a system by which the Church presented several names to the State. In 1974 when Cardinal Kominek, the Archbishop of Wroclaw/Breslau, died, the State is said to have vetoed twelve candidates before the succession was agreed. But a decade after that the State seldom chose any name but the first on the list presented by the Church.

As part of the control of Churches, the States wished to cut or at least weaken the Churches' links with bodies outside the State – the Pope for the Roman Catholics, the Ecumenical Patriarch at Constantinople for the Orthodox and the World Council of Churches for the Protestants. But in this last case, to be inside the World Council was useful, provided that the suitable people were selected or permitted to attend.

THE CHRISTIAN COOPERATORS

The more unjust the government, the less dialogue was possible between Christian and Marxists. In the Stalinist phase it was hardly possible anywhere. No Christian leader could afford to be seen to debate with torturers. Nevertheless some did, and thereby were at once disreputable among their people, though not in high Communist society.

After Stalin died and most governments grew less tough in their policy, certain rules still applied:

(1) Bishops needed to be friendlier to the State than their priests or pastors. They needed to get licences to build new churches or repair old ones or to get men into seminaries. This difference later opened a rift between bishops and pastors.

(2) Orthodox and Protestant found dialogue with the State easier than did Roman Catholics – the Pope was publicly against Communism and was believed to be the agent of imperialism and capitalism; and in ethical rules, as on abortion or divorce, Orthodox and Protestant were less hostile to law which gave the people a lot of freedom in such matters.

The Orthodox found it easier because their history consisted in managing under a hostile or unpredictable State, such as the Ottoman Empire or the tsarist Russian Empire. For centuries they were familiar with the need to bow before an unpleasant government. They found the situation almost normal.

The Protestants found it easier because within their tradition was a school of Christian Socialism, and socialism is an extensible word. Such schools of Christian Socialism were always weak in numbers and influence among Western Protestants. But their views had achieved respectability in Lutheran Germany, and among the Protestants of Czechoslovakia and Hungary, the Dutch Reformed Church, the French Huguenots, and the British Churches.

Wherever the tradition of Christian Socialism existed, the possibility of dialogue with Marxism existed: not with the members of government, who consisted of *apparatchiks*, but with the philosophy schools in universities, which perforce were atheist but which threw up some minds who thought hard and did more than parrot the formulas of Marxist-Leninism. In good times – that is, times when the government acted not too unpleasantly and when Church leaders did not need to behave too defensively – a Marxist philosopher or two from a university could debate seriously with a theologian or two from a Christian seminary. In Eastern Europe between 1950 and 1989 such dialogues were rare.

The states had a contradiction in their policy. Some Christians were dedicated Socialists; some professed themselves Christian Communists. Should the Communists encourage such people, to prove that there was nothing wrong in a Christian being a Communist, despite what Pope Pius XII had said? If they encouraged such people, were they encouraging religion, which would be contrary to Marxist theory? In every Marxist state outside Russia, East Germany and Albania an association of clergy friendly to Communism, sometimes more than one such association, was formed. The governments liked to ensure that the leaders of the Church belonged to it, though they could not always succeed in that; sometimes they subsidized it; sometimes they secretly paid its members a higher stipend; and normally State grants helped it to run a newspaper or several newspapers. Quite often its leaders were members of the rubber-stamp Parliament. In 1958 the

Vatican excommunicated three Hungarian priests who accepted seats in Parliament and in reply the Hungarian government promoted and honoured them. The priests took no notice of the excommunication. And this excommunication was difficult to justify, since before many years a Jesuit was elected to the House of Representatives of the United States. At the request of the Hungarian bishops, the Vatican lifted the excommunication. But nothing reconciled the Vatican to those organizations which were led by Catholic priests, were fellow-travelling in their philosophy and refused to accept rulings delivered by the Curia in Rome.

Everywhere the Communist states found Christians to back them. These priests did not have an easy time. The people saw them as men on the make.

Yugoslavia

In Yugoslavia, the government at first encouraged priests' associations. These were like guilds or trade unions of progressive or radical priests who had the normal instinct that it was their duty to honour bishops and simultaneously to stop them running the Church. For a time these associations were important in all parts of Yugoslavia, for, when Tito first won power, the clergy with authority were not the bishops but the former chaplains to the partisan guerrilla armies. Milan Smiljanić was Tito's chief army chaplain in the resistance. After the war he became minister of agriculture and vice-president, though still a priest. He stood at the patriarch's right hand in official ceremonies. But, as in other countries, the influence of such associations declined steadily, partly because the bishops slowly reasserted their authority in the constitution and partly because the Communist leaders lost interest in their effectiveness.

Hungary

Hungary formed a Catholic Democratic People's Party. The Party broke off relations with the Vatican. The 'patriotic priests' were much encouraged. Communist officials were given votes at bishops' meetings. There was an association called the Movement of Catholic Priests for Peace, founded by a Cistercian, Richard

Horváth, who had recently been suspended from his order for radical utterances. In a speech – we may regard it as epitomizing the socialist priests – Horváth said, 'Thanks be to God, we are in a new epoch, that of socialism. In all history there has never been a movement of men's souls so near to Christianity ... No one wants to take our faith away. They only want us to put it at the service of society. They ask us to bring God to help build socialism.'[4] As the government appointed priests to their jobs, it started to insert the members of this movement into the government of the dioceses.

Take the archdiocese of Esztergom, the primatial see of Hungary. The archbishop was in prison. His vicar-general ruled, but quickly died. The cathedral chapter then did its duty and elected a vicar-capitular, the auxiliary bishop, who was promptly arrested. The chapter then resigned themselves to doing what the Party wanted and elected one of their number who was a member of Richard Horváth's movement – Canon Beresztocy. He became a distinguished Communist, and was elected deputy chairman of the Hungarian Parliament. Later even the bishops accepted a compromise over the cooperating priests in Hungary.

Czechoslovakia

In Czechoslovakia there was an association of cooperating priests, the Priests for Peace (called Pacem in Terris after 1970). To belong to this group was advantageous to a priest: in job and in pay. Almost all the higher clergy were soon members, because otherwise the State vetoed their appointment. No one could teach in either of the seminaries without being a member. In 1982 there was a scandal when it was discovered that the State paid substantial awards to priests who were members of the organization. In this way the Church administration went on. Soon the Party lost interest in the Communist Catholic movement. But the Priests for Peace remained strong. Their members more easily found their way into canonries, deaneries or the diocesan administration.

Its tradition of clergy with a critical attitude to Rome made the Czech Church cooperate with the Communist government more actively than any other Catholic Church behind the Iron Curtain.

4. *Documentation Catholique*, 54 (1957), 274, note.

The diocesan administration of the diocese of Prague not only was a Church office, lodged in the archbishop's palace, but was a department of the ministry of culture, with photographs of party officials all round the walls. At Hradec Králové the old bishop made no trouble when government imposed on him a Priests for Peace member as his vicar-general. At Budějovice the bishop was removed by force. The chapter had three new canons forced upon it and then elected a member of Priests for Peace as vicar-capitular. Rome excommunicated him and then the government decorated him. The more 'progressive' the bishop, the more he could get his way with local party officals and therefore the more he could run – not run very effectively, but still run – the diocese. At Banská Bystrica the government did not even bother to force canons into the chapter to make the right election: they imposed someone whom they called the vicar-capitular. Since he was not 'elected', the other 'bishops' would not recognize him and Rome excommunicated him. Neither non-recognition nor excommunication made the slightest difference. In the diocese of Olmütz the bishop was still in situ but he had no power whatever: the diocese was run by the chapter, which consisted entirely of 'progressive' canons.

Olmütz was the place for the career of the most remarkable among the Czechoslovak Catholic cooperators: Josef Vrána. He was a country pastor with progressive views, so the government made him a canon of Velehrad cathedral and from there thrust him in as vicar-capitular to run the diocese of Olmütz, a feat not difficult because all the chapter there were progressive. He rose steadily, by an eager collaboration with the regime. He was political in his activity, a member of various local soviets, and after the Prague Spring was suppressed by Russian tanks he became chairman of Pacem in Terris. In the negotiations to get better relations between the Vatican and the regime, and so to get at least a few bishops of whom the Vatican need not disapprove, the Vatican finally conceded that Josef Vrána should become Bishop-administrator of Olmütz in the full sense, on condition that he resigned his membership of Pacem in Terris. He resigned the chairmanship but remained a member. He continued to receive many prizes from the State and many protests from churchmen. The Czech government insisted from 1973 that all bishops must be members of Pacem in Terris, and the Vatican insisted that no one could be a bishop who was a member, so for a few years after Vrána's election no bishops were appointed.

It will be noticed that the Communist government in Czechoslovakia really valued the clergy who were willing to cooperate. With their aid it ran the Church. It had no need of the Vatican, though it occasionally had to endure ill-feeling because someone whom it put into an office was not recognized as validly appointed. The fact was that the government had in Slovakia a country which was 90 per cent or more Catholic. It could not avoid the Church, therefore it controlled it. Some of the cooperators were no doubt men on the make, who wanted good pay and interesting work. Others were priests who genuinely believed that the only way to get sacraments to the people, or religious education, or the churches repaired, was to go along with the Party. And others, though probably not many, were people who accepted the doctrine that, ethically and socially and at bottom, Christianity is a communist faith according to which property should be common for the use of all and the State should be directed towards the equality of the poor with the rich. It is much the most probable that the second of these three classes contained the majority of the progressive priests.

And yet the arrangement did not work. The government was not popular. People could not say aloud that it was unpopular. But, not for the first time in history, the churches became places where people could show what they felt even though they were under a tyranny. Some of the ageing congregations were soon in a mood to have no priest in their parish rather than a priest of whom the government approved.

The Czechs had a Protestant with an international reputation. Josef Hromádka was born a north-Moravian peasant and spoke Czech with a Polish accent. Early in life he was influenced by socialism and Protestant German liberal theology, and he was a disciple of Thomas Masaryk the founder of the Czech state. He became the first head of the United Church of the Bohemian Brethren (membership in 1989: 200,000) and soon was professor of systematic theology in the Hus faculty – till 1948 part of Prague university – a post which he retained for fifty years. He started a long friendship with the leader of the European reaction against Protestant liberalism, Karl Barth. Hromádka was fierce against the Nazified Churches in Germany and backed the republican cause, which was led by Communists, in the Spanish Civil War.

When then the Communists took power in Czechoslovakia, Hromádka was the most famous Christian thinker in all Eastern Europe. It was weighty that he at once accepted the new State and determined that the Churches ought to work with it. He saw Marxism as a reaction against an unjust social order but not necessarily a revolt against God. From time to time he protested privately to the government about what it did. In 1958 he came out with a public protest against the government decree that teachers in schools must teach atheism to the boys and girls. He founded and for ten years was the president of the Christian Peace Conference. This was the only official Christian body behind the Iron Curtain to exercise influence in the West. It owed this power solely to Hromádka's reputation, for his Christian Socialism was truly founded in Christian doctrine and was not mere assent to the Marxist proposals for society. He taught of the evils of capitalism and of the Christian good in Communism. But as time passed he started to be criticized by his younger pupils for failing to be tougher with the misbehaviour of the State towards the Churches.

During the earlier 1960s the Czech State started to relax its heavy hand upon the Churches. It released some of the clergy in prison and eased its censorship. It even released Archbishop Beran of Prague, who was now a cardinal, on condition that he went into exile. During the late 1960s it consented to what Hromádka had wanted from the first: a dialogue between Marxists and Christians. The Prague Spring of 1968 and the coming of Alexander Dubček opened the door to religious freedom and everything changed. When Dubček was overthrown by Russian tanks and the repression started again, not quite all the freedoms of the Dubček era were lost by the Churches.

The Russian invasion of Czechoslovakia in 1968 shattered Hromádka. He had stood publicly for gratitude to the Russians and the belief that Marxism and Christianity could be reconciled. He was the only international churchman who stood for those two faiths. In his eyes nothing could excuse the invasion of August 1968. He handed the Russian ambassador a letter which said that the invasion was the greatest tragedy of his life: it destroyed the beliefs upon which he had built his life's work. Soon afterwards he died in sadness. The possibility of Christian–Marxist dialogue was shattered for the time. Afterwards, one of his own pupils blamed him in bitter language for having led Czech Protestantism towards 'moral disintegration' by his favourable attitudes to Communism in Russia and in Czechoslovakia.

Poland

In Poland there were so many Catholics that it was easier to find men of weight to cooperate with the regime. When the government arrested a bishop and needed to get a willing vicar-capitular elected to take charge of the diocese, it had no difficulty in finding men – some, though not all, of them honourable men – to take charge. The government's Ministry for Religious Affairs promoted such people to higher office.

An able man led the cooperators: Count Boleslaw Piasecki, who was alleged at an earlier time to have had Fascist connexions. He headed a movement called Pax. Piasecki was careful that the publications of Pax should be orthodox. He had a messianic idea. The Pope, and therefore the world, believed that Christianity and Communism could not be reconciled. Since Communism was the best system for just shares in the wealth of the State, Christians must come to see the moral value in the Communist structure of society. And Communists must come to see how Christianity could help them to their better goals. Most Communist countries rejected God officially; most Christian countries rejected Communism. Poland was a country both Catholic and Communist. It must become the model for the world and the Church.

Piasecki thought that he opposed an open-minded Catholicism to an obscurantist Catholicism. He called for a Church where the laity had rights, instead of a clericalized Church. He called for a Church of truth instead of a Church of superstition and illiteracy; a Church of the common liturgy instead of a Church with its centre in special cults. He pleaded that even atheists are in a measure worshippers of God by their work for a better society. He wrote a book along these lines, *Essential Problems*. The Holy Office at Rome condemned it.

The influence of Piasecki and Pax, though never wide, remained for decades. As late as 1975 Pax had about 15,000 members, of whom 1,800 were priests. It had several newspapers, including a small Warsaw daily. But its big influence faded at the Hungarian Revolution of 1956. That brought home to the Communists that they could not run the Church with their chosen clergymen. Willy-nilly, they had to get on with the official Church.

East Germany

In East Germany the idea of a socialist or Communist Protestantism was slow to form. In 1950 Christians' memories were overwhelmingly of the struggle to preserve the Christian faith against Hitler. Their instinctive attitude to a hostile Communist government was that of the 'Church struggle'. They were defensive, and pro-Western. But, as Stalinism faded, they saw that Christianity need not necessarily be identified with a Western style of life, or with a capitalist economy, or with a bourgeois society, or even with a Western ordering of democracy. Unlike the theologians anywhere else in Eastern Europe, except for Lublin in Poland, their theologians had not been turned out of the universities. There they met Marxist philosophers as colleagues. Unlike anyone else in the Communist world outside Bohemia, they could look back upon the history of ideas and see the development of the atheist denials as a necessary moment in the struggle of the European mind to find truth. Therefore they began to consider whether the right attitude to official atheism was not confrontation but an offer to help construct a more Christian, more just and more socially conscious society.

In these attitudes they were helped by a phrase inherited from the martyr murdered by the Nazis, Dietrich Bonhoeffer: 'religionless Christianity'. Though the phrase had a doubtful meaning, it gave them the argument that the repudiation of 'religion' as the opium of the people need not be identified with the rejection of 'the Christ'.

So when the State, instead of saying that Christians damaged society by their superstitions, invited them to help construct a Communist society of fair shares, and to denounce nuclear war, and to be 'socially engaged', there were some Christian leaders, and more of Christian youth, willing to accept the proffered hand.

The trouble was that the government could and did suddenly withdraw its gesture and proclaim from the rooftops that no compromise between Marxism and Christianity could ever be possible. It remained a sore point in the Churches that children must be taught materialism in school and must pass through *Jugendweihe*, and that no pious person qualified for leading jobs in the State.

In March 1978 Bishop Schönherr of (East) Berlin had a momentous interview with the glum head of the government, Erich Honecker. This sealed a new if uneasy alliance. Henceforth the State allowed a small number of hours for Church broadcasts – once a month for information, six broadcasts a year to show worship or put the religious case. It became easier for the Churches to run their hospitals, hospices and homes for backward children. It became much easier for the Churches to have bookshops at which Christian literature was sold, though the amount of Christian literature and the titles were still controlled by the State censorship. The annual Lutheran Church meeting – the *Kirchentag* – now had a certain freedom.

In 1979 the State in propaganda for consumption abroad could represent the Churches as flourishing. They had 8 Protestant seminaries and 100 other places of education, and they ran 52 hospitals with 7,000 beds and 280 hospices with 11,000 places. They had in Berlin a publishing house which brought out some 250 titles a year (but still they could mostly be sold only at the back of a church) and produced Bibles for the blind. Sunday-morning radio was directed to the sick in hospitals, and once in two months the Churches were on State television. In Dresden the Lutheran choir had an international fame. The Roman Catholics had some 2,700 monks and nuns. Most of the monks were pastors; most of the nuns were nurses. The government claimed that it did not interfere in the choice of bishops, whether Catholic or Protestant. This was formally correct rather than true in practice on all occasions.

A lot of the faithful disliked the harmonies between Church and State where they were found. The Bishop of Greifswald, Horst Gienke, treated Honecker as though he was a friend of the Church. He wrote a letter to him saying that there were no problems in the relations of Church and State. The letter was leaked to the press, and the situation of Bishop Gienke was not comfortable with his people or his clergy. Then the cathedral of Greifswald was restored and the bishop invited Honecker to attend the service of consecration. Early in 1979 Honecker came; but many of the faithful stayed away because the bishop had invited him. The bishop became so unpopular for such 'compromises' with the State that in the first week of November 1989, a few days before the Berlin Wall came down, his synod voted, by a bare majority of two votes, that he be no longer bishop – an extraordinary vote, in recent Lutheran history almost unique.

But the case of the Bishop of Greifswald was only one of numerous signs in Eastern Europe that bishops and their communities drew apart because the bishop must get on with the government and his community resented this necessity.

3

Violence

ALBANIA

In Roman days Albania was already a Christian land. Slav invaders destroyed the churches but the Albanians came again under Italian, especially Venetian, influence and by the later Middle Ages northern Albania was largely Catholic and southern Albania largely Orthodox. During the fifteenth and sixteenth centuries the Ottoman Turks conquered the country. Many Albanians fled to southern Italy, where communities of them may be found to this day.

The Turks were accustomed to Christians who were Orthodox and came under the Patriarch of Constantinople. They rather liked the Orthodox and disliked the Roman Catholics. Under Turkish rule the Catholics' churches fell down, their children could not be educated, their priests were illiterate and many leading people passed into Orthodoxy or into Islam. A curious mixture of faiths grew up – a public practice of Islam with a secret practice of Christianity in the home, all mingled with superstition. By the middle of the seventeenth century Muslims were the majority in the country. By the end of Ottoman rule in 1912–13 Muslims were two-thirds of the population. Thus Albania was the only country wholly in Europe with a large Muslim majority (1945: Muslim 72.8 per cent, Orthodox 17.1 per cent, Roman Catholic 10.1 per cent).

Like its Ottoman predecessors, the Communist government after 1945 particularly disliked Roman Catholics. The dictator was Enver Hoxha, a fanatical schoolmaster. The Catholics were only one-tenth of the population. They had a good organization, and help from Italy, but they were therefore associated with the long Fascist protectorate and were resented as imperialists or as clerical-Fascists. Archbishop Thaci of Shkodër (Scutari) died in a concentration camp; four other bishops were shot. Archbishop Prenushi of Durazzo was sentenced to twenty years' imprisonment but soon died in jail and the death is suspect. In 1951, with one of the bishops cooperating, the government forced the Catholics to become a national Church without links with the Vatican; but soon it dismissed the cooperator from his see and sent him home to his family.

The division of the country into three religions – Catholic, Orthodox, Muslim – made them all weak and made life easier for the regime.

Under Ottoman rule the Orthodox Church prospered. It was hardly affected by the Italian occupation. At first the postwar Communist government did not behave worse to the Orthodox Church than Tito behaved to the Croat bishops further north in Yugoslavia, which was badly. Church property was nationalized, some churches were closed and seized, religious education was banned. But there was a league of progressive priests which was for socialism and against the bishops, and the State paid all the priests a very small and inadequate stipend. In 1949 Archbishop Christof was deposed for being 'friendly to Fascists' and the regime appointed Bishop Paisios to be primate, for during the war he had sided with the Communist partisans. So the regime still accepted that religion had to exist and might be useful to the State. Even in 1960 some village churches were still full of worshippers on Sundays. But the confiscation of churches and the pressure on funerals and marriages and especially baptisms grew. About 1960, the former Orthodox church in a suburb of Tirana was a restaurant and on its former altar stood a chromium-plated coffee-machine.

When Paisios, the State-appointed primate, died in 1966 the State chose a successor, Damian. But that was the end. Enver Hoxha had quarrelled with Moscow and was determined to maintain a Stalinist Communism. Nowhere else in Eastern Europe were the statues of Stalin kept upon the streets. In his total political isolation Hoxha asked for and received the patronage of Chairman Mao in China. During the year when the Orthodox Church of Albania was given a new primate, the Cultural Revolution started in China. Bands of young thugs went round China vandalizing mosques, churches and temples. China resolved to destroy religion totally. Albania copied this example. Whatever survived of public religion was now destroyed. The high school in Durazzo started the thuggery of the Albanian teenagers, battering away at churches and mosques. Villages held public meetings at which simple people were made to renounce religion or to accuse their parson of filthy crimes.

In 1967 Hoxha made a constitutional change unique in the Communist states. Because Karl Marx had said that religion is someone's private affair, all the states included in their constitution an article asserting that every individual had a right to practise religion or non-religion. This article remained even though the governments did not always observe it with individuals or large groups or even whole Churches. Communist Albania built this article into its first constitution. On 13 November 1967 a decree annulled the article. The new constitution of 1976 followed this decree and did not provide for any the right to practise religion. It ordered that the State support atheist propaganda to inculcate scientific materialism among the people.

So in 1967 the Albanian government announced with solemnity that it was the first atheist State in the world.

The government arrested the new primate, Damian, and kept him in prison till he died. Five other bishops were imprisoned and some of them were probably shot. The government closed the last four religious houses and the last seminary. Any clergy still in pastoral work were arrested and put to manual labour. All places of worship, including mosques, were seized. The regime showed every sign of hating not only the Churches but every form of religion. Christmas was abolished: the feasts were to be New Year's Day and Labour Day. In February 1976 the government, now worse than fanatical, abolished Christian names and ordered everyone who had one to change it.

Suppression of religion was not altogether easy. There was quiet evidence that Christmas and some other feasts were observed by the people. There was a little evidence of house-services – a priest (legally speaking an ex-priest) celebrated the sacrament in a home and technicaly this was not illegal before 1976, but in practice it had to be kept very secret. Citizens could hardly be stopped from travel, and it was a coincidence if their journey ended at a former shrine. But ordinary people were afraid of talking to foreign visitors about religion. Priests ('ex-priests') in concentration camps were liable to be shot if they conducted services, and as late as 1976 a bishop ('ex-bishop') was so beaten for doing this that he was found dead next day.

In Albania the motive for the desire to abolish religion was plain: religion is what divides the country, therefore if Albania is to survive it must be irreligious. Alone in Eastern Europe the Marxist onslaught upon religion was here taken up as a national necessity. And the need was more than the fight for education among a largely illiterate people: in a country where nearly three-quarters of the people were old-fashioned Muslims, the place of women left much to be desired. The Muslim women of Albania still followed the prescripts of the Koran on feminine inequalities – sometimes even Christian women too, because those were the social habits of the communities. Hoxha was married to an ex-Muslim woman who when thus yoked to power became a dedicated emancipator of the female sex and held religion responsible for male bias. A modern, united, educated society with universal literacy and equality of the sexes could be achieved only by abolishing religion – that was the theory; and it took no notice of the awkwardness that educated people usually have ideas of human rights. So religion was abolished by force.

In reply to such arguments an Albanian priest in Serbia produced an Albanian catechism which was far more than a catechism. It consciously tried to show religion as inherent to Albanian culture. It drew on religious documents from Roman Catholicism, Orthodoxy and Islam, with the aim of showing that religion could unite even when religions differed.

Quite a number of Catholic refugees were looked after in Italy. There had been Albanian communities with a continuous history in Sicily and southern Italy since the flight from the Ottoman Turks. In 1986 Pope John Paul II received them and told them how the plight of the Albanian Church was daily with him when he celebrated the sacrament and that he wanted to share the martyrdom of the Albanian people. Other large numbers of Albanians lived in Yugoslavia, where they were uncomfortably nationalist among the Serbs.

Hoxha died in 1985 and was succeeded by Ramiz Ali. Europe hoped for change. As first it did not happen. Foreign visitors reported that the people seemed hardly less frightened when they were asked questions about religion. But more churches were restored as historic monuments, and Albanian literature began again to mention religion. There was a political motive for change, namely the plight of the Albanians of Kosovo, across the border within Serbia, who were divided from the Serbs by religion as well as race. The Albanian government could more easily make common cause with the Albanians in Serbia if it was not brutal to their religion. But when change came, it came through the external influence of the general collapse of Communism.

Mother Teresa

While this irreligious State misbehaved, the only Albanian whose name the world knew was one of the most famous of Christians.

Agnes Gonxha Bojaxhui was born in 1910 into an Albanian family in Macedonia and was therefore at her birth a citizen of the Ottoman Empire. A Jesuit interested her in the Italian mission. She looked for a teacher's training and found it with the Sisters of Loreto, who worked particularly to educate the poor in Bengal. She left Albania and became a postulant at the sisters' training house in Dublin. She was then a novice in the Darjeeling nunnery, professed in 1931, took permanent vows in 1937 and assumed the name 'Teresa'. She taught history and geography in a school in Calcutta.

As the years passed in Calcutta it was the conditions of the poor which took her heart, much more than the ignorance of young Catholic girls. While she was engaged in a retreat at Darjeeling, she experienced what she regarded as her second call, or second vocation: to share the life of the poorest of the poor and to serve them. This meant leaving her nunnery, which she loved as a family. She convinced her supporters and was allowed to leave her order. She was thirty-eight.

She went first to the Swedish sisters in Patna and there took a course in nursing and midwifery. In December 1948 she started in Calcutta, to collect waifs and visit the sick. After only three months two of her old Loreto pupils joined her. She needed a house and was given one, and in 1950 the nunnery was approved as a 'diocesan institute' under the name Missionaries of Charity. In 1965 it was approved by the Pope. By 1984 the missionaries numbered 1,700 sisters and 300 brothers, in 250 homes, and their founder was world-famous as Mother Teresa. All pledged themselves to the poorest of the poor. In Calcutta their concerns were the homeless, the incurable (especially lepers), the dying and the children (including the babies left to die, who usually were girls). By 1984 they had eighty-one homes for the dying.

Mother Teresa was tough against abortion and felt a special debt to Francis of Assisi, Elizabeth of Thuringia and Vincent de Paul.

It was a remarkable sign of a changing world when in March 1991 the Albanian government allowed its most famous citizen into her native land to open a little religious house.

THE 'DESTRUCTION' OF THE UNIATS

The Uniats were Roman Catholics who were allowed both the use of Eastern rites instead of the Latin rite or its translation, and certain Eastern customs like a married clergy. Some were in the Near East, especially Lebanon. Those in Europe could be described unkindly as former Eastern Orthodox who, under the pressure of the Austro-Hungarian Empire, had accepted the prayer for the Pope into their liturgy and the right of Rome to approve their choice of bishops. But this change from Eastern Orthodoxy to Rome had mostly happened a long time ago, at the so-called Union of Brest-Litovsk in 1595, from which Union the name Uniat came. The Uniats themselves resented the description Uniat: they were Roman Catholics of the Eastern Church.

When Russian armies captured Eastern Europe in 1944–5, five main bodies of Uniats passed under the rule of Moscow or its satellites. Much the largest lived in that part of the Ukraine which formerly was Austro-Hungarian, numbering perhaps 4.5 million. Next were the Uniats in modern Romania, where they mostly lived in Transylvania which was also once Austro-Hungarian; they were Romanian by race and numbered several hundred thousand. Next were the Ruthenians, once in Austro-Hungary, then in the far eastern tip of modern Czechoslovakia and in the south-east of Poland before the Second World War; now, they were partly in the Ukraine and partly, something like 300,000 people, in a single diocese of Prešov at the eastern tip of Czechoslovakia. Then there was a small Uniat Church in Bulgaria, about 10,000 people, and a larger one in Hungary, probably 200,000 or more.

The forces making for the destruction of the Uniats were two: the Stalinist State and the Orthodox Church. The Orthodox Church always believed that these peoples had, so long ago, been forcibly and unjustly separated from its communion. The Orthodox realized that the Uniat liturgy was their own; that the spirituality was theirs; that Uniat priests were married like theirs; that the Uniats need only drop the name of the Pope from their rite and take no notice of the Vatican and they would be Eastern Orthodox and they would lose nothing in religion but would end a schism troublesome in Eastern lands. The Stalinist governments of the Ukraine, Romania, Bulgaria and Czechoslovakia fiercely resented Churches which owed allegiance to the Vatican, and which they fancied to be the agent of the Americans. They found that, if they forced the Uniats to drop the Pope, they were backed by the responsible heads of the Orthodox Churches – the Patriarch Alexei of Moscow, who had stature: Patriarch Justinian of Bucharest, who had stature; and the Orthodox Metropolitan of Prague, who had no stature whatever.

The Stalinist regimes had no conception of how to achieve this Christian reunion morally, because their only doctrine of government was force. They imprisoned the Uniat bishops, killed a few, caused others to die by inhuman treatment and kept others in long terms of confinement. They held synods which they packed with their frightened supporters. These synods voted to leave the Roman Catholic Church and asked to be admitted to the Orthodox Church.

A less violent reunion by law would have had a better chance. Some able and good Uniats felt the schism between themselves and the Orthodox to be a stain on Christian charity. They regarded the mention of the Pope's name in their rite as unimportant and easy to sacrifice if some of their people found it repugnant; they preferred more local government of the Church, with less interference from Rome; they felt religiously at home within the Orthodox Churches, for their way of worship hardly changed; and they were persuaded by the State's media that the Vatican was corrupted into a lackey of warmongers. The Uniats who opted to lead the union were not all yes-men, as was proved when some of the Ukrainians who fled to the United States ended up in the Orthodox Church and not the Catholic. But under the conditions of a Stalinist union, where agreement with the State meant promotion and disagreement meant exile or worse, a lot of Uniats thought the choice to be clear. Most of them went underground. To go underground was hardly to go into literal catacombs but to attend Orthodox churches for regular services and occasionally to put themselves at risk by welcoming into the home some travelling disguised priest who was a Roman Catholic in the Uniat mode.

The Uniats in Ukraine

The Ukrainians had a national feeling which was against the Russians. They wished for more autonomy from Moscow, if not for total independence. Ukraine was the single place where, if they had not been barbaric, the Nazi occupying authorities could have created an independent state in which the people would have backed Germany against Moscow. The Uniat metropolitan at the beginning of the war, the legendary giant Szepticky, hailed the Germans as giving them freedom, denounced them for what they did to the Jews and supported the formation of Ukrainian units of the German army against Russia. As with all peoples who had no political mode of expression, the Ukrainians' nationalism was focused through their Churches.

The KGB regarded the Uniats, with reason, as an expression of Ukrainian dissent from Russia. They arrested the metropolitan Slipyj and all his four bishops for cooperating with the Germans. They faked a synod, threatened the voters at the synod and forced the 'election' of suitable members of the synod. In March 1946 the Uniat 'synod' in Lvov cathedral voted for the end of union with Rome and for unity with Moscow. The KGB used violence and long exile against anyone who dissented. The best leader of the Ukrainian movement for union with Moscow, Father Kostelnyk of Lvov, was killed by a Ukrainian guerrilla.

After more than seventeen years of imprisonment, in 1963 the

Uniat metropolitan Slipyj was released on condition that he did not talk. He went into exile at Rome. Sometimes he still wore his prison garb, to show that his was a suffering Church. In 1971, as Pope Paul VI moved for reconciliation with the East, Slipyj could hold his peace no longer, despite his understanding. He talked of the cruel destruction of his Church. They were, he said, 54 million people before 1917 and since the First World War they had lost 10 million, by famine or air raids or war or religious persecution or by the deporting of thousands. Since the Uniat Church was made illegal in 1946, and many of their people were forced into the Russian Orthodox Church, they had been able to celebrate the mass only in 'catacombs'. Speaking in Rome, he denounced the Vatican for its silence and failure to protest at the persecution of the Uniats by the Russians. Lately Paul VI sent representatives to the Moscow council to pay respects at the election of the new Patriarch of Moscow, Pimen. There Pimen had declared the old union of the Ukrainians with Rome, the so-called Union of Brest-Litovsk, to be null and void. Yet not a single Roman Catholic present protested at this speech. The Uniats did not like the new Vatican policy of 'openness' to the East because they believed that it would lead to weakness over the persecutions and repression which they suffered.

Slipyj, still no patriarch but now a cardinal, died in 1984 at the age of ninety-two. To the end he was militant against the Russians.

Meanwhile the Ukrainians, not least because of Pope John Paul II, began to take things into their own hands. They were Orthodox congregations, if they wished to be legal, so they started to exercise the power of the congregation in affecting what their priests did and who was appointed. In quite a number of places they possessed the legal right to elect their parish priest. They started to exercise it. They refused to elect Orthodox priests and chose priests whom they knew to be in heart Uniat. In this way several former Uniat churches and congregations, though nominally and legally Russian Orthodox congregations, became Uniat congregations in disguise. In the first three months of 1984 the authorities tried to stop this practice by forcibly closing thirty churches in Western Ukraine.

The Uniats of Prešov in Czechoslovakia

At the far eastern tip of the post-1945 Czechoslovak state were still some 300,000 Uniats in the rolling hills of Ruthenia. Since the Russians had abolished the Uniat Church in the Ukraine, it was important to them that the Uniats just across the border should go the same way.

In 1950 the Stalinist Czech government held a synod or pseudo-synod at Prešov which voted to abolish the Union with Rome and declared that all the Uniats of Czechoslovakia were Orthodox. A month later the Prague government gave these decisions the force of law, said that the Uniat Church was illegal and handed to the Orthodox Church (till then, 35,000 in the whole country) the Uniats' churches, manses and property. Bishop Gojdic of Prešov was condemned to imprisonment for life and died in jail ten years later. His auxiliary bishop, Hopko, was imprisoned for a few years and was then confined to a monastery. Priests who refused to become Orthodox were thrown with their families out of their manses into the street and put into labour camps.

Uniats could not get education for their children unless they declared themselves to be Orthodox. It was made illegal for the rare priests of the Latin rite to minister to ex-Uniats. More than a third of the Uniat priests became Orthodox. Where the ex-Uniat priest refused to be Orthodox, hastily trained Orthodox priests were put in and ministered to tiny congregations. Some Uniats went on as 'Orthodox' in their same church with their same ex-Uniat priest. Some attended the Orthodox services till better days might come. And some abstained from going to church.

Then came 1968, and Dubček, and the Prague Spring, and for a moment near-democracy in Czechoslovakia. In this open climate charges poured down upon the government that the 'abolition' of the Uniat Church had been a vile injustice. The Uniat Church was again made legal. One Uniat priest who returned from a forced-labour camp to his village had to marry thirty-six couples on his first Sunday.

But then, who owned the ex-Uniat now Orthodox churches and manses? And suppose a Uniat priest in 1950 said that he was Orthodox and went on in the parish and now said that he was Uniat again, should the people go back to his altar or was he a traitor? The government decided to hold a vote in each parish to decide whether the parish wished to be Uniat or Orthodox. Mostly this happened without trouble. In many parishes the people voted unanimously for the Uniats; and then, if their old ex-priest, expelled eighteen years before, was still to be found in retirement or in a lay occupation, he returned in a triumphal procession. The Uniats got the cathedral of Prešov on 7 July 1968, not before the Orthodox took away the furniture. But the Orthodox kept the bishop's palace hard by, and the seminary. In a few parishes there were struggles, locked church doors were broken down, crowds booed outside manses occupied by Orthodox priests who refused to leave. In a few cases services were disturbed – Orthodox women pelted a Uniat priest with rotten eggs during a service, windows were broken by stones during a service, a Uniat verger was stabbed by an Orthodox priest.

And meanwhile Russian tanks invaded Czechoslovakia, and in time Dubček disappeared from politics and the country was back to the harder Communist line. For a time the Uniats were again at risk as hostile to the Communist State. By October 1970 the government had decided for their legality but had handed thirty parishes (where no vote had yet been taken) to the Orthodox. The final count of parishes – voted or not-voted – was 205 Uniat and eighty-seven Orthodox, but the eighty-seven were small mountain parishes. No Uniat had been ordained for eighteen years, and the clergy were old.

There may seem to have been a lot of fuss over whether or not the Pope's name is mentioned in a church service, but underneath lay something closer to the passions of humanity: whether or not a Ruthenian people could feel free under Czechs and Slovaks.

Outside Czechoslovakia, some Roman Catholics regretted the restoration of the Uniat Church as a blow to the new ecumenical spirit, and they wanted the Uniats to feel at home in Orthodoxy. Such an attitude had no realism where a Church had been destroyed by violence. And the Orthodox could hardly be ecumenical when some of 'their' churches were occupied by force. Everything hung on the 1950 synod of Prešov – was it a synod or a pseudo-synod; was it legal or illegal?

The Uniats in Romania

Just over half the Roman Catholics in Romania were Uniats; just under half had a Latin mass. If they were Latins they were almost all Hungarian by race; if they were Uniats they were almost all Romanian by race. The Uniats were the second most important Church in Romania – 1.5 million people.

The Second World War was disastrous for both Latins and Uniats because the Romanians regarded them as likely to be traitors to Romania. On top of that, the postwar Communist government was glad to do all it could to repress religion where it could do so with the blessing of the religious-minded Romanian people.

The Uniats had an intransigent orator, Monsignor Suciu, who administered the diocese of Blaj. In tremendous sermons in the Latin cathedral of Bucharest he denounced materialism and drew crowds of Orthodox to hear him. He visited the parishes of his vast diocese and was greeted by the people like a victorious general. He collected much private money to replace the lost State money for schools.

From the end of June 1948 the press ran a campaign against the Vatican – the Church of the rich, the Church bound to the capitalists of America, the Church dedicated to exploiting the workers. To the astonishment and dismay of the bishops, 423 priests adhered to the government programme. A 'representative' meeting of nearly forty priests in the schoolroom at Cluj – where the government chose those who took part and drafted the chairman's speech and police guarded the meeting – unanimously asked for admission to the Orthodox Church. Since none of the bishops would cooperate, all six were imprisoned and all died in prison, some after having helped to dig the Danube canal. Juliu Hossu was the one who later captured the affection of a helpless West. For a time he worked down a coal-mine, but he survived. In his last years he was confined to two rooms in a monastery. Rashly Pope Paul VI sent him a secret message that he intended to make him a cardinal. Hossu pleaded that the Pope should do no such thing. So he remained a cardinal within the Pope's breast until after his death.

The Uniat Church was destroyed as a public force almost as

ruthlessly as the religions in Albania; the difference being that in Albania Christians could find nowhere to say their prayers except in the catacombs, whereas in Romania the Uniats could find a historic Christian Church which worshipped publicly and was a power among the people. Quite a number of former Uniat priests accepted new work within the Orthodox Church. In Transylvania they could move to the Hungarian Roman Catholic Church with a Hungarian liturgy, where the priest must by law be Hungarian, though they did not know Hungarian. The fate of Transylvanian Uniat Catholicism was one of the calamities to the Catholic Church which came out of the Second World War. It was a calamity destined not to last.

Since the bishops had been martyred, the underground Uniats for a time got their ministrations from five underground bishops. Each of these was discovered and sentenced to twenty-five years' imprisonment. After the twenty-five years, one was dead, one had psychological weakness due to torture, two had incurable illness and the fifth resumed his activity (in 1979) and found five active underground priests.

Just as Patriarch Alexei of Moscow welcomed the return to the true fold of the Uniat Church forcibly abolished in the Ukraine, Partiarch Justinian of Romania welcomed the return to the true Church of the Romanian Uniats. Neither of these leaders, who in other contexts did so much for their Churches, doubted publicly whether a government should reunite Churches by terror.

The Uniats Elsewhere

In 1939 Bulgaria had a small Roman Catholic population, some 70,000 people, mostly with a Latin liturgy and unmarried priests but including 10,000 Uniats with an Eastern liturgy and married priests. Generally the Roman Catholics were treated badly in Bulgaria between 1948 and 1975, and for a time the Uniats among them disappeared from view.

There were also Uniats in Yugoslavia (50,000), Hungary (200,000) and Poland (200,000 Ukrainians). These Uniat Churches were not troubled by the State more than the Roman Catholic Church as a whole. None of them was ever made illegal.

In Poland the Catholic Church had always felt the Uniats as

an intrusion, not just because they had a different way of worship and married clergy but because by means of it they stressed that they were Ukrainians rather than Poles. In 1947 a Polish official was murdered by a Ukrainian. In reply the Polish government, which badly needed settlers in its new areas seized from Germany, forced many Ukrainian Uniats into western Poland. A small number crept back later. The forced emigrants left behind 689 churches. By 1989 half or more of these churches had vanished or were in ruins; 245 of them, including the cathedral at Przemysl, were in use by the Roman Catholic Church of Poland; 28 were used by the Eastern Orthodox Church; 70 were used for various secular purposes, including 9 museums. After 1947 there was no Uniat bishop.

4
Show Trials

Nowhere except in Albania and with the Uniat Churches did the Stalinist governments think it right or possible to destroy Churches by law or decree or police action. But they thought it possible to use all those methods to help religion to die out among the people. In the Stalinist years the show trial was common. Put a famous archbishop or a troublesome pastor into the dock, produce squalid evidence about his behaviour, perhaps torture him in prison to extract a confession which could be used in court, and then control the reports of the newspapers and radio to make the maximum disgrace for the Church.

All show trials had another motive as well as propaganda. In the earliest years after the Nazis, it was not easy to distinguish a show trial from a trial thought to be just retribution. Where an archbishop was accused of Fascism during a Nazi occupation, that was useful in publicity against the Church but the motive was more vengeance than propaganda. Where it was impossible to accuse a prelate of such behaviour because he was famous for resistance to Nazis, the propaganda motive was the stronger, but there was also the motive of depriving the Church of force among its leaders and so making it cooperate with a Communist government.

There were many such show trials. Three of them reverberated through Europe: the trials of Father Tiso in Slovakia, Archbishop Stepinac in Yugoslavia and Cardinal Mindszenty in Hungary.

TISO IN SLOVAKIA

Josef Tiso was the son of well-to-do Slovakian peasants. He trained for the priesthood at Vienna and became the parish priest of

Bánovce in Slovakia. He was still the rural dean of Bánovce when
he died.

Between the World Wars the friction between Czechs and
Slovaks in the artificially created state of Czechoslovakia was
worse because the Czech leadership was Protestant and liberal
and more than three-quarters of the Slovaks were not only Catholics but rural Catholics with priests as their leaders. Tiso became
one of the political heads of a Catholic Slovak party which
demanded Slovak autonomy from the Czechs. Although he was a
politician, he remained a good priest.

In 1938–9 Hitler broke up Czechoslovakia and annexed
Bohemia to the Reich. This forced Slovakia to be an independent
state with an 'independence' conforming to German foreign policy.
Monsignor Tiso was its president and the Pope sent his blessing.
Under German pressure, Tiso's assistants liked Nazi methods. Tiso
remained President of Slovakia for its entire period of independence, from late in 1939 to April 1945 – the only time in history
that Slovakia was a sovereign state. Then he fled to Austria,
where the Americans found him and handed him over to Slovak
Communists who brought him back in chains to Bratislava. His
trial ran from December 1946 to April 1947.

The question of guilt was not simple. There were photographs
of him making the Nazi salute or having tea with Dr Goebbels,
but such were not capital crimes. When the Nazis and his own
extremists forced anti-Jew legislation on Slovakia he was the head
of an immoral government; but evidence was offered that he
wanted to resign and did not do so only to use his dispensing power
to help many individual Jews. When in August 1944 units of the
Slovak army rose in rebellion to help the advancing Russians and
murdered a German general, Tiso invited the Germans to help;
and although the repression of the revolt was marred by atrocities,
he celebrated a mass of thanksgiving at Banská Bystrica and
afterwards decorated SS officers. Hours before his death he said
to the ministering priest that he died a martyr in the defence of
Christian civilization against Communism.

The ex-partisans and the ex-prisoners of concentration camps
were determined on his death. Since he was the only head of State
that Slovakia had ever had, many Slovaks admired him and
thought him a moderate surrounded by villains and regarded his

execution as a Communist injustice. The Slovak bishops appealed for clemency, there were demonstrations in his favour in the streets, but to no avail. He was hanged on 18 April 1947. The death of Tiso was bad for postwar Czechoslovakia, for some Slovaks venerate his memory. Photographs of him were sold in the streets, with the caption 'Slovak Martyr'.

Tiso's was the most agonizing of all the cases common under Nazi tyranny. You are an official of an immoral state. Do you resign because you cannot bear it, which clears your conscience but stops you from helping? Or do you put up with horrors because you can make them slightly less horrible by staying where you are? Tiso chose the second of the two evils as the lesser. The chief argument against resigning was that then the Nazis would turn Slovakia into another Bohemia, with another murderous despot in control. And he accepted the doctrine that only a non-democratic central Europe could protect Christendom from atheist regimes. He was (it seems) a sincere priest. But it is hard not to think that most sincere priests in his predicament would have felt forced to resign whatever the consequences.

The aim of his trial was more vengeance than propaganda. But if it was supposed to alienate Slovaks from their clergy it had the opposite effect.

STEPINAC IN YUGOSLAVIA

The country of Yugoslavia was an amalgam of different Slav peoples – Slovenes, Croats, Serbs, Montenegrins and Macedonians – together with a big group of non-Slavs who were Albanians and small groups of non-Slavs who were Hungarians in the north and Greek or Turkish in Macedonia. The country was the result of throwing together a miscellany of peoples who were left stranded by the collapse of two empires: the Ottoman and the Austro-Hungarian. Parts of the country – Montenegro especially – were very poor; parts of the north, like Slovenia, had shared in Austro-Hungarian prosperity.

The Nazis conquered the country in 1941 and did the obvious

thing: they annexed the more Germanic part of Slovenia and divided the rest into a Serbian state, where the religion of most of the inhabitants was Orthodox, and a Croat state, where the religion of most of the inhabitants was Catholic.

The puppet head of the Croat state was Ante Pavelić, whose early career included that of assassin. But Croatia also had a lot of Serbs. During 1941 to 1943 communal struggles raged, many Serbs were murdered by Croats and, since the separation between the two peoples was a religious separation, the Catholic Church in Croatia was accused of being part of the pogrom against Serbs. The Croatian ustasche – a private police force – murdered some 300,000 Serbs including 128 priests and three bishops, and destroyed 300 churches. A number of Catholic priests, especially a few Franciscans, were implicated in the massacres, though sometimes as ex-priests who were now ustasche officers. Several of the worst started as military chaplains. The murders were often accompanied by sadism. It was one of the tragedies of Christendom.

Croat priests and bishops made scattered protests. But mostly they were not vocal against the murders, for they lived under a reign of terror. Archbishop Sarić of Sarajevo wrote repeated panegyrics in praise of Pavelic. He fled to Switzerland at the end of the war.

When in 1945 Yugoslavia was reunited under a Communist partisan, Tito, revenge was the order of the day. Some 400 to 500 priests retreated over the northern border with the ustasche forces and surrendered to the British. They were handed over to Tito's forces and slaughtered without trial. An unknown number of Croat Catholic priests were murdered as Tito's forces advanced. A Croat Orthodox bishop and two priests were tried and hanged, and another bishop, a Russian emigré who was a Croat Orthodox bishop, was shot. Quite a number of priests and nuns were sent to jail. These were not show trials for propaganda: they were the grim pursuit of justice or revenge. The Bishop of Dubrovnik disappeared and no one ever knew what became of him, but some time later a body in bishop's clothes was discovered at the bottom of a well. Because Franciscans had taken part in the massacre of Serbs, the partisans killed all twenty-eight friars of a Franciscan house and threw from a bridge to their deaths seven

Franciscans who had nothing whatever to do with the massacres.

The head of the Croat Church, that is the Archbishop of Zagreb, the capital of Croatia, was the obvious target to assail. The archbishop was Aloysius Stepinac. He was the primate, and he did not flee.

Stepinac was born in 1895, the seventh child of a peasant family, and won two high medals for valour during the First World War – one from each side! For a time he followed his father into farming; he was not ordained priest till 1930, after a long training in Rome. Thereafter his career was brilliant: four years after his ordination as priest he was the coadjutor archbishop with right of succession (because the king refused to accept several other names as coadjutor), and three years after that he was Archbishop of Zagreb, at the age of only thirty-nine. At that time his people regarded him as a holy and wise man who could handle the strife of peoples and Churches in multiracial Yugoslavia. He was lean and handsome and laconic.

He was in favour of a separate Croatia, and when the state was set up after its occupation in April 1941 he welcomed it. He ordered a Te Deum to be sung in all parishes and saw in Croat independence the hand of God; he welcomed German troops in Zagreb. Every year of the war – including April 1945, when Hitler was finished – the Te Deum was sung on the anniversary of Croat independence. But when the Croats offered many Serbs the choice between conversion or death, he began a series of letters to protest to Pavelic – against the execution of Serbs, against the new laws against Jews and gypsies, against forced conversions, against the demolition of Orthodox churches, in favour of just treatment for the Jews, against the mass deportations of Jews, against the shooting of hostages. He hid some hunted Jews for a time in the roof of his palace, a castle which dominated Zagreb. He refused to let Jews wear their obligatory stars in church. He got huge crowds whenever he preached in his cathedral. In December 1941 he preached a strong sermon against the terror regime under which Croatia now lived. In October 1943 he preached a sermon which caused the extremist press to attack him for interfering in politics, and shortly afterwards his brother was executed by the Germans for being a partisan. Before the end Pavelic hated Stepinac but could not touch him. He was an extraordinary man. He could make rather too complimentary remarks about Pavelić. In April 1945, when Communist armies neared Zagreb and the bishops issued a pastoral letter against Communist wickedness, Stepinac's sermon in the cathedral denounced swearing.

The new Communist government at once fell into conflict with Stepinac. It made civil marriage compulsory and abolished the civil effect of religious marriage. It shut all the Catholic newpapers, and held rival meetings at the times of masses. It confiscated the property of the Church (the Church did not possess great estates in Yugoslavia), and banned the crucifix from schools, and destroyed shrines by the roadside, and abolished school worship, and prohibited choir practices, and got some schoolmasters to teach that Jesus never existed, and expelled monks and nuns from their houses (telling the nuns to go out and get married and have children) and banned them from teaching in schools, and occupied most of the seminaries. Near Zagreb, a crowd took from the cathedral the venerated image of Our Lady of Marija Bistrica, who was the aim of a Croatian annual pilgrimage and smashed it into little pieces in the square outside. All over the place slogans were painted on walls: 'Death to the Priests!' Policemen sat in church to listen to sermons.

Stepinac and the other surviving bishops protested against all this in a joint pastoral letter of September 1945, read from pulpits. The pastoral letter angered Tito, and not all the clergy agreed to read it.

The attack upon the Churches in Communist Yugoslavia had one motive hardly present in the other Communist states except Albania. Yugoslavia was an artificial country with racial tensions: how after such massacres would it survive as one country? Perhaps, since the main lines of divisions in the country were religious – Catholic, Orthodox, Muslim – if religion was weakened this would unify the state in a common, secular, Marxist way of society.

In the winter of 1945–6 the State set up show trials of priests accused of collaboration with the Nazis. They included Stepinac's secretary and the Franciscan provincial. After nine months in jail, these two linked Stepinac's name with the collaborators. The secretary said that the archbishop's palace was a centre of terrorism, and that Stepinac's statement that his conscience was clear was not true.

At the end of September 1946 Stepinac was tried at Zagreb for alleged collaboration. Since the behaviour of the wartime Croat government had been brutal, it was easy to represent an archbishop who had stayed in office throughout its time as a compromiser. Before the trial opened, Marshal Tito said that he knew the accused to be guilty. The prosecutor charged Stepinac with blessing the terror gangs; he replied, 'I give my blessing to everyone who asks me for it.' In the last stages of the trial he repeatedly refused to defend himself; he said only, 'I did everything according to the Catholic moral law.' His address at the end of the trial attacked the government for all the injustices to the Church since the end of the war.

He was convicted of collaboration with the Nazis and of the forcible conversion of Serbs and was condemned to sixteen years' forced labour. No one in the West believed in the justice of the trial, and the Vatican excommunicated the officials who took part in the prosecution. Tito urged him to leave Yugoslavia, but he refused. In parts of the West he became something of a hero, so that in the United States church halls or high schools were named after him. In 1952 the Pope provocatively made him a cardinal. The government called him the ex-archbishop, but he said he was not the ex-archbishop but the archbishop. For the last nine years of his life he was under house arrest rather than in prison; he died in 1960.

He never compromised, and the hard stance of a man who had no power was to delay the reconciliation between Church and State. Unexpectedly the government allowed his funeral to be celebrated in Zagreb cathedral and his body to be buried behind the high altar. There it became at once a shrine for prayer. Some churchmen afterwards looked back upon this funeral as the turning-point for the Church in Croatia.

His memory remained controversial in Yugoslavia. Had he compromised more than an archbishop should under a reign of terror? Or was he a martyr? The trial festered in Yugoslav memory. The argument went on. On the twenty-first anniversary of Stepinac's death the chief prosecuting lawyer at Stepinac's trial, backed by the chief minister of Croatia, took the chance to make wild accusations against the Church and Stepinac. Kuharić, the then Archbishop of Zagreb, replied: we are deeply offended as a

Church; we need a historical judgment. Kuharic recorded Stepinac's defence of Serbs and Slovene priests and Jews. Stepinac's memory could have grotesque results. A pastor and a mosaic artist got two months in jail and a big fine because their church put in a mosaic on which visitors thought they recognized in one of the saints the face of Stepinac. The incriminated part of the mosaic was destroyed.

Until 1953 the bishops were intensely unpopular among some of the people. Their confirmation tours were marred by physical assaults upon them. A Slovene suffragan bishop had a can of petrol thrown over him at a railway station and the petrol set alight – his assailant was given ten days in prison. Another suffragan was beaten and his priest-companion was killed; the two assailants got only five months and three months. Before 1953 many bishops suffered mob violence on their tours. Age did not save them. One was assaulted though he was over eighty. After 1953 this mob violence was stopped by government policy.

MINDSZENTY IN HUNGARY

In historic tradition Hungary had a great see: Esztergom, where the occupant had a national status. It was a country with many Protestants, Lutheran and Reformed, but most people were Catholics.

Hungary was not by nature a Communist state. At the end of the war it was still an old-fashioned feudal society where a thousand families owned a quarter of the land and where the Catholic Church owned more than half a million hectares by way of endowment. The Russian invading armies behaved like soldiers out of hand, with rapes and looting and murder, so the people did not welcome their occupiers despite their gratitude for the disappearance of the Nazis. Moscow at once selected a list for a provisional government, and in March 1945 that government changed the ownership of more than a third of the land. It was a vast redistribution to peasants in small lots. The Catholic Church kept only a little over 1,100 hectares as endowment and therefore was left, for the first time in its long history, dependent on the giving of the faithful. The State continued to pay a minimum wage to the clergy out of the funds which it took. The few who would have nothing to do with the State refused the State stipend.

In November 1945 there was a general election. This was to be the freest election ever held in Hungary before 1990. It produced a majority for the conservative Smallholders party and a Calvinist pastor, Zoltan Tildy, as Prime Minister. Only 17 per cent voted for the Communists. But the election was immediately followed by one of the worst inflations in the history of the world. Russian forces exploited the Hungarian economy for the sake of Moscow, the West was in slump, every penny of Hungarian savings was worthless – the experience killed whatever chances of democracy remained. Under the umbrella of the occupying power, the Communist Party under Rákosi, in control of the police, hunted out former officials, attacked the bourgeois, controlled the press and much reduced the number of Protestants by driving out 240,000 Germans. By 1948 Rákosi, still with only a minority to back him, had total control and had instituted a regime of terror. The state was a colony of a Stalinist Soviet Union.

Cardinal Seredi, the primate during the war, was already dying when he welcomed the Russians. Pope Pius XII appointed to succeed him the most extraordinary prelate of the twentieth century. It was a choice with long consequences.

Jozsef Mindszenty was a political priest in the Hungarian Revolution of 1919 and was at that time a hostage of the Communists. Between the wars he won distinction as a parish priest in his home countryside. In March 1944, ten days after the Nazis occupied Hungary, he was made Bishop of Veszprem, aged fifty-two. He protested against the shutting of Jews in ghettos and against the Nazis continuing to resist the later Russian onslaught to the useless devastation of Hungary and was put into a cell where he heard Nazi shooting of hostages nearby. Just before Easter 1945 his guards vanished and the Russians arrived. Immediately he began to protest against what the new authorities did to the Churches. This stalwart stance drew the attention of Rome. He became primate in October 1945 and a cardinal a year later. His sermon at the enthronement could hardly be heard in the cathedral because a storm howled through the windows shattered by shellfire.

The question was whether in a government of terror a Church did better or worse if it compromised with the State. To get sacraments to the people it needed a legal status. To have a legal status it must do what the State wanted and not criticize the policy or the leaders of the State. If this was humiliating, a prelate must sometimes put up with humiliation or the necessity for flattery of politicians because the higher good was that the people should get the sacraments and the faith which they needed. Patriarch Alexei in Moscow, Patriarch Justinian in Bucharest, Patriarch Kiril in Bulgaria, the Lutheran Bishop Schönherr in East Berlin and the Lutheran archbishops in Latvia and Estonia all helped their Churches by a certain willingness to play along with the State; that is, to make the best of a bad situation, to get such freedoms for the Church as were still allowed, and in return to lay on courtesy or flattery for the State leaders, so that the State regarded the Church, however lamentable and backward, as a help to it in being accepted by some of the people. At its best the policy hardly corrupted integrity. At its worst – Justinian's successor Justin in Bucharest, or Nikodim of Leningrad – it was felt to be scandalous among the clergy and the people. Is it really the higher good to be silent in the face of injustice?

Mindszenty had no compromise in his nature. The experience of being a hostage of both Communists and Nazis left him without an intellectual (as distinct from a physical) fear of policemen. And, in a country forced into the extreme left of politics, he was a traditional Catholic Habsburg-minded monarchist. He believed in his historic place as primate, the crowner of the kings. His appeals to the West helped the starving people against inflation and famine. Soon he was a symbol of strength for all the anti-Communist yearnings in the country, which included most of the people. He was vastly popular and not in the least conciliatory. The country experienced a religious revival, because of its desperation and its antagonism to Marxist materialism. Vast numbers, Protestants among them, marched on pilgrimage to the Catholic shrines. Religion was very near to politics. Mindszenty was the figurehead. He was the most dangerous foe of Rákosi's regime. He publicly said that the government was the worst in the history of Hungary.

The controlled press started to concentrate venom upon him as a Fascist, a former ally of the Nazis. He was arrested just after Christmas Day 1948, accused of spying, treason, and manipulating currency. In prison he was tortured ferociously and beaten into signing a confession, though not the 'full' confession which the police desired.

His trial was a spectacle. He admitted everything. He was sentenced to life imprisonment. The Pope and the United Nations condemned this trial. Thousands of students marched through Brooklyn in his support. The bishops still at liberty reached a weak agreement with the government in which the Church approved the Communist regime and in return was given a subsidy from its own former funds. Citizens who professed religion publicly began to lose their jobs; the religious houses were dissolved with inhumanity.

In October 1956 the memorial service for a former Communist minister executed with gross injustice turned into a student demonstration. A colossal statue of Stalin in the park was pulled down. When police opened fire, a demonstration turned into a revolution. There was fighting with Russian tanks in the streets.

Mindszenty's guards released him without orders. The country people, most of them Protestants, crowded in to kiss his clothes. He at once drove to Budapest. The journey was delayed because at each village he had to speak to a crowd and write autographs till four o'clock in the morning. On 31 October he was escorted into Buda by a triumphal procession and peeling bells. On the evening of 3 November he made a radio broadcast to the nation. He backed the fight for freedom as a great act of the Hungarian people, he asked the Russians to desist, and he called for a free election under international control.

Immediately after the broadcast, news came that the Russians were pouring back into the city in strength. Zóltan Tildy, the Calvinist, rang him from Parliament to ask him to come. At Parliament he found nothing but confusion, and Tildy running up a white flag. He left, but the place was already ringed by Russian tanks. He hid his cassock under his coat and between two lines of Russian tanks reached the American embassy. The West was appealed to and said that it was helpless. Pope Pius XII condemned the repression of the Hungarian Revolution.

Mindszenty remained in the American embassy at Budapest for fifteen years. He refused every chance to move. John XXIII offered him a post in the Curia. Mindszenty said that he wanted to be among his people. In a little apartment at the American embassy he lived on, a standing reproach to the regime and a standing embarrassment to anyone who wanted reconciliation.

In 1971 the Americans told Pope Paul VI that Mindszenty needed care and that his presence in the embassy hampered friendship between Hungary and the United States. The Pope ordered Mindszenty to come out. He went to Rome and then to the Hungarian seminary in Vienna, to be just across the frontier from his people, and wrote his memoirs. The Hungarian government pointed out that for him to publish his memoirs would break the agreement under which he had been released. He took no notice. He sent a copy of the draft to the Pope, who said that he loved it but that to publish it could aggravate the predicament of the Hungarian Church. His speeches in the West against Bolshevism caused some Hungarian bishops to ask Rome to silence him. It was clear that he intended to publish. Mindszenty, said Cardinal Casaroli, 'is like granite, and he can be just as disagreeable as granite'.[1]

On 1 November 1973, therefore, the Pope asked him to resign the see of Esztergom, saying that this would provide for the care of his diocese and would enable him to be freer about his memoirs. Mindszenty refused. He said publicly that he could not resign because of the situation of the Hungarian Church. And, if he resigned, a Bolshevik government would control the choice of his successor.

On 5 February 1974 the Pope declared the see of Esztergom vacant and nominated an apostolic administrator for the diocese. This was a high-handed exercise of papal prerogative, but had precedent from the days of Napoleon. There was anger at the Pope from Hungarian exiles and other anti-Communist Western Catholics. An Italian newspaper talked of the Pope offering Mindszenty's head on a platter to King Herod. Demonstrations against the Pope disturbed the inside and the outside of St Peter's at Rome.

1. Quoted in J. Közi-Horvath, *Cardinal Mindszenty* (English trans. 1979), p.100.

Mindszenty then published his memoirs. They are the most readable book written by a bishop in the twentieth century. They are the only autobiography of a cardinal to end with an attack upon his Pope. They were much translated. On 6 May 1975 he died at the clinic of the Brothers of Mercy in Vienna. He was the supreme symbol of the fight of Eastern Europe against Communism. No one except the Holy Office did more to dig a gulf between the Communist Party and the Churches.

The high-handed act of Pope Paul VI in dismissing him helped the plight of the Catholics in Hungary. From the disappearance of Mindszenty, Rome and Budapest found talking a little easier. Early in 1990, during the age of perestroika, they thought it safe to consider whether Mindszenty might be rehabilitated. On 8 February 1990 they celebrated a requiem mass for Mindszenty in Esztergom cathedral. And then the main square of Esztergom, outside the palace of the archbishop, was renamed 'Cardinal Mindszenty's Square'. The acting president of Hungary, speaking at the renaming ceremony, said that Mindszenty's trial was 'a show trial' and its justice was to be investigated. Early in May 1991 they solemnly restored the exiled body to a grave in Esztergom. Mindszenty was only a partner in that diocese for less than three years, more than forty years before. Yet it felt like a coming home.

5

The Effects of the Marxist Attack

The results of the attack upon Christianity in Eastern Europe are impossible to assess in terms of success or failure. If religion is belonging to a church and going to it, Eastern Europe was less religious in 1985 than in 1945; but so was Western Europe, and that was nothing to do with Marxism. People could be against Churches for many reasons which were nothing to do with Communist governments. In Poland the Catholic Church was so powerful that it generated anticlericalism among people who were frightened of an excess of Church in politics. In Yugoslavia the religions were so involved in the tensions which divided the people that intellectuals who wanted a unified Yugoslavia might be against religions. In Prague or in Budapest or in East Berlin, philosophers might reach conclusions which rejected Christianity as well as Marxism, the difference being that they could speak the denial of Christianity but had to be silent on the denial of Marxism; but the repudiation of Christianity by such minds was nothing to do with Marxism, except that they became a little more influential in the State because governments liked them.

In all countries there were fewer clergy; the average age of a priest or pastor rose steadily (but this was in small part because the average age of men and women rose steadily); many more old churches were closed than new churches were built; fewer people attended services (except in Poland). But all these things happened simultaneously in Western Europe, where no one discouraged the young from attending church or forced scientific atheism into them during school or told them that to become a priest was to make oneself useless to society. We cannot take a statistic of 1985 and compare it with a statistic of 1945 and say with any certainty a decline has been caused by the power of Marxism.

All over Europe, West as well as East, many members of the intelligentsia rejected religious faith or greatly revised inherited religious axioms because they now saw the Bible as only one historical document among others or because their science made them think that miracles did not happen. But in the West religion was respected by a lot of intelligent people who were not religious, as an experience, or as an emotional element in the make-up of many men and women which they could not themselves share, or as an idealism with good moral effects. In parts of the East, especially in the Soviet Union, the irreligious had been trained to despise religion as a human illusion which was like witchcraft or superstition, and they were also trained not to regard the moral ideals of the religious as other than harmful because they led to the oppression of the poor. The prevailing mood in the universities of Europe was secular; but in Eastern Europe, except in the Catholic University at Lublin in Poland, its secularity was more anti-religious. The systematic teaching of materialism to young children in the schools will have had consequences for the future which are unknown, even though a lot of this teaching was ineffective.

By about 1975, several Communist societies had the feeling that the campaign against religion had not achieved the success for which its founders had hoped. The reason for this feeling was the admission that religion is not the necessary ally of the capitalists, or of the oppressors of the poor, or of the supposedly imperialistic Americans. The attribution of these demonic qualities was seen by a younger realism to be itself an illusion. And if religion is accepted as not doing the harm which was imagined in the crisis of society after the Second World War, why bother with all the militancy, and the expenditure on atheist lecturers, and the locking up of recalcitrant pastors which only makes martyrs? It was recognized, everywhere outside Albania and Czechoslovakia and the Soviet Union and perhaps Romania, that aggression did not pay.

Kasimir Kakol, the Polish minister for Church affairs, discussed in 1976 how to fight Polish religion. 'The State', he said, 'must avoid aggression. If the Church is attacked too violently it puts itself forward as a besieged city and wins popularity. And such aggression is bad for the nation and society because it cuts the people into two.' After the fall of Khrushchev, the Russian leaders asked themselves whether his persecution of the Church had been a success. They had doubts. Churches had been closed but the congregation had, so to speak, gone underground. A public congregation is easier to control or to influence than a private. Without priests, a congregation is more easily open to the radical and the fanatic. If the closure of a church, as in more than one place in remote Siberia, has the effect of encouraging a congregation of Jehovah's Witnesses, that is not a gain for the State. And at this time was the first glimmer of a perception, slow to form in a Russia that revered Lenin who hated religion, that it was not intelligent to put a lot of simple believers against the State unless that could be held to be a necessity.

ACTS OF AGGRESSION

This more pragmatic attitude did not mean that acts of aggression were not committed still against churches and church people, in some countries more than others. When they happened, they were usually taken to be another proof that aggression does not pay. Here are three examples out of many: from Yugoslavia, the Soviet Union and Poland.

Medjugorje

After the death of Cardinal Stepinac in 1960, the relation of Church and State in Yugoslavia grew steadily more 'normal', with quite a lot of liberty for the Churches and not much nastiness to religion by State officials (except for a time in Bosnia-Hercegovina) and in 1966 an agreement with Rome (called not a concordat but a protocol). There still remained the materialist education in schools, though, and the exclusion of pious persons from higher posts.

Probably it was important that the crisis of Medjugorje happened in the state of Hercegovina. In 1981 the Virgin appeared several times as a slim lady on a hill to six children aged eleven to eighteen. Quickly, more quickly than usual, pilgrims gathered at the place. The Bishop of Mostar thought nothing of the visions but ordered an enquiry. His commission included nine theologians and two psychiatrists. Two said the appearances were genuine, eleven said they were not. However, the bishop's endeavours to suppress the cult were frustrated by the police. They had the children examined by psychiatrists, arrested the pastor of the parish where it happened, put a cordon round the hill, imprisoned some Franciscans who printed the story in their magazine and banned the magazine, with the result that the pilgrims were far more numerous than before. A ham-fisted State helped to make a doubtful shrine acceptable to the people. The effect on the local people was a marvel: fervent religious practice, 500 at mass every morning, 2,500 at mass on Sundays and half of them young, and many applications to become monks or nuns. As with other shrines, there came a time when the truth or otherwise of its origin ceased to matter. People who came there found peace and joy and an invitation to holiness and did not care how it started.

Zagreb television calculated that, by 1987, 8 to 10 million pilgrims had come to the shrine. This gave the Communist Party a problem of conscience. Their financiers wanted to make money out of so much travel. Their men of principle said that you must not make money by encouraging superstition. However, they started to allow hostels for the pilgrims.

Dudko in Moscow

As the illegal samizdat literature grew during the 1960s and 1970s, the old Russia spoke again, through duplicated or badly printed paper, but loud and clear for all that. We sit on the ruins of the churches they destroyed at the Revolution and weep at our downfall. Yet, a surprising thing is happening. The sons of the Communists are becoming Christians. The Russian soul bears God within it. What has atheism given? It has taken away our history and our culture. Can you build anything on it? Let us go back to our classical literature and remember the bells of our churches. Atheism will soon become a swear-word in Russia.

The worst moment of those years was the recantation of Dimitri Dudko. This was a sign both of the increasing liberty which churchmen enjoyed and of the sudden cruelty if they tested the State too far.

Dudko had a State record in that even while he was a theological student he served more than eight years in a labour camp. He was ordained at last in 1960 and two years later was a priest at St

Nicholas of the Transfiguration in Moscow. There he made a mark, as preacher and confessor. The people loved him as a man of affection and wisdom and depth of spirituality. There were lots of young people.

Eleven years later Dudko felt strong enough to start after services a meeting for questions and answers. As a brains trust of one, he was gifted. He taught Christian doctrine and referred to ethics if the subject came up and associated atheism with the devastating immoralities of Russian life. But he did not attack the regime or talk politics. In thirteen years he thought that he had baptized 5,000 adults. St Nicholas's church became the talk of Moscow.

Dudko's influence was too threatening and the crowds too numerous for the authorities to stomach. In May 1974 Patriarch Pimen dismissed him from the parish. He was moved to a village church fifty miles from Moscow. People in Moscow came fifty miles to join the village congregation. After eighteen months he was injured in a lorry accident that might have been engineered, and after two years he was dismissed from the village parish despite the petition of the congregation. He was moved to another village about the same distance from Moscow and there started the first ever parish magazine in the Soviet Union. Instantly State pressure to make the congregation dismiss him began. There was local vandalism, the names of young people who came to him were taken, his mail was interfered with, his son was forced to be examined by a psychiatrist when the boy was found to wear a baptismal cross, a service was interrupted by police who took the names of all present. The crowds persisted, but some of the young could not bear the tension and started to leave him. He lost a lot of sympathy when he called for the canonization of Russian martyrs of the twentieth century, especially Tsar Nicholas II and his family.

It took the State more than four years to decide to arrest Father Dudko. This was a big parish priest, with a numerous following, and of a stature not lessened because his sufferings made him famous in the West. The arrest (on 15 January 1980) produced a wave of petitions from Orthodox Christians in Russia and eminent churchmen outside Russia.

On 20 June 1980 Dudko appeared on Soviet television to recant his errors: 'I renounce what I have done and I regard my so-called struggle with godlessness as a struggle with Soviet power.' The next day he was allowed to return home. A few months later he was appointed to a large and rich parish twenty-five miles from Moscow.

The recantation shocked both the West and his spiritual children inside Russia. Some said that it could not be genuine, it was not his style, it was drafted by the KGB and he had accepted it only under threats to his family. His flock deserted him. No longer did the crowd make the journey from Moscow. He was alone, and felt it a suffering that he was alone. 'I cannot forgive myself for my weakness, and my heart is torn asunder seeing your confusion and hearing garbled interpretations.' The recantation of Dimitri Dudko was the loud success of the atheist State against the Orthodox Church in all the years between the death of Patriarch Alexei and the coming of glasnost. And yet it was no success. For by it the Soviet Union told the world that, despite all its lip-service to human rights, it was still willing to threaten with death someone merely because he tried to do good to the people in a way which it did not like and which had nothing criminal about it; and therefore that barbarism still reigned among its higher councils.

Popieluszko in Warsaw

Jerzy Popieluszko was the most vocal of the priests in favour of the Polish trade union Solidarity. He had a bond with the workers, and several thousand at his services. Several times he was arrested, his house was vandalized and explosives and pamphlets calling for armed uprising were planted in his room. During the summer of 1984 he attacked from the pulpit, as an injustice, the various Communist pressures upon the Church. In July 1984 he was arrested and charged in court, but was released after a month. He believed that his life was in danger. Two days later he went back into the pulpit and demanded a true dialogue between the State and Solidarity. Seven weeks after that he was taken away by three security police and his body was found beaten and roped in a reservoir.

The murder of Father Popieluszko changed the situation. The State put the policemen on trial and gave them long sentences. But country and Church were outraged at the policemen and therefore the State. Rule by the Communist Party never recovered its reputation after this martyrdom.

OPINION POLLS

In 1972 and four years later, and again in 1987–8, polls were conducted into the attitudes and religious practice of young people in Hungary.

As in France, some areas were found to be more religious than others; that is, some old tradition of religion lived on and kept many of the community to their faith and worship. This was mostly in the lands west of the Danube, where religious practice was more common than in the east. Such a difference in geography has been proved in France to be due to deep roots in the past history of the region.

It was found that villages, especially the smaller villages, were likely to practise religion more than the towns. In Western democracies the churchgoing groups were the middle classes, who mostly lived in the suburbs of towns. In the Hungarian countryside the old peasant faithfulness continued.

The statistics proved that more than half of the young people received no religious instruction from their parents. But only about 13 per cent could not remember God ever having been mentioned or talked about by their parents. About half came from homes where the Bible existed or could easily be got – but that means 50 per cent of the people or more came from homes which had no Bible. The remarkable thing was that one in five of the young people had a Bible of his or her own. There was evidence that the number of Bibles was growing. This was partly due to the authorities making it possible for the shops to sell more Bibles. It was partly due to the easing of attitudes during the 1980s, so that a book which was formerly hidden as not quite respectable might again be brought out on to a table in the sitting-room. And it was partly because during the later years schools were again allowed to teach about the Bible. It was also remarkable that the biblical knowledge of some young people was not small. One in ten could

answer correctly when asked the age of Jesus when he was crucified – a percentage which must be higher than would be achieved
by such an enquiry in Britain. Three out of four knew the name
of Jesus's mother. School influences account for the result that
only a half or a few more than a half were sure that Jesus was a
historical person and not someone in a romance.

Many of the young people found religious believers among their
friends at school, and the polls showed that they were less likely
to meet professed atheists than to meet believers there.

A third of the young people had never been inside a church.
But more than a third of them went to church every Sunday or
more often.

The number of people being confirmed was smaller even than
twenty years before. So late as 1965, nearly three-quarters of
baptized Catholics received confirmation and first communion,
and over half the baptized Protestants. By the 1980s this figure
was down: well under a half of the baptized for Catholics and
fewer still for the Protestants. Nearly two-thirds of the young
people therefore had received no confirmation or first communion.

When the enquirers got on to the question of the existence of
God, most of the questioned were not interested. Rather more
than a third believed that 'science' had disproved the existence of
God and rather more than a third believed that 'science' had
disproved nothing of the kind. About a third of the young professed
belief in God. Nearly one in five thought that God is love and that
He is manifested through the person of Jesus. This was a statistic
which might disturb the bishops but would even more disturb old-
fashioned Marxist managers of anti-God campaigns who believed
that, while religion could not be eradicated from the old, it could
be and should be eradicated from the young.

Not many of those questioned believed in life after death (one
in four would not rule it out finally, but only about one in seven
professed to believe it).

Nearly 37 per cent of young married couples still had a church
wedding. Thus more than half of the people who married chose
not to be married in church.

Almost more revealing than any of these questions, for seeing
how successful or unsuccessful was the atheist policy or campaign,
was the answer to the question, 'Does religion keep people in

ignorance?' For it was fundamental to the anti-God campaign to show the young people that it did. A quarter of the Hungarian young agreed that religion did keep people in ignorance, but three-quarters of them thought that it did not. A still more pointed question – 'Do you believe that the front line of class struggle is between believers and non-believers?' – received an almost unanimous negative. Whatever else the anti-God campaign had done, it had not persuaded the young that religious people were bound to be the props of bourgeois and capitalist society.

Three-quarters of them also gave a 'No' to three other pointed questions: 'Do you believe that religion is for the weak and the dependent?' and 'Do you believe that religion is good for very simple people only?' and 'Do you believe that religion is an obstacle to social progress?'

Nearly 88 per cent of them agreed that it is no one's business whether a person is religious or not, but only 70 per cent agreed that no one should prevent a religious person from getting a responsible job.

A Hungarian sociologist examined a parish of nearly 4,000 where the religion of the majority was Lutheran. The Lutheran services were attended by about 150 to 180, a majority old and a majority women. Only 6 per cent of the children registered for voluntary religious education, most of them girls. By far the majority of weddings and funerals were religious, but baptisms grew steadily fewer. The educated young had little use for religion. But then they had little use for Marxism or atheism. The existence of an atheist State served only to make the handful of atheists feel good. In nine years there were eight baptisms by the atheist rite offered by the State.

At Brno in Czechoslovakia, the Institute of Scientific Atheism conducted an enquiry in 1984 – though we have no check on the number in the sample. Thirty-six per cent of the population were found to be religious, most of them Catholic; 30 per cent of the 10 million Czechs, 51 per cent of 5 million Slovaks; women more than men, peasants more than industrial workers, pensioners more than teenagers. A separate enquiry found only 3 per cent of university students who said that they were religious.

A similar body in Bulgaria, the Academy of Sciences, held an enquiry into 42,644 people in 1962. No religion 64.4 per cent;

some religion 35.5 per cent. But – half the babies were baptized
in church, a third of the brides were married in church, and four-
fifths of the funerals happened in church. The enquirers were
gloomy about the success of the atheist campaign. They said that
it reached only those who were already atheists.

Soviet sociologists studied religious practice in a series of enquiries. Most of them had to produce answers unfavourable to religion,
but there is no reason to suppose that they fudged. Their samples
produced the answer that belief in God grew steadily less common
among ordinary people. Two-thirds of any congregation of any
denomination were women, and about half of the total were
illiterate or of little education – but with wide variations, for the
Evangelical Baptists in Byelorussia (for example) produced a lower
average age and a higher standard of education. The sociologists
also observed a link between religion and nationalism: in Voronezh
in 1965 7.6 per cent of the region were Ukrainians; among Evangelical Baptists in Voronezh city 43 per cent of the congregation
were Ukrainians.

In Yugoslavia the censuses of 1931 and 1953 asked questions
about religion. The census of 1953 showed that atheism had
become the third most numerous religion in the state: 12.3 per
cent of the nation were atheists, more than were Muslims. But this
was just at the end of the bad time, when people did not like to
record too honestly on official documents. Censuses were less
reliable than opinion polls, because people were unwilling to put
down the truth on a form which the police could see, and very few
censuses asked for information about religion. Opinion polls in
Zagreb (in 1966 and 1984) produced the surprising result that the
atheists had fallen by 6 per cent and that young people were
turning towards the Churches. But the number of professed atheists
was still high by European standards – 18 per cent, plus 18 per
cent no interest, plus 19 per cent, don't know. This left 45 per cent
who said that they were believers.

During the 1960s the Institute of Social Sciences in Belgrade
conducted three such enquiries. The largest sample was 4,000
students. Nearly 20 per cent said that they were religious, a
percentage higher among Catholic and Muslim families than
among Orthodox. The proportion who belonged to a religion
varied by region – the highest, for Catholics in Croatia, was 33

per cent; the lowest, for Orthodox in Montenegro, was 8 per cent.

In the Slovene university of Ljubljana, the Party discovered with dismay that half the students went to church. It asked itself how its education was failing.

In Poland the percentages looked different. In a poll of teenagers, conducted by the university of Lublin over ten years to 1979, nearly 87 per cent said that they were religious, 72 per cent said that they were regular at worship, 70 per cent went to confession once a year, and 30 per cent said that they would live together without a church wedding.

It is therefore certain that during the Cold War religious practice in Eastern Europe declined. (For example, figures for Roman Catholics in Hungary were: 1949 (an official census), 67.8 per cent; 1971 (Church estimate), 60.8 per cent; 1978 (Church estimate), 50 per cent.) But such a fall was happening in Western Europe. Therefore it does not follow that it was due to the Communist attack. It could happen because the country workers moved into the towns as all Eastern Europe industrialized, or because women went to work, or because the language of the liturgy changed and some people for a time were unsettled – that is, the fall could be due to the reasons supposed for the decline in the West.

And yet it is impossible to think that the Communist system of education did not contribute.

From time to time Communist leaders consoled themselves for the partial failure of their endeavours. They saw religion declining in Western Europe and argued that as, in time, their policies created prosperous welfare states, nothing would do more to kill the people's need for religion. They took it for granted that the alternative to their management was not a religious sort of State, for they were sure that Churches were too backward-looking to command the assent of or even to have a lot of influence in a modern society.

CHRISTIANITY AND THE HISTORY OF THE NATIONS

All the Eastern European States made grants to historic buildings. Almost all the historic buildings were cathedrals, churches or monastic chapels. Even Albania restored some historic churches for the tourist – but as museums. In this way the Soviet government restored the church of St Basil the Blessed in Red Square, or the cathedrals inside the Kremlin, as museums. A church so magnificent as St Basil the Blessed would have been impossible to restore without the State, and the Church was not discontented that it should be a museum.

Most Western tourists, and some Eastern pilgrims, found historic monuments more appealing when they were still used for worship. Santa Sophia in Istanbul, one of the historic churches of Christendom, was taken by Ottoman Turks in 1453 to be a mosque, and under a Turkish republic was turned (1934) into a museum. The museum lost half the marvel. The Communist States, outside Albania, had an interest in allowing church people to use the churches, because then the church people provided the vergers and the care and had to raise the money to maintain them. The painted monasteries of northern Romania, one of the Christian wonders of Europe, received State aid but the irreligious State was glad that monks and nuns cared for them. Probably the most important monastic house in all the Communist states was that of St John of Rila in Bulgaria, for it went back to the tenth century and he was the national hero. Church and State celebrated the millennium of St John of Rila. The Patriarch Alexei came from Moscow, and the Bulgarian dictator Georgi Dimitrov, who was the son of a working-class Protestant and had once been accused by the Nazis of setting fire to the Reichstag, made a speech in which he talked of the historic service of the Church in bearing the national consciousness of Bulgaria during the years of Turkish rule and then went on to attack the members of the synod for being blimps with ossified brains. In 1961 Chervenkov's government turfed the monks out of St John of Rila and called it a national monument. Three years later his wiser successor summoned back the monks.

This memory of the past, which made the Churches a little less disreputable in the eyes of some regimes, could lead to the oddest alliances of Church and State.

In 973 the Prince of Hungary married a Christian wife. His son, Stephen, not only made Hungary, he made it Christian. The millennium ought to have been celebrated in 1973, but the State insisted that it be celebrated in 1970, to coincide with the twenty-fifth anniversary of the Hungarian Revolution, and that the celebrations be in a low key. Even the Minister of Education and the Minister for Cults attended the mass in Budapest cathedral.

In 1966 the Polish Church celebrated its millennium. It was a national feast. The government arranged football matches to coincide with the special Church occasions, which the media disregarded, and children were taken away on trips.

Why the attitude to history changed was the rise of a new generation. The Communists of 1948 were afraid. They thought of history as a shackle to that past from which society must be freed. But they also wanted their young to be educated. The young could not get educated without wanting to know the history of their people and the literature and culture which they inherited. For decades the Bible was banned from schools. In about 1980 – it took so long – Hungarian education authorities insisted that no one could understand culture and literature without knowing something about the Bible; and that when history was studied it was impossible to miss how the Churches contributed to the nation's history, and impossible to leap over the Reformation, and wrong only to describe how Churches exploited the working class. A longer perspective was on the side of the Churches.

This mellowing happened with the reputation of Martin Luther. In the Stalinist years Luther's name was muddy, the bourgeois slayer of peasant rebels. But Luther was too potent a figure in German folk memory for this to catch with the people. They still revered Luther; and, as history mellowed, Luther came back into favour, as the opener of the way to the social and intellectual liberties of Germany.

This change can be marked by the two Luther anniversaries of 1967 (450 years from the Ninety-Five Theses) and 1983 (500 years from his birth). In 1967 the governments were not at all helpful. In East Germany, where was Wittenberg, which must be the heart of any celebration, the State allowed the Church to invite speakers from the West to lecture in various places – an unheard of concession so soon after the building of the Berlin Wall. But when the Western speakers were on their way in an aircraft, the government cancelled their permits for the places where they were due to lecture; and in Wittenberg the State celebration happened at a different time and place from, and with a less colourful procession than, the Church's celebration. The 1983 celebration was much easier but still not without its awkwardness between Church and State. Where the 1983 celebrations really helped the Churches was in Latvia and Estonia and Hungary, for foreign speakers came: the small Protestant Churches were for the moment on the national map.

Not all such historical occasions were liked by the State. On 7 July 1985 it was the eleventh centenary of the death of St Methodius, to whom with St Cyril the Slavs first owed their faith. One hundred and fifty thousand pilgrams turned up at his shrine in Velehrad in Moravia, but several cardinals, including Hume of Westminster, were refused visas. The Party sent out instructions that schools should counter the Christian view of the alleged history, organized a historical conference on the *real* origins of Czechoslovakia, set up exhibitions to show how false was the clerical view of the past and ordered officials to encourage strife between the denominations. The Minister of Culture attended the celebrations at Velehrad. In his speech he talked of the *political* achievement of Cyril and Methodius and was hissed and booed by the crowd, who gave Cardinal Tomašek of Prague, aged eighty-six, an ovation.

The Russian millennium of 1988 was more important, for by 1988 Mikhail Gorbachev had been in power for three years. But before he appeared, the coming millennium began to help the Churches. Even in 1983 the government returned to the Church, as a new headquarters in time for the millennium, the Danilov monastery in Moscow, which had been used by the State as a prison and a warehouse and a factory, and was now restored at great expense to become the centre of the patriarchate. It dated from the fourteenth century and contains the tomb of the founder of the Kremlin. This was the first time since the Revolution that the Church possessed a monastery in Moscow.

The State allowed these celebrations of the millennium to be theatrical. In the Bolshoi theatre (!) in Moscow, massed choirs of Zagorsk Academy and Moscow Cathedral sang the glory of God with an audience from State officials to nuns from Riga and Kiev. It was broadcast on television. The millennium was a feast of the Russian people as well as of Russian Christianity.

At last many more Bibles were being imported. The Bible was never banned but it was unobtainable. There was a small amount of printing and some legal imports, but the combined printing and imports came to fewer than a million Bibles over forty years for some 60 to 80 million people who might want them. This meant a high price for Bibles on the black market. A few people tried producing illegal editions, but some of the printers were imprisoned. From 1968 the Baptists had an illegal printing-press; the first press had gears from a motor bicycle and an electric motor from a washing-machine, and ink was made out of burnt rubber boots and boiled moss.

The millennium opened the gates. During the eighteen months after January 1988 nearly 1 million Bibles and 1.5 million New Testaments were imported into the Soviet Union; and already leave was given for the import of a large number more during the next few years. The new concessions did not apply to the Bible in Ukrainian.

DIVISION IN THE EAST EUROPEAN CHURCHES

It is a rule of Church history that Churches have parties like any other body of humanity, and it is a rule of history that an institution with parties sometimes becomes so tense that it divides into two. The normal line of division is between the conservative and the radical: in Church terms, between those who wish to be faithful to the inheritance of the past and those who see that their Church is in many respects failing and want to reform it drastically. Just such a schism happened in Western Europe during this age.

It is a rule of Church history that persecution brings parts of the Church to a tighter feeling of community as the members unite against a common antagonist, the State.

But it is also a rule of Church history that persecution brings nearer the risk of division: the situation is more anxious, consciences are more acute, fanaticism can be round the corner. Was that bishop wrong to cooperate with an anti-Christian state? Can we trust that pastor, who wrongly cooperated with the State and now confesses his error, with his old pastoral care? If he goes back to his parish, will the people go near his church? The Bolshevik Revolution in Russia had generated a schism in the Russian Orthodox Church. Hitler had generated a schism in the German Lutheran Church. It was impossible that the pressures of the Communist States should not produce here and there a division in the Churches.

Deep within the Christian soul was a tension which existed among religious people throughout the world but was more obvious in a world officially against Christian souls. It was the pull between rejecting the world and doing good to the world: the old argument between Martha and Mary, between the active nun and the contemplative. But in this case the argument was imposed from outside. The Communist governments said that no Church can be political, it is intolerable if Church leaders try to influence politics, we shall lock them up if they do. But the Communist governments also said that the importance of religion, if it has any at all, is not to disappear into the clouds of a dream world but to back social reform, and fair shares for all, and the conscientious duty of Christians to be loyal citizens in a Communist state. With one voice the Churches were told that they must never be political, and with another voice that they must be very political indeed – provided that they were political in the right way. This was hard for Church leaders who often had to tread so sagging a rope. But it was not only a difficulty for the diplomats. It could be felt at times to be a worry in the souls; for it was a particular and heightened form of an argument which afflicted religious men and women through the centuries, not only under Communism, that they lived at once in eternity and in time.

The experience of schism in Eastern Europe was no worse than the experience of schism in Western Europe in the same generation.

The Churches could not freely use publications to battle against each other. The State's heavy hand disliked competing sects as sources of trouble or disloyalty. But underneath these apparently united fronts could be heard, as always, inward murmurings.

A nation determined to be its own nation, and unable to be so in politics, insisted on autonomy in its Church. Bulgaria owed allegiance to the see of Constantinople. But the patriarch there, Athenagoras, came from America and was Western-minded and against Communism. The dictator of Bulgaria, Chervenkov, was nasty. But in 1953 he saw the need to free the country from this Church subjection and made the see of Sofia into a new patriarchate, so that Kiril became the first patriarch of Bulgaria; not at first recognized by Constantinople. Kiril was an exceptional person and no yes-man; he was revered in the Church and slowly achieved a *modus vivendi* with the State. He was a historian who was elected a member of the Bulgarian Academy of Sciences in his own academic right, a unique distinction for a patriarch.

In the same way, in 1967 Macedonia broke away from its allegiance to the Serbian Patriarch and set up its own archbishop, in the see of Ohrid, whom, for a time, no other Orthodox leaders would recognize. This was an act of pure nationalism.

Within Macedonia was a special problem: that of language. This was spoken and written in varied forms, some of them in Bulgarian Macedonian, some of them in Serbo-Croat or Romanian Macedonian. The Church, with its liturgy in Church Slavonic, was the unifying force of the people. The Bulgarian occupiers of 1944 ordered a Macedonian language and script; and because this was needed it caught on, and for the first time the Bible could be translated properly into Macedonian. The New Testament appeared first, at Skopje in 1967.

Where the State behaved particularly badly, some church pastors went underground. A catacomb bishop was much less controllable by the State until they caught him, but he could do little for his Church except as a pastor wandering from home to home among the faithful. And he was also much less controllable by the Church authorities – that is, a wanderer hardly needed to bring with him a certificate that he was authentic as a representative of his Church. Felix Davidek was a Czech whom some unknown bishop secretly consecrated to be a bishop during the

1960s. He ordained a lot of priests and most of them were married and went on with their secular occupation, and he justified this by the plea of necessity. Among the Ukrainian Uniats can be found traces of the same difficulty.

The classical situation that breeds schism – classical because familiar in the early Christian Church – is the gulf between those who play along with the atheist power and those who refuse. Suppose the State arrests a chief pastor and then puts into his chair a more compliant successor. Should Christians recognize the successor? Such a schism did not happen with the Catholics in Hungary only because no one would appoint a successor to Cardinal Mindszenty so long as he was still nominally archbishop, even while he was locked up. But it happened with the Hungarian Lutherans along just those lines. The State threw out the Hungarian bishop Ordass and put in a more pliant bishop: first Dezséry, then Zoltán Káldy.[1] Most Hungarian Protestants regretted this but carried on: Bishop Káldy was not scandalous; the work of the Church had to be done. Some, though few, could not bear to recognize Káldy as a true bishop, for their true bishop was outed – hence a long strife within the Lutheran community, still not quite settled. And even though it did not happen with Mindszenty, this type of situation lay just under the surface and exploded into placards carried through the streets of Rome: that the Pope was a traitor when he ejected a reluctant Mindszenty from his see.

The same basic situation was found among the Uniats at the tip of Czechoslovakia. The State said that Uniats were illegal and all Uniats were Orthodox. Some pastors with a minority of the congregation became Orthodox. The rest of the congregation kept away from pastor and services. Then from 1968 the State said that the Uniats were legal. The pastor and the minority at the church said that they were Uniats again. Should the rejecting majority of the congregation now forgive and come back to church? In several congregations the majority refused to have anything to do with their former pastor, whom they thought to be corrupted. And when the acting bishop tried to transfer the pastor to another

1. Born 1919; a fine evangelical preacher; by 1952 defended 'political preaching'; banned Ordass from pastoral work; developed a 'theology of diakonia' to rally the Church for socialist ideas.

parish, his minority said that they would become Orthodox if this happened.

This was a classic situation in a time of persecution, to which the experience of primitive Christians had made Christendom accustomed.

The worst clashes came in the early Stalinist years, when States inherited pastors whom they had not chosen – Wyszyński in Warsaw, Mindszenty, Stepinac, Stefan in Bulgaria, Dibelius in Berlin. But as time passed all the Church leaders were likely to be gentler, perhaps weaker personages. This the faithful did not like. Mindszenty's successor, Lékai, was criticized because he was not Mindszenty; Wyszyński's successor, Glemp, was criticized because he was not Wyszyński. A cardinal and his hierarchy, a chief Protestant pastor and his presiding committee, must somehow get along with the State's ministry of Church affairs.

This was bound to produce a gulf between the hierarchies and some ardent laity or younger priests. Such gulfs especially occurred where the hand of the State was heavy. The Russian government preferred sycophants among its Church leaders. The young and ardent regarded these sycophants as betraying the cause by baptizing an unChristian regime. Big Russian Orthodox priests – Yakunin, Dudko and many another – suffered and Patriarch Pimen made no open protest but cooperated in shutting their mouths. This same gulf can be discerned in Czechoslovakia; and even in Poland, with the friction between a very Catholic working-class Solidarity and Cardinal Glemp of Warsaw with his bishops.

In various States there came into existence groups which in Hungary were called 'basis-groups'. These were bodies of laymen and laywomen, with a friendly priest or several, who set up their own system of prayer and retreat and worship. Their origins lay in the underground of the Stalinist period, and several of the leaders had languished long years in jail and some had experienced torture. They were like the old pietists, with private readings of the Bible and an intensity of faith, and with some experience of healing and of the charismatic gifts; and at times they were not without the defects of the old pietists, in self-isolation and a touch of the self-righteous and with a conviction that the spirit-led soul needs no other guide. But there was one prelate towards whom most of them looked back with veneration: Mindszenty.

The only way for the Church leaders to cope with such groups was to try to draw them back into the mainstream of Church life and give them the chance of Church work. Neither the State nor senior clergy were happy at giving authority in the Church to young disobedient laity. Yet, in the shortages of priests, the only way they could run congregations or educate children in religion was by using lay people. And when, as happened in Hungary, the bishops sacked or suspended priests who took part in such basis-groups, the gulf grew wider rather than narrower.

In Protestant Latvia, uniquely, a basis-group won authority in the Church. The archbishop (Baltic Protestants had an archbishop, though he had no bishops under him) was Erik Mesters, who had fought in the Red Army and later was Lutheran chaplain in Moscow and was approved by the State and wore (it was noted as an innovation) a mitre at his consecration. A big quarrel blew up because he ordered all parishes to celebrate the anniversary of the Bolshevik Revolution. Then he backed the State side in a battle between a free-speaking pastor, Modris Plate, and the local Party which was trying to oust him from the parish. Plate founded a revival group for Latvia, called Rebirth and Renewal, and this group began to be entangled with resurgent Latvian nationalism against Moscow. In April 1989 the general synod raised the members of the group Rebirth and Renewal to authority in the Church.

Persecution fostered extremism, and extremists were divisive. In western Ukraine in 1956 there appeared an underground sect of Penitents (*Pokutnyky*) who combined secret forms of religion – night prayers in homes, strict observance of fasts, pilgrimages to a place where the Virgin appeared – with a total rejection of the Soviet State.

The most successful though the most agonized of all these dissenting groups were the breakaway Evangelical Christian Baptists in Russia. The Russian Baptists were increasing in number. Early in the 1960s a group split from them and set up their own body because the United Baptist Council failed to protest against gross interference by the State. They were popularly known as the *Initsiativniki*, because their protest was led by an 'Initiative group'. Most were working-class, most went to prison or camps. They maintained themselves courageously, with a flourishing under-ground literature.

ORTHODOX CHURCH LEADERS IN EASTERN EUROPE

Alexei of Moscow[2]

The modern history of the Orthodox Church in Russia began in 1943, when Russian armies began to advance against Germany. During the 1930s Stalin almost destroyed the Church or drove it underground, with the murder of many bishops and priests and with thousands of others in concentration camps. The war proved to Stalin that he needed the Church. To fight a desperate war he needed to reunite the people and therefore must reconcile himself with the Christians who were so historic a part of the Russian inheritance. Moreover the German occupying governors won sympathy from Russian peasants and much sympathy from anti-Russian Ukrainian peasants because they allowed churches to be reopened.

In 1943 Stalin made an agreement with the then senior member of the Orthodox Church, Metropolitan Sergei, who agreed to do all he could to support the Soviet cause and in return was allowed to recreate the Orthodox Church and the patriarchate (extinct since 1925). This did not mean the end of the obligation on Communists to make propaganda for atheism, but now the obligation consisted of abuse and argument, and was not usually carried into vandalism against church buildings or far worse. The Marxist duty to foster the end of religion remained. But Alexei, the patriarch from 1945, was allowed to reconstruct the Church. In return he only had to provide words – that Stalin was a military genius and a wise and noble and gentle ruler, that the Americans were warmongers, that the Vatican led people into darkness etc. –

2. Born Sergei Simansky, 1877; studied law at Moscow University; monk 1892; Bishop of Tivkhin and vicar of Novgorod 1913; Metropolitan of Novgorod 1932, of Leningrad 1933; Patriarch of Moscow 1945–70.

but he also had to accept with a good conscience the forcible incorporation into the Russian Orthodox Church of the Uniat Church in the Ukraine and Ruthenia.

Alexei was the last of the tsarist bishops: courteous, charming, sincere, aristocratic, European. Whether or not he tortured his conscience is not known. Fortunately for him he had a chief assistant, Metropolitan Nikolai, who was willing to be still shriller in his anti-American speeches. Some who knew Alexei think that probably he chose with a fairly serene mind an evil which was sore but which was the lesser of two evils. His willingness to compromise made it possible to reconstruct his Church. Certainly he cared with sincerity about the depth of spirituality in the Church, and about the power of the liturgy among the faithful, and about the right education of his clergy.

This last was not easy. Many of the best of the pre-war clergy had been murdered. Some of those who lived had survived because they were not the best. A new generation, almost a new type, of clergy needed training.

The theological academy at Zagorsk was allowed (from 1946) to function properly. One other higher college and eight other seminaries were opened. The Church was allowed to print a journal and other Christian publications. Parish life became easier in many parts of European Russia. There was no shortage of ordinands to fill the places at the seminaries, though those places were not enough to staff all the parishes. Older churches were repaired. It was still difficult to get a licence to build a new church – one at Samarkand, the cathedral at Tashkent, and a few others. (But the building of the cathedral at Tashkent helped to cause the dismissal of the archbishop.) The cathedrals or churches which were handed back were delivered as the ruins they had become and had to be repaired at the congregation's expense. The cathedral of Vladimir, for example, was handed back full of ice and piles of rubbish. In the great cities nothing like enough churches could be opened. This meant huge congregations in the churches that were open. In the Lent of 1947 the cathedral at Leningrad was calculated to have had 400,000 communicants. The first of the new generation of bishops, Mikhail Chub, was consecrated in 1953. He was a person of exceptional intelligence and wide reading and of far too independent a mind to be allowed

promotion to the highest sees. From that time onwards all the new
Orthodox leaders had grown up in schools with an officially atheist
course, which told them that religion is fantasy and that its aim is
to keep the masses as slaves. They had also grown with a materialist
environment in their community. This difference distinguished
them from someone like Alexei, who had grown in an assured
world where society took Orthodoxy for granted. Therefore they
were more like 'converts'. They were clergy despite society, rather
than because of society. And their younger origin took away from
the State a hoary argument: that these bishops and older clergy
were but survivals of a class-ridden world.

1961 was the most difficult of all the years after the Second
World War. It was a year of massive closure of churches, of strident
propaganda in favour of atheism and of harsh measures against
people who insisted on trying to go to church. In the years 1955–7
Alexei and his bishops believed that they had come so far in
more freedom that they must be able to go further. The hope was
frustrated.

Despite his repudiation of Stalin, Khrushchev started in 1959 a
steady new campaign against the Churches. Some 15,000 churches
were closed on one excuse or another, on occasion with mob
violence but usually by refusing to license a priest and then, when
no services were held, declaring the church redundant. Alexei
tried to show the Russian people that the Church was an integral
part of Russian nationality and the growth of Russian civilization;
that, so far from being an instrument of enslaving the masses, it
was a force to the ending of slavery; that it had created the great
historic monuments of Russia and that it was one of the chief links
for peace among the nations. A speech which he made in Moscow
along these lines was heckled scandalously.

In 1961 Khrushchev forced Alexei and a synod of bishops at
Zagorsk to amend the statute of the Church about parishes. Alexei
summoned the bishops without telling them the agenda. Three
State officials attended the meeting and watched. A useful resolution agreed that the Russian Orthodox Church should be a
member of the World Council of Churches. But a resolution on
the parishes deprived the parish priest of all power over his church
and all canonical leadership in his congregation. The running of
the parish church was put into the hands of a committee of three

laymen who were selected by twenty who were elected not by the congregation but by the whole community. The three laymen, with the leave of the local Communist Party, could do anything – close the church, sack the priest – whether the congregation wanted it or not. Their appointment of a new priest needed the bishop's 'blessing' and the sanction of the local civic authority. The local Communist Party was urged to make sure that the right sort of people were elected to the church council.

Afterwards Alexei was much blamed for so easily consenting to this revolution in parish life. But such a plan – where there was no hard and fast division between the Christians and the non-Christians in a parish so far as responsibility went for the church, and where the lay majority had the right of deciding what the congregation should do – had theoretical attractions for others in Europe besides those under the pressure of a ruthless political party. In addition the State was then making the best of its onslaught upon the Church by prosecuting some clergymen (including two archbishops[3]) for misuse of the funds of their churches. To free the priest from responsibility for the spending of money was in one way a protection. It was not difficult for Alexei to make the best of what he could not prevent. However, this made it easy to close country churches which, as the population declined, could not be kept in repair.

The willingness of the hierarchy for silence was attacked by some of the people and especially by radical priests. The attitude could not have been expressed better than by a holy bishop who died in 1975 – Josif, the Metropolitan of Alma-Ata in Siberia. He was already a monk in tsarist times. After the Revolution he spent twenty years in labour camps. From 1955 he was allowed to rule his distant diocese and was beloved by the people. He was once asked why at a synod he kept silent when he disagreed with the resolution before them. He said:

I often ask myself, are we doing right to remain silent, not exposing what

3. Archbishop Iov was imprisoned for six years; Archbishop Andrei Sukhenko of Chernigov for eight. Iov on his release was instantly reinstated by the Church to a diocese, so it was clear that the Church did not believe him guilty. Andrei (whose real offence was refusing to close a convent) was also given a new diocese at once, but the imprisonment had affected his mind and he had soon to be retired.

is happening in the Church …? Sometimes I get sick of it and want to throw it all up and retire. When that happens, my conscience objects. It says, you cannot abandon the faithful. You cannot abandon the Church. If I speak up and say all, even if I criticize publicly, I should be out and nothing would be changed. So – while I have strength – I do what I can and work quietly for the Church.[4]

It must be said that the State's ministry of Church affairs wholly approved of Metropolitan Josif. And his attitude had its difficulties which were more than personal. On the one hand it kept the sacraments and the faith among the people. On the other hand it seemed to make the Church leaders irrelevant to the people who were struggling for justice and freedom in the State. Patriarch Alexei had a background and a personality which made it impossible to disregard him, until he grew too old to affect matters. His successor, Pimen, had neither the background nor the personality and was soon regarded by the radicals as an irrelevance.

The worst problem was shortage of clergy. The number of priests fell by nearly a third between 1961 and 1974 and the average age was high. There is reliable evidence of a certain contradiction: (1) to be a first-class priest was to risk or even invite dismissal or suspension; (2) some priests therefore took care not to seem too successful, and some did little for their people; (3) the people preferred a bad priest to no priest, for if they had no priest the church would be closed;[5] (4) the religion of the parishes and congregations was alive and devout. For all its hierarchy, Orthodoxy was a very lay religion.

Justinian, Patriarch of Romania 1948–75

The Romanian Communists picked for their patriarch an able widower of fellow-travelling convictions and a partly Western education, Justinian Marina. Under him the Orthodox Church

4. Quoted in Jane Ellis, *The Russian Orthodox Church: a contemporary history* (1986), pp. 23–4.

5. In one area of the Soviet Union, Georgia, the doctrine *better a bad priest than no priest* produced scandal. During the early seventies a corrupt patriarch of Georgia linked himself with corrupt local policemen to milk the Church of money and property. The patriarch was at last ousted, a reforming patriarch (Ilya II) was put in, and the Georgian Communist Party (Shevardnadze) coped with the policemen.

flourished; though it was a condition of flourishing that it should at no point oppose the State. Sibiu was the largest seminary in all the Orthodox Church in any country – in 1973 it had 780 members. That year there were 12 Orthodox dioceses, 19 bishops, 8,627 priests and deacons, 56 DDs, 62 monasteries, 30 nunneries, 28 hermitages, 540 monks and 1,443 nuns. All the great historic buildings of Romania were Orthodox monasteries, and the State wished to help to maintain them.

Justinian was a Christian Socialist by conviction, with a notion of the 'apostolate to society', and was moved by Jesus the Carpenter and by the place of the Church in honourable labour. He was not afraid of the arguments over dialectical materialism.

The high point of amity between Church and State came in 1968. In that year the Russian army invaded Czechoslovakia and overthrew the Prague Spring in which Dubček was trying to get a more humane sort of Communism. The new Romanian dictator, Ceauşescu, was the only Eastern ruler to denounce the Russians. Since this took courage, and some Romanians were afraid of a Russian threat to themselves, the Church rallied round the dictator wholeheartedly and on grounds of freedom. Justinian at that moment won admiration from many Westerners.

But Ceauşescu grew, or diminished, towards megalomania. He invented a National Unity Front, to make the people of Romania more Marxist. At its first Congress (1974) Justinian could be observed sitting on the platform, and his second-in-command, Metropolitan Justin of Jassy, lauded Ceauşescu for giving them all complete freedom. Henceforth adulation was to be the order of the day if the Church was to get along.

Justinian could not control all his priests. Father George Calciu spent fifteen years in prison for preaching too frankly, but when he came out again he went back to his pulpit undaunted. The case became a long-running strife between Church and State.

In 1977 an earthquake damaged nearly 500 Orthodox churches. A fortnight later Patriarch Justinian died and the Church was nervous about what would happen. It was taken for granted that Justin of Jassy would succeed, because he was believed to be a dedicated Marxist, but it was thought uncomfortable that he should receive his office from the dictator Ceauşescu. In the last year or more of Justinian two famous churches had been destroyed – for what reason is still unknown – so it was taken for granted that Justin must deal with a dictator more unfriendly now to the Church. However, Justin's election and enthronement happened with due solemnity. And his start was marked by important concessions to the Church – the giving of a monastery and a piece of land to create a theological institute and an ecumenical institute. Justin had taught theology as a layman for many years and was ordained deacon and priest and received the monk's tonsure, all within a few days, only in order to become an archbishop. The Church publications gave always more space to Ceauşescu, so the Church was obviously under pressure as the dictator's megalomania grew. The Church press printed sycophantic remarks by Justin about Ceauşescu.

Father Calciu was still preaching and was rearrested in 1979 and sentenced to ten years in jail. He went on hunger strike and was forcibly fed. His case was taken up internationally. But in the case we hear, not for the first time, of a body in Romania with a remarkable name – 'The Committee for Freedom of Religion and Conscience'. And beneath the top hierarchs the Church still flourished. Its theological standard was rising all the time. There was no difficulty in finding priests. Romanian representatives at ecumenical conferences were heard with respect. But Father Calciu was finally unfrocked by the Church (obeying the police) and was exiled to the United States.

The Latin bishops, who were Hungarian in Transylvania and not Uniats, had at first a bad time as the State tried to cut the links with the Vatican and threw out the nuncio. But slowly one of the bishops, and then another, won the right to act. One of them survived and became a hero to his people. Aron Marton was a Hungarian by origin who became in 1939 the bishop of the Latin Catholics in Cluj, where he was revered, not least for what he did when trying to rescue the Jews. Like the rest of the Roman Catholic bishops he went to prison in 1949 and after that into hard labour in the mines. He was released six years later, tried to restart his work as a bishop and was at once put under house arrest except that he was allowed to go the few yards between his house and the cathedral. Yet he ran the diocese, and his people were freely allowed to visit him. In 1967 he was freed, though now with poor health. He went on for another thirteen years, until resignation

just before his death. He did everything he could for the illegal
Uniats. His successor was approved by Ceaușescu and therefore
was not so approved by the people.

German of Belgrade[6]

From about 1955 the Serbian Church was freer than most Churches in the satellite states, Tito's Yugoslavia being no longer a
satellite of Moscow. From 1952 Christmas was openly celebrated
in Belgrade. German, the patriarch from 1958, was a man of
quality who ten years later was elected one of the presidents of the
World Council of Churches. Quite a number of State decorations
of a high order were awarded to distinguished and cooperating
bishops. The Church had a modest right to sell a few Christian
books, even in the State bookshops, and it had good seminaries
which were not destroyed and which trained good Church
musicians as well as pastors (but there were capricious closures of
seminaries for alleged misbehaviour of staff or students). Church
marriage was illegal if it preceded civil marriage, but if it followed
no one mocked it. In the countryside there was an unusual charismatic movement of devotion, to which even one of the bishops
belonged. One of the strengths of Serbian religion was not in
church but in the home: the festival of St Sava, with a home altar,
and many candles, and sweetmeats passed round, and hymn-
singing, and the head of the family leading the household in
prayer. In the churches the icons, especially certain icons of the
Virgin, still attracted much devotion from the people. The most
beloved of the icons was the Virgin at Peć.

By the eighties the Orthodox Church began in a modest way to
flourish. This was because after Tito's death the various nationalisms of the federal State became ever more vociferous. Because of
the history of Turkish occupation, Serbian nationalism was bound
up with the Orthodox Church. The nationalism of the Serbs was
something much more profound among the people than their
Marxism. The Marxist doctrines, taught in schools and universities
over so many years, had made many Serbs cheerfully irreligious.

6. Born 1899 in Serbia; educated at Belgrade University; bishop of three sees
in succession, 1951–8; patriarch 1958. Too ill to act 1990 and the see was declared
vacant.

But they began to help the Church, and not only because that was good for tourists from the West.

In 1980 the Orthodox bishops in Croatia dared to ask the State for the return of the precious objects which had been seized from churches during the revolution and were now stored in museums. The Croatian government agreed to this, though there was a time proviso. In June 1989 Patriarch German blessed the new cathedral of St Sava in Belgrade, topped by a forty-five-foot golden cross, and quite often he was reported in the newspapers as opening new churches.

The Church and Serbia began to be seen once again to be bound together. This was in part due to the Albanians. In the southern Serbian province of Kosovo, on the Albanian frontier, lived a majority of Albanians who, as the nationalisms of the State re-arose, became vocal and on occasion violent. Because their violence and their speeches were sometimes directed against the Serbian Orthodox Church and its presence in Kosovo, Patriarch German was the first to stand up in Belgrade for the rights of the Serbians who lived in Kosovo. In March 1981 unknown persons burnt to the ground the historic monastery at Peć, a sacred place to the Serbian Orthodox Church. There were other Albanian attacks upon Serbian churches and worshippers in the province of Kosovo. The Serbian bishops got no help from the State, so they published a documentation of all they had suffered in Kosovo since 1968: thefts of monastic woodland, thefts of beasts, breakings into monasteries, destruction of Serbian village churches which had stood empty after their people left in fear, public abuse, attacks on monks and nuns, pollution of Serbian cemeteries.

Slowly the State in Belgrade swung behind the Church in a united antipathy to Albanian nationalism. This was a fact in liberalizing the policy of the Belgrade government towards the Orthodox Church.

Let us take Nikanor, the Bishop of Karlovac. In 1947 he was made bishop of the see where his predecessor had been murdered by the ustasche six years before. For his first four years he worked in impossible conditions, of State hostility, and public abuse, and injustice to the clergy. In 1955, moved to Novi Sad, he rebuilt a church for the first time; and after fifteen years he had restored sixty-three churches and built seventeen clock towers and restored all three of his monasteries. By the 1980s most bishops were able to follow this example. Much depended upon the local heads of the province, or even of the commune. Nothing changed in Bosnia-Hercegovina to ease the tension between Church and State. In Croatia, where the Church had suffered, the old guard of Communists in the government, with their dogmatic Marxism, were thrown out of high office after Tito's death and younger and more pragmatic people ran the government, with better results for the Church.

State education was still materialist. The clergy were highly taxed, but both bishops and a trade union of the clergy hammered away at trying to get reductions, not without a measure of success. At the nunnery of Mesić in the Banat the police refused to protect the place from illegal violence when a father collected a band of thugs to attack the nunnery and seize his daughter who was a novice. In Slovenia in 1986 the Roman Catholic archbishop was allowed to give a Christmas message on the radio and the government made it easier for holidays to be taken on Christmas Day. This caused agitation in Serbia for Patriarch German to be allowed to broadcast a Christmas message.

CATHOLIC CHURCH LEADERS IN EASTERN EUROPE

Wyszyński in Warsaw

The primate who held the uncomfortable seat which corresponded to the sees of Mindszenty or Stepinac was Stefan Wyszyński.[7] Fortunately for himself he had not been a bishop during the war, and fortunately for the Polish Church he was not by nature quite so tough against Communism as Mindszenty and Stepinac. Earlier in his life he was suspect for left-wing opinions.

7. Born 1901; priest 1924; studied in France, Italy, Belgium; doctorate at Lublin University in sociology and canon law; founded Christian Workers University 1935–9; barely escaped Nazis 1939; rector of seminary 1945; Bishop of Lublin 1946; Archbishop of Gniezno and Warsaw, and primate, 1948; cardinal 1953, arrest 1953–6; a friend of the Second Vatican Council; died 1981.

In July 1949 came out the papal decree against Communism. The Polish government reacted furiously, with savage abuse of the Vatican, and confiscation of church property, and clapping many clergy into jail. Not without friction and a charge from his own right wing that he compromised too much with the atheist regime, Wyszyński reached an agreement with the State. The Church would back the new regime, and its policy over making collective farms, and its policy to maintain its western lands annexed from Germany (an annexation of which the legality was in doubt). In return the State would allow religion to be taught in schools and keep faculties of theology, and religious orders, and chaplains in the army, and chaplains in hospitals. The Vatican disliked this compromise, and it was proved to be right when the bargain soon collapsed. It collapsed because the State would not keep its undertakings, and also because some of Wyszyński's clergy were not willing to be prevented from criticizing the regime and its Marxism.

In September 1953 a State court condemned Kaczmarek, the Bishop of Kielce, to twelve years in jail. On 25 September Wyszyński, who by now was a cardinal, defended Bishop Kaczmarek in a crowded church. That night he was arrested and disappeared for three years into secret places of confinement (actually a monastery). For a time the Poles hardly remembered him. He was not yet a legend.

But the conflict of Church and State grew ever more acrimonious. The State took power to control all Church appointments. By 1954 some 2,000 priests were in prison. In 1954–5 the government felt strong enough to abolish the theological faculties and the teaching of religion in elementary schools, and to seize all the property of the religious orders. The power of the Catholic Church in Poland should already be observed: it took the government four years longer than any other government behind the Iron Curtain to adopt the measures generally normal in the Communist states. And although the government abolished all the theological faculties, the State continued to allow the Catholic university of Lublin, which received no State money and depended on Church endowments. From 1950 Lublin was the only officially Christian university in Marxist Europe. And though the State took the property, it did not stop people from becoming monks and nuns.

The effect of Stalin's death (in 1953), and then of Khrushchev's repudiation of Stalin, was dramatic in Poland. In 1956 popular demonstrations forced a change in the head of State to Gomulka, a Communist known to believe that Poland must go its own way and not Russia's way. Peasants collectivized the collective farms (which were not numerous). And the Church got back its cardinal.

To a Polish people already in movement, the Hungarian Revolution of October 1956 came as a shock. The danger was that Poland would rise in revolution and then that Russian tanks would roll on Warsaw as they had rolled on Budapest. Gomulka judged that the Church leaders could help him to keep the people from a flaring of patriotism which must end in blood and neo-Stalinism. He thought that Cardinal Wyszyński, still confined in his monastery, could help save him from street demonstrations. He sent a cabinet minister to Wyszyński to beg him to return. Between them Gomulka and Wyszyński almost certainly saved Poland from the fate of Hungary. Such a result of an alliance between a Communist dictator and a cardinal was unique.

It was still the State's business to get rid of Christianity. Of adult graduates, 19 per cent said they were atheists – a very high figure where Catholicism and nationality were in such union. Clubs of Young Rationalists – 2,000 such clubs by 1974 – were surprisingly popular unlike the dreary state of most atheist clubs in the Russian Empire outside Bulgaria. The Communists were not in a hurry to secularize. Haste had failed. They believed that secularization would happen by industrialization, and they thought that they could afford to wait.

The contrast with other Communist states was extraordinary. Statistics tell the story. In 1965 there were 4,000 ordinands, 7,000 monks, 2,600 nuns, more than 70 bishops, plenty of priests (19,456 priests in 1976) and 30 and more seminaries; attendance at mass was very high (about 55 per cent of the people) and catechetical instruction was almost uncontrolled. Pilgrimages were plentiful. In 1975 there were one and a quarter million pilgrims to the chief shrine of the nation at Czestochowa.

Intellectuals started to be interested in the Church: sometimes in Christianity more than in the Church; sometimes in the Church more than in Christianity. For there they could see a freedom of the mind and heart in this stifling state.

The Churches began to experience a very rare pastoral problem. Artists, journalists, writers sought a freedom, which they could not find from the State, inside the Church. Some of them took up again a membership which they once had in childhood and then dropped; others came into the Church without any background. But whether they returned or came for the first time, they were trained by a Marxist view of the world. How the Churches should meet this intellectual movement towards them was a question which had not confronted bodies of bishops for some centuries.

Towards the end of his life, Cardinal Wyszyński, now a legend, was backed by the trade-union movement Solidarity, which, with its leader Lech Wałęsa, expressed its antipathy to the Party by a devout Catholic adherence. Poland was the only country in Europe where religion was a binding force in a trade-union movement engaged in fighting its government for the sake of the workers' rights. In the near-bankruptcy of the country, the Communist government had to keep wages down. On which side should the Church leaders stand?

In 1978 the election of a Pole to be Pope caused a fervent wave of patriotism and even nationalism among the Poles. It was a sign that Poland was not at the fringe of European culture but at its heart.

The election was greeted by the non-Catholics in Poland, Orthodox or Protestant, with a certain apprehension. It was so deeply ingrained in most of the Polish people that Pole equals Catholic, which was an axiom that much affected their work, that non-Catholics were nervous of an event which made the equation even more axiomatic. They did not like some of the effects of the wave of emotion – for example the illegal seizure by local Catholics of some Protestant Churches in what had been southern East Prussia and their failure to get them back by a process of law. They thought that some of the Catholic pressure on Protestants in Silesia stank of the methods of the Counter-Reformation. Not being linked with the workers' movement, their relation to a government which was non-Catholic, even if hostile to religion, was happier. Their members were more likely to join PROM, 'the Patriotic

Movement for the National Revival'. All the Protestant Churches recorded an increase in numbers.[8]

The Catholic bishops sat uncomfortably. They believed that too radical a programme must lead to national bankrupty or Russian invasion, either of which would be calamity, and therefore they must support the government. They saw the danger of civil war. They also believed that, in the dire state of the Polish economy, strikes made everything worse. Wyszyński had to assure the workers of the backing of the Church and yet beg them not to go on strike. The bishops' main supporters, the working men of Solidarity, blamed them for having the least relation with the government. The government blamed them for encouraging anarchy; the workers blamed them for being a prop of government. The concessions went on – in 1981, for the first time, there were religious services in prisons and freedom to hold them in summer camps and then in hospitals.

Wyszyński died in 1981. His statue, pensive and in mitre, now looks down upon the main street of Warsaw, with the face of a giant who thinks profoundly. The Poles look back upon him as one of the great bishops, one of the great Poles, whom they have known in their national history. Conservative though he was in doctrine and ethics, he focused their aspirations for liberty. By a mixture of courage and wisdom, and with the aid of a Polish Pope, he prepared the way, step by step, for the return in Poland, after nearly half a century, of a government with Christian ideals.

Matulionis in Lithuania

There were two archbishops in Lithuania: of Kaunas and of

8. In 1982 they had an interesting commemoration. Julius Bursche was a Lutheran who helped to build the independent Polish state in 1918 and after. He tried to persuade the makers of Versailles that Ermland and Silesia and Masuria were Polish and not German, but in vain. He thought that if Poland had been fully constituted it would greatly raise the numbers of Polish Protestants. When the Germans conquered Poland, Bursche was the Lutheran bishop in Warsaw. They put him in Sachsenhausen concentration camp, where he suffered much. He died in 1942. So he did not live to see that his dream was fulfilled in 1945 and that Silesia and Masuria and Ermland became part of Poland and that his hopes of a bigger Protestant Church failed because the conquering Poles ejected the Protestants westward.

Vilnius (or Vilna). The Kaunas archbishop fled to the West. The other bishops in office were all deposed but one of them was shot after a trial and the other archbishop and another bishop went to prison. The only bishop who was allowed to survive in his see was Paltarokas of Panevèžys, who was the first bishop of the see and went on till his death in 1958. The reason why he was allowed to survive seems to have been that he was the only bishop to tell the Lithuanian partisans to lay down their arms. After his death there was no full bishop in Lithuania: all dioceses were run by apostolic administrators or auxiliary bishops or vicars-capitular, all of whom had to have the approval of the State and many of whom were sent off to prison camps not long after they had been allowed to take office.

During the 1960s Rome was able to provide, though with difficulty, apostolic administrators to perform bishops' functions. In 1955 Steponavičius was legally consecrated an assistant bishop, but he was soon put out because he refused to forbid his priests to teach religion to children.

Now help came from one of the released bishops. This was Matulionis, who had the most extraordinary career of any European bishop in the twentieth century. At the revolution of 1917 he was serving in Russia. Six years later he was a defendant in a great show trial but got only three years. On release he kept being rearrested and put into camps. In 1929 he was secretly consecrated a bishop in Leningrad; this won him a sentence of ten years. But four years later he was exchanged with some Communists whom the Lithuanians held, and he started to serve the Church in Lithuania. In the middle of the Second World War, under German rule, he was made Bishop of Kaisiadorys, the smallest diocese. From 1946 he was therefore again in prison for ten years. On his release he was not allowed to be a bishop, but he secretly consecrated Sladkevičius to run his own diocese. He died finally in 1962, at the age of eighty-nine. Thus this confessor was exceptional: an active priest about twenty-four years, and some five years in prison; as a bishop, nine years active, fourteen years in various prisons, six years of forced retirement. The evidence is that he was a good man. The career showed how little and yet how much a bishop of the catacombs could do.

This illicit origin of Sladkevičius's orders made it impossible for him to do much for many years. But in about 1977, to everyone's surprise, he started to appear at services. The result of this paucity of bishops was that when confirmations happened they were huge – 2,600, 3,000, on occasion more.

PART TWO

═══

WESTERN EUROPE

6

The West and Marxism

For a lot of people in the West between 1945 and 1956 the reputation of Russia, and therefore of Stalin, was golden. They had saved the world from Hitler; now they were saving Europe from American capitalism. The ideals of the radical socialist, which were strong in Eastern Europe though always a minority, were also strong in the West, though with a smaller minority. Some of these radicals believed that a Communist system was the only way to rescue the working man and the poor. If the faith of the extreme left was put like that, it was inevitable that some Western Christians would be sympathetic. In addition the Western alliance began to make a lot of noise about the need for nuclear bombs to defend itself against Russian onslaught. Some of the Christians most sympathetic to the Communist regimes in Eastern Europe, like Hromádka in Prague, believed that Communism stood for the demolition of an immoral mode of war or defence. And anyone in the West who talked about the need for nuclear deterrence was likely to make some radical Christians sympathize with the Communist East.

In the French Church, one of the most influential minds was the Dominican M. D. Chenu. He had been a regent of the pontifical university at Saulchoir but was ejected for his radicalism in 1942. He was attracted to the Soviet system, and partly because of nuclear war. He found in St Thomas Aquinas a morality of work and the working man which made him conceive of a Christian theory of labour and of the proletariat which had room for sympathy with a Communist theory of society.

The experiment of 'worker priests' – that is, priests who seek to Christianize the society of the factory by accepting employment as factory workers – started during the war, when French labourers were carted off to Germany. Secretly the bishops sent some twenty-five priests to share their labour and to minister to them. One of them was Henri Perrin, who kept a diary of what happened and so made the idea of a worker priest famous. The experiment rested upon the belief that industrial humanity was alienated from the Church, which was part of the structure of a bourgeois society, and therefore the Church must send its ministers to the work-bench not merely as chaplains to factories but as identified with the workers and able to share their outlook. In Marseilles a Dominican, Jacques Loew, was working as a docker. In the immediate postwar years several French religious orders sent men into industry to be worker priests in the great cities. Such people quickly overcame the suspicions of the workers and began to build little Christian cells.

But the workers were members of a great union, the Confédération Générale du Travail, which was dominated by Communists. Could a worker priest engage in union business and adopt the notion of a class war shared by some of the leaders of his union? As the priests worked side by side with the labourers, they discovered cases of inhuman working conditions and grew to share the workers' political radicalism. Chenu was the chief theorist of the movement. He wanted to make the priest part of this pagan but idealizing world in order to insert the Church into its structure.

There was beginning to be a conflict which was not only a difference of political views. What was the relation of the worker priest to the priest of the parish? The worker priest was persuaded that the parish priest had no comprehension of what was needed. The parish priest, and behind him the bishop, saw an overturning of the parish system. Chenu and his people saw the worker priests as a kind of religious order which ought largely to be exempt from the control of parish and bishop. And bishops did not like it when a few of 'their' priests were arrested for taking part in an illegal strike or being part of a violent demonstration. Were the priest-workers more workers than priests?

On 23 September 1953 the new nuncio to France, Marella, announced that Pope Pius XII abolished the worker priests because they were a cause of scandal. Henceforth they must not work in a factory more than three hours a day – an order which made their work impossible. The worker priests were ordered by the bishops to submit. Seventy-three out of ninety signed a declaration that they could not submit because they would not abandon their struggle for the working man.

In the event some forty worker priests resigned their secular job.

The rest were reorganized so that their work could be only part-time. The entire group of French Dominicans was for a time under threat. Three of their provincial heads were dismissed.

When John XXIII became Pope, the French cardinal Feltin tried to persuade him to reverse the decision of Pius XII. Pope John only confirmed it: to work on a building-site or a factory was not compatible with the vocation of the priest.

On the one hand, ministers needed to be workers among workers and therefore to share their axioms: in so doing, they made the Church and all society aware of the alienation and the need of the industrial worker. On the other hand it was argued that work in a trade union is political and should therefore be left to lay people; that the minister has a calling to minister to all humanity and should not identify himself with a particular class within humanity; and that a worker's soul was no different from anyone else's soul – the home and the family were much nearer the heart than was the workbench. And when so many parishes were short of priests, could the Church afford to give up so many man-hours to a very specialized area where there could only be modest results?

The Second Vatican Council cured the legal tension by its decree *De Presbyterorum Ministerio* in December 1965, accepting that manual labour could rightly be part of the work of a priest. By 1975 there were some 500 French priests and some 300 Italian priests at least in part-time industrial work. Unlike their predecessors they tried to keep out of politics. (This was not true in Latin America, where the idea of the worker priest spread rapidly and where it was associated with the 'theology of liberation' – even with the need to baptize revolution.)

In the Church of England and Lutheran Germany the same experiment was tried, but in small ways and with far smaller numbers engaged and with far less controversy – though not without some controversy.

One link between some Christians and the radical left in France was found in the 'student revolution' of 1968. When all the world's youth was emotional, French youths were in as much turmoil as American students. Throughout France the seminarists or Protestant theological students were as disturbed as any other group of young men and women. Idealism went wild. Some of the young people saw a chance to overthrow a capitalist order of society and to institute justice and equality. A Dominican preached a Lent course in that year in which he urged that a true Lenten penance would be to start a general strike. Chenu was one of the leaders to urge the Christians to join the students in a struggle for a better society and to cause revolution.

In May 1968 a group which named itself Christians and Socialist Revolution formally approved the Marxist analysis of society. In Paris and Berlin there were student demonstrations in church services and interruptions of preachers. This was the age when Chairman Mao in China was revered by some Christians of the far left, and Castro in Cuba received a respect little short of that given to Mao. At Rennes, in Brittany, the seminarists declared themselves militant Maoists and transferred to the faculty of arts. There was arson in the cathedral of the Sacré-Cœur at Montmartre. And some of the left engaged in practices which were radical in church: they held communions without any priest, and celebrated them in the middle of an ordinary meal, and abolished all distinction between clergy and laity.

In France, a body of workers separated from Catholic Action because they thought it too bourgeois and made a separate Workers' Catholic Action. Their annual meeting of 1971 accepted the class struggle and agreed to aim at demolishing capitalism in all its forms, and to fight for a socialist society, and to aim at the total liberation 'to which Christ calls all men'. They sent a delegation to the Pope, who listened with friendliness and begged them to go on with their work.

The curious thing in France was the steady politicization of French Protestantism. The Reformed in Hungary were very socialist in politics, but they needed to get on with their masters. The Reformed in France had no such motive for identifying religion with social reform. Their members were mostly not working-class, except in Alsace-Lorraine; they were highly educated, and were free. But they said much the same sort of things as the Hungarians. There came to be a certain gulf between clergy and laity: the pastors determined to show their commitment to society, the lay folk wanting them to be quiet men of Bible and prayer and not to be political. In 1972 there was a shock when an official committee issued a document asserting that the real Christ was a revolutionary, or at least a daring radical in his political and social objectives, and accusing the officialdom of the French Reformed Church of shameful truckling to capitalist power. When the media treated this effusion as if it were a Protestant encyclical, the debate grew passionate and there was almost a split in the Church.

If, then, we find French Reformed pastors preaching a social gospel and identifying it with anti-capitalist social change, we must ask whether the Lutheran bishop Káldy in Hungary was justly accused of kowtowing to a Communist State when he did the same, or whether there was a deeper common problem in the relation of Christianity to industrial life.

THE SECOND VATICAN COUNCIL AND THE COLD WAR

John XXIII

Angelo Roncalli came from a peasant family near Bergamo, below the Italian Alps. Not since 1590 had a Pope come from so simple a family. He was the first future Pope to serve as a conscript in the army. He had experience as a pastor in the north, and taught church history. From 1925 he was sent off to a sort of exile as apostolic delegate in Bulgaria and later Istanbul, for nineteen years which he used to get to know the Eastern Orthodox Church and to develop an ecumenical mind and, during the war, to help the Jews. This last drew the attention of Pius XII, who in 1944 moved him to Paris – a still unexplained promotion from obscurity to the centre – to cope with the very difficult scene where so many French bishops were accused of cooperating with the German occupying forces. He handled the French government excellently. In 1953, when he was seventy-two, he was made Patriarch of Venice and a cardinal.

Roncalli was elected Pope (1) because he was old and the cardinals would be able to have another election soon, (2) because at Venice he showed that he treated Communists more moderately than had Pius XII, (3) because after so shut-up a Pope the cardinals longed for a jolly, outgoing man. He astonished everyone by his first act, when he chose a name which had not been used by Popes for five and a half centuries and was last used in some particularly troubled circumstances.[1] (There was a John XXIII in 1410, during the Great Schism, but no one quite knew whether he was a valid Pope or not.)

Only three months after his election John XXIII announced that he was summoning a General Council. It had been assumed that the first Vatican Council of 1870, with its elevation of the Pope into the supreme ruler of the Church, had made General Councils unnecessary. Most of the Roman Curia thought that. The Church was much more efficiently run by a civil service with experience than by a crowd of bishops from all over the world. The effect of a Council must be, at least for the time while it was sitting, an unwelcome intervention in the normal processes of administration. Even the Italian bishops distrusted what an unpredictable Pope had decided to do. But in the world at large, among nearly everyone who was not responsible for organizing it or finding the money or housing the bishops who would come, the announcement was greeted with excitement. The Pope seemed to have no particular agenda – except renewal: summon apostolic men from all over the world, let them listen to God and each other, and regeneration will come. All over Europe the word *aggiornamento* became a word of every language, to mean bringing the Catholic Church up to date. The word came to symbolize the hopes of the Protestants and of the Catholics who thought that their Church lagged behind the times.

It took three years and eight months of work before the Pope could open the Council, in St Peter's at the end of October 1962. It met till December, when he adjourned it for nine months. He did not survive to see the second session.

1. He also showed a disregard of precedent by abolishing the rule from the sixteenth century that the maximum number of cardinals should be seventy. He made fifty-four new cardinals in only four years, more cardinals than had elected him. By the time he died they were eighty-seven. In 1973 his successor brought a little order into the future by ruling that the number of cardinal-electors must not exceed 120 and by enacting (in 1970) that after the age of eighty a cardinal lost his right to vote in an election. This made the cardinals' college more international, and less liable to domination by the Italian cardinals, and was the precondition for the election of a non-Italian Pope twenty years later. It was also likely to make some later elections more difficult, because the number of possible electors almost doubled.

Meanwhile he issued a series of encyclicals and created bodies to carry the Church outward. The most important of these bodies was the Secretariat for Christian Unity (1960) which, under Cardinal Bea, adopted an outgoing attitude to the Protestants. The most important of the encyclicals were *Mater et Magistra* (1961), because it demanded the help of the richer nations for the poorer, and *Pacem in Terris* (1963), because it jettisoned the very ancient Christian idea of the just war on the ground that in a nuclear age just wars are not possible. Its attitude to the Cold War and the possibility of reconciliation impressed the Russians. A more open outlook towards Eastern Europe secured the release of the Ukrainian Uniat metropolitan Slipyj, who had suffered in a Russian gaol for over seventeen years and now came to live in exile at Rome.

It was a short pontificate. No Pope since Pius IX, who died in 1878, more influenced the history of the Church. No Pope was more beloved and trusted by so many Protestants. The Church had fought a battle during the sixteenth century and got stuck in a defensive posture. The fight against the Italians in the nineteenth century had frozen the defensive posture into a fixture which hurt the Church in the modern world. But we cannot say that John XXIII single-handedly drove the Church out of defence and into a quest to serve the world, for he could not have achieved what he did unless his utterances met a vast subconscious yearning within both the Catholic and the Protestant worlds.

Paul VI, Pope 1963–78

Giovanni Montini had worked in the Vatican Secretariat of State since 1922 and therefore knew the international Church better than any of the survivors from pre-war Rome. He also chose an unusual name as Pope, for the last Paul had been elected almost 350 years before. He was the first Pope to be able to use international airlines, and so further transformed the image of the Pope from the man of the sanctuary to the man of a public evangelism. He went as pilgrim to the Holy Land and to Fatima in Portugal, and said prayers in Santa Sophia in Istanbul, and made a speech to the United Nations, and visited Bombay.

To succeed John XXIII was not easy. Paul VI suffered at first from the contrast of their personalities: from the overflowing to the restrained, from the peasant's heavy child to the frail intellectual. But the world liked a Pope who was troubled about the world. They admired the gravity and the sense of inquietude and the feeling that the personality had mystery. His magic did not reach far – he could hardly communicate to a crowd. He made dramatic gestures, but usually they did not win hearts. He gave his tiara to the poor and more than once offered to take the place of hostages seized by hijackers. His giving of the bishop's ring to Archbishop Ramsey of Canterbury and his public kissing of the foot of the emissary of the Patriarch of Constantinople cast aside centuries of Protestant and Orthodox fears that Popes were arrogant. He did not quite win the world. But anyone who talked to him individually knew that he, the visitor, was the only person in the world who then mattered to Paul. At the personal interview Paul was a genius.

He felt his duty to be a heavy burden. He had almost no talk that was not spiritual and religious, even when he walked for refreshment in the garden. He worked long hours. He read many books. And he found all that was happening in the Church a disturbance – so many nuns giving up their habits, Dutchmen putting on jazz music in church, American priests writing about the rightfulness of homosexual behaviour. He did not exude happiness. But he did exude compassion and kindness. There was nothing bitter in him. He did not easily take decisions. He postponed, and postponed, while the problem grew worse.

Each autumn of his first three years the Vatican Council met for another session. Paul's greatest feat was to bring the Council to an end within reasonable time. It finally closed on 8 December 1965. He had altered various of its texts on his own authority but it accepted the alterations.

RELIGIOUS LIBERTY

One decree of the Council was directly affected by the Cold War, and its final version was in part caused by the Cold War. This was the decree on religious liberty.

It was Catholic dogma that there cannot be liberty to teach error. The doctrine said that where Catholics were in a majority the government of the State had the duty to encourage them and to discourage Protestants or unbelievers. Where Catholics were a minority, the government of that State had the duty to give them the freedoms of religion which they needed. This doctrine looked hard to defend morally. To meet the times and yet maintain what seemed like a platitude – that there can be no *right* to teach *wrong* – it was modified thus. Where Catholics were a majority – Spain, Portugal, Italy, France, Austria, for example – the State had in principle the duty to discourage error. But there might be considerations – the welfare of all the people, or the contentment of social life – which would make it expedient, for the time, to tolerate the teaching of error. This justified France giving Protestants total freedom and Spain giving Protestants some freedom.

To the Vatican Council came two different groups of bishops determined to overturn this grudging toleration even if what they wanted had been condemned by past Popes.

The first were the convinced democrats – especially the American bishops. Democracy meant free religion for everyone. Their observation of what happened in Eastern Europe strengthened their conviction that democracy is the best, the most moral, perhaps the only Christian form of constitution. They had this conviction built into them as children of the United States. The Americans were backed by several groups of West European bishops, of whom the most influential drafter was De Smedt, the Bishop of Bruges in Belgium, for in Belgium they were long used to marrying a Catholic majority of the people to a democratic constitution.

It is not certain that the convinced democrats would have got their way if they had found few allies. The Italian cardinals were still the most powerful cardinals in the Church and they largely controlled the business and procedure of the Council. Most of them could not see anything wrong with the traditional doctrine of the Church. The Spaniards were almost solid for tradition.

The argument was hard fought. There were suggestions that, since no agreement could be reached, the council would do well to drop the plan to make a declaration on religious liberty. But the eyes of the world were on the Council. Archbishops like Spellman of New York or Cushing of Boston could hardly fly home to America with heads aloft if the Vatican Council did not demolish the idea of liberty for Catholics only and declare that the Church wanted liberty for everyone.

The vote was supposed to be taken in 1964, but the Pope postponed it and caused anger in the defenders of liberty. So it came to 1965.

It was in these debates that the key allies of the Americans were manifest. The bishops under Marxist governments had even more reason than the democrats to know that you can only truly claim religious freedom for yourself if you concede it on principle to everyone else. The Cardinal of Cracow, Wojtyla, a future Pope, was influential in this sense, and he was not the only Polish bishop; Cardinal Slipyj, the head of the Uniats of the Ukraine, who had served many years in a Russian prison and whose flock was still illegal in Russia, was on the same side; and some witnesses thought that the most decisive of all was Cardinal Beran of Prague. As he was only lately released from sixteen years of prison, his words moved the Council as the speech of a confessor of the faith. The long Czech experience, he said, ever since the burning of John Hus in the fifteenth century and the forcible re-Catholicizing of Bohemia in the early seventeenth century, had 'taught that oppression of conscience, even when intended for the good of the true faith, was pernicious ... History warns us ...'[2]

These Easterners, some of them refugees from behind the Iron Curtain, in effect said to the Council, you must help us with our Marxist governments and you will help us most by declaring that religious freedom is a fundamental human right.

2. Beran's speech in *Acta Vat. II*, iv, i, 393.

The Declaration on Religious Liberty was finally accepted on 19 November 1965, by 1954 votes to 249 votes – which in the circumstances was not a little minority. It expressed the biggest change in Christian attitudes wrought by the Vatican Council. It transformed the possibility of friendship between Catholics and Protestants. And it directly affected the conditions under which the Churches worked with Marxist governments.

THE COUNCIL AND COMMUNISM

One more declaration by the Vatican Council affected the issue. In its final form this had the first words 'Gaudium et Spes' (joy and hope), and as such it became the best-known title to come out of the Council. It was intended as a pastoral constitution on the place of the Catholic Church in the modern world.

A lot of bishops thought that the urgent thing for the Church to do was solemnly to condemn Communism. Many Italian bishops wanted this because in Italy they faced the largest Communist party in the West. Many Spanish bishops wanted it because they were grateful to General Franco for protecting them from Communism and remembered the massacres of their Civil War. They were backed by people who suffered under Communism – a former bishop of Nanking in China, a Jesuit bishop (Hnilica) who had been ill-treated in Czechoslovakia and was now in exile in Italy, a Yugoslav bishop of Split, an exiled Uniat from the Ukraine, an exiled Ruthenian Uniat. The Ruthenian told the Council that dialectical materialism is the dragon of the Book of Revelation. One of the Portuguese (Archbishop Soares de Resende) demanded that the Church condemn police states, especially those under Soviet domination. So when the draft appeared and had no crisp mention of atheism, these bishops were dismayed and militant.

But the drafters did not want such a condemnation. They did not want the Council to put all its backing behind the decree of the Holy Office of 1949 which excommunicated anyone who helped the Communists. They wanted to be peaceable: to recognize that 'Marxism' and 'Communism' were words with various interpretations and that blanket condemnations were clumsy and would be due more to the atmosphere of Cold War than to serious thought. And they wanted to help the Christians in the Marxist states: they must not drive deeper the wedge which divided those citizens from their governments. Their mood was that modern atheism is a phenomenon which must be understood, in its social and historical context. They wanted to encourage dialogue with Communism, and not to force Communists to declare that they were not Christians. These were the liberals of the West – not, mainly, American, for the Americans feared Communism and were therefore divided, but Cardinal Alfrink of Utrecht, the leading French and German theologians, Cardinal König of Vienna, who was making the Christians in the former Austro-Hungarian empire his especial concern, and one or two Arab bishops. They were backed – it was truly important – by the leaders among the bishops from behind the Iron Curtain who had been allowed to come to the Council. The weightiest of these was Wojtyla of Cracow, the future Pope John Paul II.

The draft on atheism said, after some moderate language, that the Church laments and reprobates the pernicious doctrines which are contrary to reason and experience. A new clause was added by the conservatives, saying that the Church not only reprobates but does it as it has always done it; and then a footnote added references to the tremendous condemnations of Communism in the past. The moderates consoled themselves that footnotes have not the authority of the decree and that even this footnote did not mention the excommunication of Communism by the Holy Office in 1949.

7
The Way of Worship

One change enabled Protestant and Catholic to draw closer together. Both altered their ways of worship, radically and almost simultaneously, and the result was to make Protestants feel more at home in Catholic worship and Catholics feel more at home in Protestant worship.

The Second World War, and resistance to Nazism, left a mood of conservatism, of preferring to stand in the old ways. But from the later 1950s and in the 1960s it was clear that the old forms did not hold or attract the young, who wanted experiment and freer forms of worship. Therefore the reconstruction of liturgy in those years was the most radical since the age of the Reformation. All Western Christendom, apart from the free services of the Protestant left wing, radically changed its forms of worship between 1955 and 1980. These changes always divided Churches between those who loved the old language and those who saw a necessity for the new. What the 1960s and 1970s proved was that the old idea of an absolutely fixed liturgy was dead, whether among Catholics or Protestants. Language changed too rapidly to make any words final; and, above all, the movement of peoples made the old heritage of a language unfamiliar to immigrants. Newcomers to Germany wanted to understand German and knew nothing of Luther's archaic German. Newcomers to Britain knew of English as an international language, not as the literature of Archbishop Cranmer or Shakespeare. The same movement of peoples made the historic acceptance of Latin services in the Roman Catholic Church equally doubtful: the old inhabitants of Europe had been brought up on Latin, but to the newer inhabitants of Europe the language was not only dead but very difficult.

The Churches faced a task such as they had not met for 400 years. A way of worship needed to be felt to be not 'invented'; that is, it had to stand in a tradition of a past inheritance so that the worshippers were linked to the ways of their parents and beyond them to the Christian centuries. It had to be felt to be 'objective' and not just 'what I like'. There had to be found words and rituals that were rooted in history and yet were new enough to be used by young people as words that spoke to and within their souls.

Because change was in the air, radical pastors or priests tried every sort of innovation, or even gimmick, in order to make their services live and not be the formal recitation of dead language. Very radical experiments did not last, because they were found to require hours of preparation if they were to succeed, and could not be 'put on' in church every Sunday.

The changes of language carried certain other changes. They allowed a bigger participation in the rite to a lay people, who now understood far better what was being said and done. The new liturgies all allowed a much larger scope for lay people to take part in reading, or conducting prayers, or sharing in ritual acts.

The Catholics sought to make their new liturgy truly congregational. This idea of a congregational liturgy was the ideal of the Protestant Reformation. But the Protestant Churches had not succeeded in putting it into practice, because the lay people were always too passive, or because the ministers were too clerical and dominated the prayers. And now the Protestant Churches struggled to adapt their liturgies to the modern age, and a big part of that endeavour was to make their liturgies such that the people took more part. The great Churches were engaged on the same endeavour in reforming their ways of prayers. It was natural that the result should bring them much closer together.

A piece of scholarship helped this process. Historians gained more understanding of the ways of worship in the primitive Western Church during the earliest days of Christianity. This new knowledge affected those who drafted both types of liturgy, Catholic or Protestant, and made them less far apart.

In all the main Protestant Churches the prayer-books were being altered between 1955 and 1980. The Lutherans of Germany redrafted in 1955–64, the United Churches of Germany in 1956–63, the Church of England in 1960–80 (the Alternative Service

Book, 1980).[1] The new forms, valued by some as a release from obsolete words and an enrichment by new words, ran into criticism from both sides. Lovers of an old liturgy could not be content with the loss of words which had spoken to their souls. The Bavarian Lutheran Church approved a new liturgy, but many congregations went on with their old. In the Roman Catholic Church of France and Switzerland it came to a schism, under Archbishop Lefebvre, when the conservatives refused to accept what Rome decided. In England the lovers of the old prayer-book were numerous, and many congregations preferred to remain in the old ways.

On the other side, some young people found the new ways still too 'remote'. Several groups of young German Protestants offered other forms of service. They wanted more freedom from ritual words and actions; they focused their attack upon the words of the creeds and later upon the words of psalms and hymns; they wanted more political and social engagement, so that the Church should be felt to be less distant from modern needs; they wished for modern music; and they wanted to turn the sacrament into a more evident common meal of brotherhood. But all these proposals broke the law that a ritual needs to be felt to be a link with past generations, and they had little success.

The Catholic liturgy was rooted in the earliest texts of the second and third centuries AD. By the eighth century the Roman liturgy had already a long tradition. It then had a further period of

---

1. The Bible readings were part of worship. In what language should they be read? The same age saw modern translations take the place of the historic Reformation translations which had helped to form the vernacular languages and their literature; the Luther Bible, the King James Version in England, the Kralitzer Bible in Czech, the Karolyi Bible in Hungarian, etc. The Herder Bible of 1965 was revised as the Jerusalem Bible, 1966. There were problems over the colloquial. If you meant to be understood, did you follow the Swedish translator Grönlund (1962) and make Salome dance striptease and turn the scribes into professors and the high priests into archbishops? Most successful in the English colloquial was the Good News Bible (1976); most scholarly in the non-colloquial, the New English Bible (1970). It was a sign of the ecumenical age that Catholic and Protestant translators helped each other and used each other's versions. Each side conceded a point. To help the Protestants, the Catholics allowed the Old Testament Apocrypha to follow the Hebrew Old Testament. To help the Catholics – and also to help understanding by people who were puzzled by such words as grace, or baptism, etc. – the Protestants conceded that limited comments on the text were permissible.

growth, but these changes were designed to help the piety of the clergy more than the understanding of the people. In the sixteenth century the criticisms of the Protestants caused the Council of Trent and the Counter-Reformation to make changes which yet maintained the old Latin language and the substance of the older form. This way of worship laid down in the Counter-Reformation was accepted as a sacred inheritance and was thought to be valid for ever.

The piety of the Counter-Reformation which stamped the words sounded strange in modern devotion. In those days the piety of the people was centred less in the mass than in other forms of religiosity – pilgrimages, special prayers, statues, saints. Then came the industrial world and the pressure of materialism on the environment in which people's minds grew up. If they were to be helped to apprehend another world, they needed a way of worship which was not to one side of their lives. They needed to be able to share in it, and understand it, and feel that they could understand what was being done. The arguments for dropping Latin were overwhelming – except for an overwhelming argument on the other side: that this was the sacred language of the liturgy, that it linked the Catholic Church because everyone of whatever language could join in when they went to church, and that people whose souls were formed by the use of historic words would suffer religious and not only aesthetic damage if the words to which they were accustomed were to vanish, to be replaced by what? Who shall in a moment construct a range of vernacular liturgies which will carry the depth and the poetic feeling of the words which the Catholic Church attained after centuries of Latin usage?

Unenthusiastically, the Second Vatican Council allowed the liturgy not to be in Latin. The momentous decision was approved narrowly. Until the day before the final vote, the draft said that the sacramental words – for example the words of administration of the bread and wine – must be in Latin. The decisive fact in making an eleventh-hour change seems to have been the argument of the missionary bishops. Some of them lived among a people where magic was a danger. What would those people infer if the supreme sacramental moment suddenly went into a language which to them was as unintelligible as abracadabra?

This change, which Pope Paul VI carried out whole-heartedly, was what made the Second Vatican Council valued within the Catholic Church. Many older people regretted and resented the loss of the historic and sacred words. These were educated people, the middle classes who once knew something of Latin, people whose souls associated the old language with high aspirations or memorable experiences. The attitude was different among the pastors who looked after young people, and among the bishops who wanted to revive their churches. It was surprisingly different among the working classes. The Italian rural peasantry, who were a historical backbone of the Catholic Church, might have been expected to resent change in anything to which they were accustomed. They almost wholly approved of the Vatican Council. An enquiry discovered that the reason why the great majority liked it was because they could now understand the language of the mass. Polish bishops spoke against the change at the Council. Anyone who afterwards heard a Polish congregation praying in Polish, with emotional corporate fervour, will know that the common people were not on the side of the conservatives.

Archbishop Lefebvre

The existence of religious regret at the dropping of a lovely old Latin liturgy, together with the existence of widespread Catholic unsettlement at the nature of authority in the Church, combined to produce a conservative reaction. Mostly this was healthy – a rallying round, a defence of what was best in tradition. But as the radicals produced extremists, so the new conservatives produced extremists. And one of them set up a schism in the Catholic Church.

Lefebvre was a Frenchman who had retired from being Archbishop of Dakar in West Africa and had formerly been Bishop of Tulle in France. It took him a few years to meditate on his course of action. On 21 November 1974 he issued a strange declaration. He adhered with his whole heart to Catholic Rome. He rejected the new modernism and new-Protestantism of the Second Vatican Council. All the so-called reforms were ruining the Church, ruining the priesthood, destroying self-sacrifice and the love of the sacrament, weakening the call to be a monk or a nun to the danger of the religious life disappearing, and accepting evolutionary

teaching in universities and seminaries. Soon he denounced Pope
Paul VI himself, for modernism and liberalism and friendliness to
Protestantism. At the end of 1974 he opened his own seminary, at
Ecône in Switzerland, to train clergy as he thought they should
be trained. He felt an urgency. He believed that the Church was
dying by its readiness to conform to the modern world.

In normal circumstances Lefebvre would have dropped into
oblivion as an eccentric old man who had lost his way. But many
Catholics, who would not have dreamt of attacking the Pope and
discarding the Second Vatican Council, were unsettled. They
admired Lefebvre's courage in standing up for the old ways which
they valued. They loved Latin in their prayers and knew that he
asserted its necessity and the wrongness of the Church in dropping
it. He found a surprising number of supporters. In 1975 he was
able to lead a pilgrimage to Rome and celebrate the sacrament in
two Roman churches with several thousand pilgrims, and with
150 Ecône seminarists in cassocks and surplices. In France a few
parishes had fights over the possession of the church between
priests faithful to Lefebvre and priests faithful to their diocese.

On 29 June 1976, St Peter's Day, the incipient schism was
carried a stage further. At Ecône, Lefebvre ordained thirteen
priests and thirteen deacons, in the presence of 1,800 people –
mostly French – and in his sermon he declared that the Latin mass
was sacred and that Paul VI had no power to abolish it. Three
weeks later Paul VI removed from Lefebvre the right to celebrate
sacraments. These acts caused widespread emotion in France. A
French opinion poll produced a disquieting result for authority –
if a Lefebvre mass was nearby, 35 per cent of people said they
would go; though when it was asked whether if it came to a total
rupture they would side with Lefebvre or the Pope, only 18 per
cent of Catholics and 5 per cent of practising Catholics sided with
Lefebvre. Five is a small number but 5 per cent of practising
Catholics in France was a lot of people. The fact was clear:
Lefebvre, though he fought against Popes, had a wide body of
support which derived largely from the loss felt at the dropping of
Latin from the way of worship. A further question produced the
startling result that slightly more French Catholics thought that
the Second Vatican Council had done harm than thought it had
done good; but, when the same question was confined to practising

Catholics, those who thought it had done good were almost twice those who thought it had done harm. Still, to have nearly a third of practising French Catholics thinking that the Vatican Council had done harm was formidable. It was not surprising that Lefebvre had such support.

He blessed a chapel at Rouen and founded a French seminary and opened a priory in the diocese of Bordeaux and a chapel in Glasgow. In Belgium he set up a Carmelite house. In Madrid he lectured before a great crowd which afterwards sang the Falangist hymn – for Lefebvre also held opinions at the extreme right in politics. In the diocese of Cannes there was disorder in several churches and the curés had to summon police help. On 27 February 1977, after the Sunday mass, his people occupied the Paris church of St Nicolas-du-Chardonnet and no one could get them out. They used it as their Paris centre. The clergy and the parishioners went to court and with difficulty got a judgment in their favour, but no police authority wanted the scandal of shifting by force a large congregation – 3,000 to 4,000 every Sunday – out of a church, especially when the police knew that the general public was often on the side of the occupiers, and the Lefebvrists remained in St Nicolas for years.

On St Peter's-tide 1977 Lefebvre ordained at Ecône fourteen priests: nine French, two English, one American, one Hungarian and one Swiss. Some of these priests later left him and became priests of the Pope's Church.

All negotiations with Rome for some kind of settlement were in vain. When John Paul II became Pope he was believed to be more conservative, but again negotiations broke down. In 1986 he shocked Lefebvre by attending prayers at the synagogue in Rome, and even more by going to Assisi with the Dalai Lama and Archbishop Runcie of Canterbury and representatives of non-Christian religions and engaging in common prayer. In that November Lefebvrists occupied for a time the church of Saint-Louis de Port-Marly, and there was violence between them and the people. In 1988 Lefebvre made the schism worse by consecrating a bishop to ensure his succession. He died, excommunicated, in 1991.

NEW FORMS OF PRAYER

Were vestments necessary for the priest at the sacrament, or a surplice or a gown needed for the Protestant pastors? Young pastors wanted to feel near their young men and women and did not want to feel divided from them at the sacrament, so some of them started discarding the use of vestments. This was ruled to be wrong, for it was the custom of so many centuries which was broken.

It was the custom for the Catholic communicant to receive the host at the sacrament into the mouth. But to take into the hands was primitive, and more people now knew this and wished to follow that example. In 1969 Rome ruled that the local bishops could permit it.

Since the eleventh century it was Catholic custom for the laity to receive only in the one kind of bread and not to receive the wine at the sacrament. But Catholics now knew that this also was not primitive and some wanted to follow the earlier custom of receiving the wine also. The Second Vatican Council sanctioned it; though local rules might prefer intinction, that is dipping the wafer into the chalice rather than taking the chalice directly.

Among the experimental acts in the new liturgies, one of the most interesting was the dance. In Europe it would never be other than exceptional, but in parts of Africa it was a natural mode of divine praise and the congregations wanted it. Many Protestants tried it. Rome was not narrow about it. It knew of precedents among the saints, even Teresa of Avila. It knew that when Fra Angelico wanted to paint heaven he showed the angels and saints dancing. It knew that the body joins with the soul in worship and that it could be said that the body also prays, and can express itself in movement.

Yet dancing had never formed part of a liturgy, officially, and a series of councils had condemned it because it led to disorder. But Christendom was engaged in the belief that Christianity could foster all that was best within different cultures, and in some cultures dancing and worship were inseparable. Even in the

Eastern liturgy there was a ritual dance during the rite of marriage. The European Churches generally thought that by folk custom dance is linked with sensuality and if it were brought into religious services it would bring with it profane associations. They usually preferred that it should be used outside the liturgy.

Other experiments were made with modern music – sometimes too much music. Country villages, or even town churches, did not always find it possible to discover an organist. Since canned music was now easy to provide, they started to use tapes and discs, and later audiovisual aids during the liturgy. Already many churches used microphones, and the invention made an enormous difference to the intimacy of worship in the larger churches of all denominations. In historic Anglican cathedrals the microphone changed the feeling and the intelligibility of the spoken parts of some great service. No longer did a great preacher need a mega-voice as well as special gifts of mind and heart. The microphone also was a boon to the deaf, who for centuries had worshipped on their memories of what they had once been able to hear. But everyone was concerned lest large machines on pillars hurt the beauty of a church.

Pictures and photographs of holy works of art also began to be used to accompany services. The authorities were worried about taste – that pictures might be of sentimental or absurd quality and not reputable as works of art. The best of this new approach was to project texts on a screen or a wall. But some French experimenters began to use films and had to be told that this was not suitable for a sacramental service of worship. They also had to be told that films criticizing society are not suitable for any form of worship.

In 1978 there was held a European meeting on how to 'interiorize' the liturgy. There was discussion of the need to help people to 'adore'. Were words the best way? Was the formal ending of the collects a help? Was the sermonette, which in the 1960s and 1970s was finally driving out the sermon, a help? It was clear that long exhortations were no help at all. Ought they to examine more carefully other forms of communication which were not in words? It was impossible to do without words, or the Word, but the new liturgies showed that continual changes in words were no help. If the aim was to encourage quiet meditation, this was fostered by words that were well known, not by phrases that were unfamiliar.

The meeting was agreed that, despite the words and the readings and the music and the movement, a way of worship must be 'penetrated' by silence; and especially the president, who had to say most of the words, must be 'penetrated' by silence.

The experimenters wished pastors or priests to drop the wearing of clerical costume outside church. Instead of feeling that it was necessary to their mission always to be seen to be a minister, they felt that the need for sharing in everything with their neighbours made it better for them not to be distinguished from their neighbours. Rome repeatedly insisted on clerical dress outside church. It no longer minded if young ordinands did not dress up in cassock or have their heads shaved, but they said that the abandonment of clerical dress 'secularized' the priest and was like an abandonment of his mission. Paul VI felt this as a personal pain in the heart, as though he witnessed the loss of a sacred vocation. But the feeling of many ministers of all denominations was too strong, and the abandonment of clerical dress outside church advanced steadily, even or especially among Roman Catholics. Anglican bishops put off the gaiters and aprons which had been the rule since the eighteenth century; cardinals walked in far less purple. Pope John Paul I refused to be crowned as king of his state; Archbishop Ramsey of Canterbury travelled in the least impressive of cars.

Wherever the people were conservative, they wanted their priests to look like priests. In Greece, a considerable number of Orthodox priests, observing what was happening in the West, demanded that a priest might abandon his cassock and tall black hat outside the liturgy, and go about with less flowing robes, like a Western clergyman. The official journal of the Greek Church criticized them severely. It said that they were moved by the spirit of this world and that their innovation would be ill received by the people.

The habits of the Catholic priest, apart from his clothes, began to change. In the old world every priest was under an obligation to celebrate mass every day. That obligation remained in theory. It produced lots of little altars round a cathedral or a church or an abbey, sometimes with several little masses said almost simultaneously, so that each priest might celebrate his mass. This was out of keeping with the ideals of the liturgical movement, which centred in the corporate service in which everyone shared. On a vast occasion the old rule became absurd. At the centenary of the shrine at Lourdes in 1958, the millions of pilgrims were accompanied by thousands of priests. Where were they all to find altars?

The old rule was married with the new by the practice of concelebration, where even fifty priests together could join with the principal celebrant in consecrating at the mass. This was an Eastern custom which was put forward by a Maronite at the Second Vatican Council. It had been a general custom in the West only at the ordination of priests. The intolerable situation of monasteries which welcomed the ideals of the liturgical movement and yet had many priests among their monks was put forward at the Council by a German abbot. Therefore the Council sanctioned concelebration, though it left freedom to any priest to celebrate his private mass provided that he did not do it at the time and place of the concelebration.

This made a change in devotional feeling. The individual mass in the early morning was a central part of a priest's devotion; among the best of them it was the glory and the anchor of the priesthood. To share in a great mass was much more akin to primitive Christianity, and to the Protestants' ideal of the holy communion. The Catholic mood of the age believed that this was the right way to go. The number of priests who continued to say an individual mass declined. This is proved by a statistic. In 1976, 82 per cent of French priests celebrated mass daily. But if their age was more than fifty it was 94 per cent; if they were under fifty it was down to 61 per cent.

A second plank in the priest's life of devotion, Anglican as well as Roman Catholic, was the regular recitation of the daily offices in the prayer-book or breviary. This was regarded by many in the Church as a moral obligation. It had the help of regularity and of a glorious sequence of psalms. It had the demerit of taking time, and some of the younger priests did not find so many words a helpful mode of prayer. This was proved by an opinion poll in Tournai (Belgium) in 1975: 65 per cent of the older priests regularly kept the obligation, but only 15.5 per cent of younger priests. That was a change even more dramatic in habits of devotion than the change over the individual's mass.

Throughout Western Europe in the 1970s one change was sad. Unless the tradition of the country was Reformed (Presbyterian), churches in towns or in the countryside used to stand open all day for any visitor to pray or to peer. In the big cities churches had attendants to protect them from petty thieves, but country churches needed no attendants and seldom lost their furniture. By the 1970s this was no longer true. Whether it was the use of drugs and so the need for money at any cost, or whether it was the rising numbers of burglars, the decline of the family or the decline of the Churches, the furniture of country churches ceased to be so safe. In France and Britain and Germany many more churches were kept locked in 1980 than in 1960. One statistic: 409 statues or other objects of devotion were stolen from churches in Lorraine between 1974 and 1984.

8

Charisma

Pentecostalism started in the Middle West of the United States after 1900 as a new interest in the biblical experience of 'speaking in an unknown tongue'. The speaking of unintelligible words under religious emotion was accompanied by convulsions and sometimes by healings. One group thought that the gift of speaking with tongues was the proof that the soul was baptized by the Spirit of God. At first no one meant to create a new 'denomination'. But once Pentecostalists were numerous they needed ordering, and several denominations were formed. All the American Pentecostalists were rigidly fundamentalist – that is, they accepted every word of the Bible to be literally true. They practised healing but did not reject ordinary medicine. They were usually 'perfectionist' – that is, they believed that conversion made the soul morally holy. They had nothing formal in their liturgy, but much singing and some personal witness; the sermon was important, and they kept the two gospel sacraments.

Missionaries went out to Europe. The first Pentecostalist groups appeared in Norway, where by 1957 there were 250 congregations, the largest of the small non-Lutheran denominations. They drew on Methodist teaching about perfection, and were influenced by the Baptist doctrine of the need for adult baptism. By 1960 more than 9,000 Swedes were Pentecostalist, and that despite or because of scandalous onslaughts upon them in the press. The Swedish congregations were special in the high quality of their music.

But during the 1960s the charismatic experience spread from these special denominations into the main Churches: first in America – Lutheran, then Roman Catholic, then Anglican – later among the Lutherans of West Germany. In all the main Churches the effect of the charismatics was less divisive, because they were more like the old groups of pietists within the main body.

In 1966, students at Pittsburgh in the United States who were

Catholics experienced the charismatic outpouring and speaking with tongues found among Pentecostalists. Catholics began to have the same speaking force, courage and sense of an immediate gift of the Spirit that was found among some more extreme Protestants. When this moved into an older Europe it offended people's feelings, in that gifts of healing and speaking with tongues and prophesying in church were not what old Europe was used to – except that gifts of healing were found at shrines like Lourdes. In the materialist society there was a longing, especially among some of the young, for a truer spirituality, and a sense of the free spirit, and a feeling that religion is creative and not only receptive, and a yearning among solitary spirits for an authentic community such as the conventional Churches did not seem able to provide.

In 1971 was held the first international convention of the movement, in France, in the Ardèche, with 200 evangelical Protestants and two Catholics. By 1973 there were as many Catholics as Protestants at such a meeting, and two years after that the Catholics were in the majority. One of the famous Catholic charismatics in France was a mystic, Marthe Robin, who bore the marks of the stigmata on her body and died in 1981.

Sometimes those who practised contemplation among the Carmelites were drawn towards this spirit-filled type of expression. Sometimes the charismatics repudiated urban civilization; sometimes they were in the midst of the city, trying to help the outcasts and the drug-ridden who fell through the net of the welfare state. They usually took little notice of denominations, because the Spirit blew wherever it listed and took no notice whether they were Catholics or Protestants. But sometimes they revived some old shrine regarded in the conventional Church as almost obsolete, like the cult of the Sacred Heart at Paray-le-Monial.

In all Churches authority reacted first with scepticism and then with caution. But the movement had aspects which commanded respect – immediacy of religious experience, moral power and openness, sense of dependence upon divine Spirit. In Belgium the movement won the total assent of an influential cardinal – Suenens of Malines-Brussels. In 1975 Suenens led a charismatic pilgrimage to St Peter's in Rome and held there a charismatic act of worship. At the moment of holy communion the sound of glossolalia – unintelligible words in a 'tongue' – echoed through the church and was taken up and sustained by the instruments of a little orchestra and then by the organ, and there was joyous shouting. Never before had St Peter's seen such an act of worship. Paul VI did not come to the service but he came to them and gave an address calling on them to give the world a soul. He embraced Suenens before the shrine of St Peter and thanked him for what he had done for the Church.

This blessing by a Pope did not mean that authority among both Protestants and Catholics was not nervous. Christendom had had trouble with such sect-generating movements in past centuries and remembered the experience with pain. The Christian Church confessed that it believed itself filled with the Spirit, and so the Churches themselves were 'charismatic institutions'. On the other hand they distrusted sensationalism, and were afraid of a movement which might have a conscious quest for the marvellous; they wanted to keep saying that charity is a bigger thing than prophecy or miracles. They were also afraid of the Pharisaism that easily grew among such bodies – 'unless you have this special experience you are not a proper Christian' – and they were afraid of the conviction that an emotional experience of God is the only experience of God. Some charismatics rejected the intellect as irrelevant in religion. The Churches had spent many centuries defending the place of the intellect in religion, though sometimes half-heartedly.

No Iron Curtain could keep charisma out. In East Germany the charismatic manifestations happened; among Protestants in Russia the authorities of the Soviet Union were troubled; in Romania there were some 80,000 members by 1972. A Siberian Baptist, Voronaev, escaped to the United States and was affected and in 1920 returned to start founding Pentecostalist churches in Russia. They put him in a labour camp, spread the rumour that he had apostasized, released him, rearrested him, and we do not know his end. But by 1961 there were half a million Pentecostalists in the Soviet Union.

PILGRIMAGES

A people saw visions. In France, Spain, Austria, southern Germany, Poland, Yugoslavia the experiences were reported and drew enquirers or pilgrims. The historic sites of famous visions which had won their way to the heart of the faith, as at Lourdes or at Fatima, drew ever more pilgrims as travel became easier. Usually there was a pattern strangely like that at Lourdes or Fatima. A child or children saw a vision, usually of the Blessed Virgin, and usually with a simple message. The vision was mocked by local sceptics, but others were persuaded when someone was healed at the site. The local priest was forced to enquire, then the bishop. It was necessary to distinguish between people whose sole motive was religious and people who for reasons of lucre wanted to encourage pilgrims to come to the village. It was necessary to distinguish a vision from a fable or an illusion. In a majority of cases the Church authorities refused to recognize such an experience as authentic and refused to recognize that a place of cult was justified. But in a small number of cases that refusal was very hard. And quite often, when the Church condemned, the local people took no notice of the condemnation but persisted with the cult.

Let us take the case of Kerizinen in Brittany. The vision came not to a child but to a woman of twenty-eight as she watched cattle. The Lady came as the Lady of the Very Holy Rosary. She appeared fifty-eight times after 1938, the last time in 1965, and Christ appeared twenty-eight times. The people built an oratory at the spot, and in summer many visitors came to say their prayers. The rosary was said there every day. It was a message for a nuclear age. There will be a terrible mortality, the world is on the edge of an abyss. Then the Church will rise renewed in triumph, and France will be reconverted; and the Blessed Virgin spoke of her love for Brittany and for France, the eldest daughter of the Church.

Two bishops of Quimper in succession banned the cult and ordered the clergy to keep away. It continued as before.

The experiences occurred powerfully in conditions of illegality. We saw what happened at Medjugorje in Yugoslavia. Uniats in the Ukraine saw a vision of the Blessed Virgin above the church at Hrushiv. Police went to see what the excitement was about, authority talked of delusion, and the pilgrims kept coming to witness and to say their prayers – 80,000 a day according to *Pravda*.

Lourdes, near the Pyrenees, was far the biggest shrine. At the centenary, in 1958, the place attracted at least 6 million pilgrims. Bernadette, the girl of the original visions, was a saint: her language and her way of devotion might sound outmoded, of the mid nineteenth century, the little peasant of Bigorre; but she was authentic, with a quality above time. Then some healings, though of course a very small number in comparison with the millions who sought healing, were authenticated by the most sceptical of tests; the place was accepted and blessed by Popes; and it became the heart of French Catholicism.

In 1978 an enquiry was conducted into the kind of person who goes to Lourdes and for what reason.[1] It took as base the year 1977, when there were 4 million pilgrims. Nearly a quarter came in organized pilgrimages. Nearly half of these came from French parishes. Therefore pilgrimages organized by French parishes were only one eighth of all the pilgrims. Most pilgrims were retired people, with leisure. There were also a lot of young people. People in the middle of their lives were far fewer. More of them came from the countryside than from the towns.

When they came, they talked about a variety of concerns. Workers talked about unemployment. The poor talked about family life, and the way their young people seemed not to care for the Church or not to obey the ordinary code of morals which their parents accepted as necessary for a healthy society.

Some people, but not a majority, came wanting to be healed because doctors could do nothing, or came in search of a divine intervention in some terrible problem of their personal life. Some were naïve and wanted success in business, or success in passing an examination. People felt they could pray with fervour at the shrine. They loved the rites, the candles, the piscina, the procession, the grotto, the kissing of the rock. Usually such people were traditional in their Christian way and were disturbed by the

1. See *Documentation Catholique* 78, 333.

recent changes in the Church. Normally they were very attached to the Blessed Virgin as our Lady of Succour.

Others were active and instructed Christians who in their home parishes were regular churchgoers. If they looked for a miracle, it was rather that of conversion, or of deeper faith. They knew about Bernadette, and loved the simplicity of a direct vision of God.

Others were the interested, who believed not at all in healings, and regarded the rites with detachment and suspected the sentimentality which often went with them – and wanted to see the piety of the crowds rather than to share it; and yet they were half-sceptics with sympathy, wishing to share even if they could not.

Others went only because crowds went. They had no interest in the Blessed Virgin and knew nothing about Bernadette and thought nothing of the rites. They did not know what they wanted to find and usually they did not find anything. Such critics were usually young, educated and middle-class.

And lastly there were a few that came because they were hostile and wanted to see superstition so that they might know how to batter at its ramparts. And there were a few who were just 'marginal', as the marginal gather at every place where there are crowds.

But the evidence was that the people's feeling was not one of superstition. The place affected souls because it was a place where devotion happened, where people said their prayers, where they found a vast corporate act of Christian witness. They also found a welcome, and especially if they were sick or maimed or handicapped. And such people themselves were a source of the witness of the place, the discovery of happiness and courage amid suffering. That was more important than the sermons that were preached and than the advice which was given to those who went to the confessional (which very many of them did, and it was a problem to find enough confessors).

Another European focus of piety was the shroud of Turin. Until 1204 it was exposed every Friday at Constantinople; then it disappeared in the sack of the city. A century and a half later it was exposed at a house in central France and thence came into the possession of the Dukes of Savoy and was kept at a chapel in Chambéry. In 1578, during the French Wars of Religion, when every sort of relic was at risk of destruction, it was moved to Turin.

In May 1898 they took the first photograph of the shroud and were astounded that it showed the outline of a face which was hard to ascribe to a known artistic tradition. Four years later there was a serious scholarly attempt to prove its authenticity as Christ's shroud. During the 1960s and 1970s an argument over the shroud made it the most famous devout object in Europe. The dispute was finally settled in the 1980s, when modern dating methods proved that its origin was medieval.

SAINTS

The wave of criticism and reform touched the commemoration and the making of saints. For it entered the head of modern reformers that a basis for reform must be accurate information, and the one certain information was numbers. And when they collected the statistics about the making of the saints, the numbers bothered them.

Originally the saints of the calendar grew up by popular devotion. Ordinary people wanted to remember a man or a woman who had served humanity or at whose grave miracles were believed to happen. The cult of a saint began among the people who knew the person or the relics which he or she had left. At first such a person's quality was plain to the people – he or she had died for the faith. But when martyrs were less frequent, other signs of sanctity were revered by the people: like dedication to prayer and the simple life in a hermitage, or like eminent leadership of Christendom. Often the devotion never spread further than a small area. But where crowds collected, or amazing events happened, and fervour grew, the knowledge of the saint spread to other areas and provinces. The bishops would be asked whether this was a cult which their Church should take into its calendar. Hence, early in Christian history, came the need for regulation by authority. Bishops must see that the devotion of their people was directed towards persons that were truly holy and not show-saints, or towards relics that were not faked, or towards shrines that were not corrupt.

The temptation to corruption among the guardians of the shrines of saints was ever present. The stature of a saint brought pilgrims. Pilgrims brought money. Then the guardians could restore their church, or build a great shrine. It was not in their economic interest that the stature of *their* saint be diminished or questioned, even by the discovery of truth. Historians were not welcome personages to the lovers of historic saints. And did the historians matter? Simple people came to say their prayers at a tomb or icon or image where prayers had been said for centuries. Why should this piety and this prayerfulness be thrown into doubt by professors from universities or by learned Benedictine monks?

There was a particular class of Christian who had the best chance of being revered as a saint. This was the founder of a successful religious order or of a surviving monastery or nunnery. To be a successful founder a rare combination of qualities was needed – spirituality with a power of organization, together with magnetism to attract men or women as disciples to that way of life. But more important was the existence of the order, which owed so much to its founder. The order was a permanent body that did not die, with a corporate memory, and an interest that its founder be venerated. All the founders of great religious orders came into the Church calendar as saints.

Sometimes political motives entered. King Edward the Confessor was a good man but he became a saint partly because he founded at Westminster an abbey which was important to the English and partly because he was the last English king not to be a Norman and therefore he was a symbol for the people. Such a political motive for making a saint entered even in the twentieth century.

In every century it was easier to become a saint if the person was ecclesiastical – counting nuns among ecclesiastics. Most laymen or women not nuns did not have time for much prayer. More lay persons were canonized in the nineteenth and twentieth centuries than in all the previous centuries of the Church put together. Many of these modern laity were saints because of martyrdom rather than of quality of life before death – for example the canonization in 1964 of twenty-two Ugandan martyrs (perhaps a touch of political motive also entered here). Even in the twentieth century, which tried hard to bring the laity to share in the Church, the numbers of new saints (to the end of 1984) were: ecclesiastics 140, laity 36.

For a man it was four times easier to become a saint if he was a monk; for a woman it was twice as easy if she was a nun. In the year 1975 among the cases being put forward at Rome for people to be made saints, 77 per cent of those for whom applications were made were members of a religious order.

Statistically it was also more than four times as easy for a man to become a saint as for a woman. Why? There were more women than men in the Church. Women on average have more years to become saints than do men. No one doubted the gifts of spirituality found in women. Everyone knew that women were among the most valued saints in Church history. Yet as saints they were far fewer. Perhaps political motives were more rarely present, or perhaps until modern times it was harder for a woman to organize a religious order. Was it anything to do with the fact that the process of a canonization was conducted solely by men? Questions needed asking about the making of saints. Yet as the laity took a larger share in the Church, and therefore women took a larger share in the Church, the number of women saints grew. More women were canonized in the twentieth century than in the ten previous centuries.

Statistically it was easier if one was French or Italian. Even in 1975 among the candidatures for a canonization as saint, almost half out of those from the whole world were Italian and French.

The modern numbers of new saints were large by the standards of previous centuries. Why were the numbers growing? Did modern weaponry mean more murders and more murders mean more martyrs – such as Maximilien Kolbe, the martyr of Auschwitz who gave up his life to save another, or Edith Stein, the Carmelite murdered at Auschwitz and canonized in 1987?

Numbers of new saints:

  6 sixteenth century
 30 seventeenth century
 33 eighteenth century
 81 nineteenth century
176 twentieth century (to 1984)

What was the meaning of this? Just possibly it was due to a greater *historical* consciousness among ordinary people.

The permanence of religious orders had the effect of allowing changes in the ideals of sanctity to take their effect as the decades passed. In the fifteenth century the friar Savonarola of Florence, a preacher who stirred the city to puritan moral reformation and political change, was burnt at the stake as a heretic. In 1983 the Dominicans asked Rome to consider making him a saint. In the West Indies of the sixteenth century Las Casas was the passionate protector of the Indians against the European conquerors, and no one was ever more unpopular among his contemporaries. In 1983 the Dominicans also asked Rome to consider making him a saint.

With such rapid growth in numbers of saints, it was necessary to consider what was happening. Was the calendar to be flooded with saints' days?

The new Roman calendar of saints was published in 1969. It failed to reduce the numbers drastically. There remained 158 saints' days – among them more than half (89) for saints from Italy or France or Spain, and more than a third of them for people who belonged to religious orders. Local provinces then took a selection of these general days and married the list with their own local saints.

A new Anglican calendar was published in 1980 in which much the same principles reigned.

These calendars ousted obscure early martyrs and reduced the clutter. They introduced other names whom the Churches wished truly to remember – the Anglicans brought in Richard Hooker and Lancelot Andrewes and George Herbert and John Keble and others, including names which an earlier generation would never have allowed into a Protestant calendar – Sir Thomas More and St Francis de Sales. The last name was a sign of a certain bias in favour of 'mystics' in the calendar – no fewer than eight persons were famous 'mystics', and five of them were named as such by the calendar. 'Mystic' was a new word in any calendar, and a word which formerly was not complimentary as a description.

The Anglicans also showed how ecumenical was the age when they brought into their calendar names of persons who either dissented from the Church of England or acted in such a way as to deny its discipline – for example, John Bunyan and John Wesley.

The principles were good and made a far better calendar; and yet they were not easy to follow consistently. *Get rid of saints of whom we know nothing* – but could they get rid of St Nicholas, who was Santa Claus, or St George, who was the patron of the English nation? Both were kept. The day and the symbol were more important to the people than the person. With St Cecilia, the patron saint of music, the opposite happened. The historians said they knew nothing about her. The calendar did her out. It did not work. The musicians continued to celebrate her day. The people wanted her whether or not she existed. Her day and symbol were more important than her person.

In the Anglican calendar, omitting groups, there were sixty-six men and ten women. About 21 per cent were monks or nuns or friars, about a fifth, which is a lot for a Protestant Church but hardly an excess in relation to the Christian centuries. Just under half of the men were bishops, and bishops were never half the members of the Church. But this was a sign that what the people really wanted to remember was less sanctity than a power of Christian leadership, in which sanctity might be one element.

Of the women, three had been married. This was pointed, for it was difficult to find even three. In order to secure that result, it was necessary to insert one woman of whom nothing whatever was known (which was contrary to principle) and another woman only after controversy whether she should be there. This showed the inadequacy of calendars except as representative. No one doubted that among mothers were some of the best Christians ever. But if they were good mothers they were sure not to be known and therefore could not be commemorated. The best of all the saints were people of whom no one had ever heard. Anyone who used a calendar had to be aware of a multitude of unknowns and to remember that they were recognized only in another place.

The tradition of the Reformation was for a long time not happy with the commemoration of the saints, except the saints of the Bible or Luther or Calvin, and it distrusted calendars. That changed during the Nazi years. The Nazis banned one calendar of Lutheran saints as an attack on the Nazi ideal of life. After the Second World War, some people wanted to remember martyrs under the Nazis like Dietrich Bonhoeffer. Such people were more likely to be remembered in street-names or on stamps than in a church, but churchgoers started to feel a lack. The American Lutherans created a calendar of witnesses to the faith. The Germans created a draft calendar which at last (in 1966) won from the Church governments the right to be used in church. Although it was not five years since the erection of the Berlin Wall, it was used in both Germanies.

This calendar was amended in 1984. A quarter of all the names were martyrs. More than 100 names were shared with the new Catholic German calendar.

In Istanbul there was a moving little ceremony in 1972, when the Ecumenical Patriarch celebrated a saint, Lydia. Of her it was known only that she traded in purple cloth at Philippi, and listened to St Paul, and asked to be baptized, and pressed him to stay in her house. This meant she was the first European ever to be a Christian. At that moment it was Christian Europe which mattered to the Patriarch Demetrius.

9

The Ministry

During the Reformation, all Western Churches except the Roman Catholic accepted the rightfulness of the marriage of priests, though not without hesitation at the change of custom, especially in England.

The Eastern Church had always allowed married men to serve in parishes; but it would not allow priests to marry, and since all bishops had to come from the monastic order all bishops had to be unmarried. Occasional movements arose to allow bishops to marry, on the grounds that a division between married priests and unmarried bishops was bad for the clergy, and because the choice of bishops was thus limited. There had also been pleas that the Orthodox priest might marry after ordination as well as before. These movements were always very weak. The people would not countenance the idea of any such change of custom.

But in Western Roman Catholicism a movement to allow married priests was historic. It arose in countries where Catholics lived among many Protestants, as in southern Germany or Holland. It had two arguments. The Roman Catholic Church was the only Church which did not allow married priests; and yet it did allow married priests, because in the Uniat Churches of the East, where the people followed Orthodox customs although they were Roman Catholics, they followed the Eastern custom of married priests and unmarried bishops. Therefore there was nothing wrong in a Roman Catholic wanting married priests and at any time the Church could decide to allow married priests. This encouraged pressure for change from those who thought the rule to be a mistake.

But celibacy had been a Roman custom since the fifth century and a Western custom since the eleventh or twelfth century. And many pastors and lay people in the Church valued celibacy as a part of that self-sacrifice which made the high ideal of the minister:

the surrender, for the sake of a pastorate, of one of the highest goods known to humanity – the life of a family.

Yet the people needed sacraments and many countries were short of priests: France, Holland, even Austria of the European countries. Some of the Third World countries, especially in Latin America, had a desperate want of priests. Since the people needed sacraments, and since unmarried priesthood was a matter of discipline and not of doctrine, why should not the deficit be made up by allowing married men?

The subject arose at the Second Vatican Council. The Pope said that he did not think this a suitable subject for public debate. He promised an encyclical on the theme in due course. This encyclical (*Sacerdotalis Caelibatus*, 1967) insisted on the celibacy of priests and was tough in its language and was much criticized, by those who wanted change as a document inadequate to the theme.

In Holland the argument – married priests or not – produced a turmoil which had repercussions far outside Holland. The Dutch Roman Catholics were now educated and many of them were liberal-minded, and the more liberal wanted to pursue the openness of the Council far. And this radical desire for openness met a conservatism which grew more obsessive as the radicals grew more extreme.

In Holland it did not come to schism because – but only because – the Dutch happened to have a great man as cardinal, Alfrink. But the argument devastated the Catholic Church in Holland. To this day the gulf that formed is no mere matter of history.

To bring priests and laity into the government of the Church, the Dutch created a sort of synod (108 members) to advise them and called it the Pastoral Council. They believed that thus they carried out the intentions of the Vatican Council to make the laity share fully in the Church. One of their problems was the desperate shortage of priests. (Dutch ordinations: 325 in 1950; 48 in 1970 – some 8,000 priests in Holland.)

In January 1970 this Council resolved, almost unanimously but with all eight bishops abstaining, that priests be no longer celibate of necessity; that under some conditions married priests could be brought back into the ministry; that married men might be ordained priest. Rome, and the Pope personally, was shocked. They were even more shocked when a fortnight later the Dutch bishops passed a resolution supporting the Council. The effect all over the Catholic Church was explosive.

The tense argument was debated at the Rome synod of 1971. Cardinal Slipyj, exiled from the Ukraine, who being a Uniat was used to married priests, argued that many Ukrainian married priests were excellent and had done very well under persecution. The argument that the unmarried man can more easily stand up to persecution, because he cannot be got at through his dependants, had been found by the experience of persecution not to be true. The Dutch Cardinal Alfrink argued for the ordination of married men, and was backed almost unanimously by the Canadian bishops, some of whom believed that unnecessary suffering was caused to priests by the discipline of celibacy. The Latin American bishops, who were desperate for priests, thought that controlled experiments with married priests ought to be tried. The head of the missionary religious order of White Fathers, Van Asten, demanded understanding for priests who left the Church and he held high the moral and personal value of the affection of wife and children.

To the contrary, the Italian bishops, who were present in the largest numbers at the Rome synod, were unanimous in favour of maintaining the rule of celibacy. So were the Sri Lankans. The United States bishops, in spite of the view taken by more than half their clergy, voted to keep celibacy. But it was Cardinal Enrique y Tarancón, from Toledo, who best expressed the reasons against allowing married priests. They are argued for as a way of solving the shortage of priests. But they do not solve the problem. Churches which have married clergy are also short of clergy. Therefore celibacy is not the reason for the shortage. The married man has less mobility than the single. The permission to marry will not increase the number of ordinands, at least not of good ordinands, because it will diminish the call to self-sacrifice which is what attracts the idealism of ordinands. The Church would be able to afford fewer priests, because married men are more expensive to maintain than single. And in countries where the Church is persecuted the Church would lose its force of resistance, because the priest would need to consider the effect upon his family as well as himself. And some of the fathers sang the ideal of celibacy – its commitment to the people, its spirit of abnegation, its vigilance, its mistrust of honour.

Finally, however, the synod voted to allow the Pope to allow married men to be ordained, in exceptional circumstances. That was an important vote.

Still, priests were leaving, if not their priesthood, at least their active priesthood because they wished to marry, and while the debate went on this grew more common and sometimes it affected eminent people.

The abbot of the famous Belgian Benedictine house at Maredsous, Olivier Du Roy, resigned, because his plans for the future of the abbey included non-celibate monks. The head of the order of the White Fathers, Van Asten, now resigned in order to marry. Various opinion polls in France, where priests were in short supply, showed (in 1973 and 1976) that a comfortable majority of French Roman Catholics thought that married persons should be able to be ordained and a smaller majority thought that priests should be able to marry. But when the opinion poll distinguished between French Roman Catholics and regular churchgoing Roman Catholics, the numbers were quite different: some 40 per cent of the practising Catholics thought that priests should be able to marry – nowhere near a majority. The same sort of difference was found in the United States, where nearly 80 per cent of Catholics were in favour of married priests but when practising Catholics were asked the result was different. Yet when the opinion of the French priests was asked, a vast majority were in favour of the ordination of married men – 86 per cent for and only 9 per cent against.

In Holland and France at least some married priests continued to celebrate sacraments and regarded themselves as priests in the full sense. In Holland, twenty-five married priests taught in four of the five institutes of theology.

Rome did all it could to reconvert the now radical Dutch Church to conservatism. Its method was to wait for a vacancy in a bishopric and then appoint someone who was ultra-conservative – Simonis to the see of Rotterdam in 1971; Gijsen to Roermond two years later (and Gijsen was famous for his hostility to the liberalism of the Dutch bishops). These appointments were the final touch which destroyed the good atmosphere of the Dutch Catholic Church and left a heritage of division to this day.

There happened in Holland what also began to happen in France. Since there was a shortage of priests, more and more parishes began to be run by women pastoral workers, and more and more places at seminaries were taken up by women, or by married men who could not be ordained but intended to be parish workers. These in effect were unordained curates. In 1984, when only thirteen men were ordained, there were 324 women pastoral workers in France and the bishops began to worry that the women were becoming an unordained clergy.

The Debate in Greece

The tension at last affected the so conservative Orthodox Church. In Greece, 264 Orthodox priests and monks petitioned the government that priests be allowed to marry after their ordination. They said that the law – no marriage after ordination – was a purely civil law from the code of Justinian and ought to be changed. The Greek synod rejected the plea with resolution.

The Debate in France

During the 1970s the French Church passed through its worst crisis since the French Revolution. The reasons were not only celibacy and marriage of priests and attitudes to sexuality, but these were part of the crisis, and some of its bitterest forms were expressed publicly because of them.

The years from 1958 to 1968 were a serene time for the great French Church. The French were always among the more liberal-minded of Catholics and they had disliked the last conservative years of Pope Pius XII. The war and its aftermath had almost made the historic French anticlericalism disappear, and under the blessing of General de Gaulle the Church was an influential part of the French State. It loved the *aggiornamento* and the Church coming out into the world. When Montini became Pope Paul VI he was a person influenced by the best of the French Catholic philosophers. The French helped the Pope to apply the Vatican Council and make its ideals practical. The Gallican strand which lay concealed within their Church made them like the idea of collegiality as contrasted with a dictatorship of the Pope. The influence of the French inside Rome and within the Curia grew steadily. In 1969 Paul VI astonished the Italians by appointing a Frenchman, Cardinal Villot, as Secretary of State.[1]

In that same year the French bishops had a meeting at Lourdes with clergy to discuss the rule of celibacy. It was agreed that the subject was a delicate subject because it touched the heart of a priest's life. Contemporary human scientists, especially the psychologists, put forward the importance of sexuality to the full human being, and this had modified the relationship between men and women; and the women's movement had created a new image of woman and a new understanding of the sexual relationship. This new understanding at its best had brought a more profound spiritual dimension to the relationship between man and wife.

The celibate priest who was not a member of an order had always lived something of a solitary life when he retired to his vicarage, with his company the woman who kept house for him – often his mother, sometimes an unmarried sister, often a housekeeper who might or might not be good as a companion but who on occasion might be a common-law wife. Suddenly the television set brought to his fireside a varied and extended company of friends or enemies. It did what it did for solitary widows and for everyone who lived largely alone. Mostly that was likely to be a help. But it was argued by some that to have so many visitors to the fireside for no pastoral reason must increase the influence of the general world upon the priest and his way of life.

Confronted by the arguments, the French bishops by an enormous majority (107 to 6) voted that this was a bad time of unsettlement to be thinking about changing a historic discipline of the Church; that even this sort of discussion caused an unsettlement among celibate priests; and, further, that the need for change was not proven – for the moment parishes could be looked after by other methods: deacons, the ministry of women, monks. They said

1. Never before was a group of French thinkers more influential in Rome: Congar, de Lubac, Daniélou and the Swiss-French Journet. All those except Congar became cardinals.

that the argument for ordaining mature, married men was not convincing.

In France this produced the misuse of a term. In some country villages the holy communion would be administered to the people by a lay man or woman from a reserved sacrament, with due readings of the Scripture and prayers beforehand. It was natural that French congregations should call these services 'mass without a priest'. But there was no mass, there were only prayers round a reserved sacrament, because there could be no mass without the presence of a priest. French bishops were disturbed at this popular usage and protested against it. They were also disturbed when they found that the rite accompanying the holy communion looked like the rite of mass – what they called a 'plagiarism' of the mass – and they ruled that it should not do so.

The new situation produced cases of conscience. Someone lives in a village where there is no priest and therefore no mass but there is holy communion. He has a car. On Sunday, should he get into the car and go to a village where there is a mass, or should he go to holy communion at his own church because that is where his community says its prayers?

THE ORDINATION OF WOMEN

In the ordination of women, Lutheran Denmark led the way among the traditionalist Churches. The Danish inheritance was more open to variety than any other Lutheran tradition. From 1946 its Church polity was a democracy, in that each community could choose its own pastor. In the following year a Danish parish elected a woman as pastor.

The Danish Church divided. There was talk of schism. Was it legal? Was it possible in an orthodox Christian Church? The government brought in a law to ensure its legality (in 1947). But her ordination needed to be conducted by the bishop. The bishop of that area was not willing to ordain her. The government brought in another law (in 1948) allowing a congregation which wanted a woman as pastor to go outside its area and find any bishop who was willing to ordain her. This was regarded by many Church people as gross interference by government in the discipline of the Church. Accordingly, when the first women were ordained, the bitterness reached the pitch of demonstrations, not without violence.

It took twenty years before there was no longer any bishop unwilling to ordain women as pastors. Twenty years after that, half the parishes had women as their pastors. This was one way of helping over the problem in the liberal states of finding the people to minister in the parishes.

The other Scandinavian Churches were affected by this decision. Liberal governments had a tendency to clear away all discrimination against the female sex; and if it was possible for a woman to be a pastor, as the Danes had ruled, then a government had a duty to make it possible in law. But in Sweden the government was more the ruler of the Church than was the Church Assembly. In 1957 a bill came forward to allow women to be pastors. It was referred to the Church Assembly, which threw it out. Next year the government forced it upon the Church. This led to controversy, in which the rights or wrongs of women's ordination were mingled with argument over the power of a government to do such a thing to a Church without its leave.

Because Sweden was the most traditional of the Churches which arose directly out of the German Reformation, this decision caused a sensation among other Protestant Churches which were allied with the Swedes – not least among the Old Catholics of Utrecht and Germany and in the Church of England, which had full communion with the Swedes and started to ask whether it could have full communion with a Church that allowed women to be ordained priests.

Norway followed Sweden soon afterwards. The radical Bishop Schjelderup ordained a woman to a parish against the wishes of the other Norwegian bishops.

The Reformed were attracted by the developments, especially in France. Some of the Reformed Churches put off the decision as too controversial. Behind the Iron Curtain the small Reformed Church in Poland, very short of ministers like all the Eastern Churches, considered the ordination of women anxiously and decided against it – there was no principle against it, but at the moment it ought not to be done. The Lutherans and the Reformed in Hungary, both very short of pastors because of the pressure under which they lived, trained more women in theology. Both denominations decided, as late as 1980, that they could use women as assistant preachers but would not, for the time, put them in independent charge of a parish. But some Protestant Churches with quite a Catholic tradition followed the Scandinavian Lutherans. In Czechoslovakia, under a regime where no Church could flourish, the Czechoslovak Hussite Church began to use women largely as parish priests. In 1982 it had 296 pastors and 96 of those were women. In Prague alone that year 22 out of the 35 pastors were women.

Meanwhile the women's movement developed apace during the sixties, especially in America but with impact on all the Churches, not excluding the Roman Catholic Church. In April 1963 Pope John XXIII issued the encyclical *Pacem in Terris*, which called the world to the recognition of human freedoms and appealed for an end to the Cold War. It included a text which cited the emancipation of the female sex as one of the good features of the age in which they lived. But it was rare to find Roman Catholic theologians who taught that there was no barrier to the ordination of women as priests. In 1965 a pastoral epistle of Pope Paul VI rejected all discrimination against women. A few years later Karl Rahner, a Jesuit who was much respected as a Catholic theologian, declared to a Lutheran pastor of the Bavarian synod that the practice of the Church not to ordain women to the priesthood had no compelling theological reason. He said that he did not expect a quick change in the practice of the Church but the custom was not a dogma, it was based on a social situation which was valid in the past but which was changing fast.

Pope Paul VI admitted women as hearers to the last two sessions of the Second Vatican Council. Five years later he did something more dramatic: he made two women saints, Teresa of Avila and Catherine of Siena, into doctors (that is, topmost teachers) of the Church, a rank hitherto occupied only by males. In the same year Uta Ranke-Heinemann, the Catholic daughter of the (Protestant) German president Heinemann, became a professor of theology, the first female professor of divinity in a Catholic university.[2]

2 Professor at Essen University, 1985, she lost that chair two years later because she doubted the virginity of the Blessed Virgin.

This did not mean that Paul VI came anywhere near the idea that women would be ordained priests. That he thought to be contrary to Catholic teaching and practice.

The next step was taken by some of the Anglicans. They were a Church with a High Church tradition and links not only with the Reformation but with Eastern and Western Catholics. Anything that they did was bound to add a little pressure to the desire for change within the Roman Catholic Church.

During the Second World War, Hong Kong was occupied by the Japanese. To get sacraments to his bereft people, the Anglican Bishop of Hong Kong ordained to the priesthood a deaconess in Macao, Florence Li. Her ministry was valued. After the war she was persuaded to retire on the ground that her priesthood was irregular, though the Church did not presume to say whether it was invalid. But twenty-five years later this precedent of a war emergency meant that Hong Kong was the place where change came first.

In 1971 a committee appointed by the Lambeth Conference from the whole Anglican communion met at Limuru in Kenya to advise on this question. It resolved by a majority of one that if a provincial Church of the Anglican communion ordained women as priests, the other provinces should not break communion with it. Fortified by this decision, Bishop Baker of Hong Kong ordained two women to the priesthood at the end of that year. He did not have the approval of the Archbishop of Canterbury, but afterwards the archbishop (Ramsey) showed no sign of wishing to put him out of the Anglican communion for his act.

It looked therefore as though any Anglican province had the chance to ordain women, if it thought it right, without losing communion with other provinces and without committing other provinces to its action. The feminist movement within the United States was already producing not merely pressure but demonstrations. In 1974 four bishops without any authority ordained eleven women to the priesthood at Philadelphia. The act was illegal in the Church and the ordinations were declared invalid. But when such a demonstration could occur, the pressure on that side of the Atlantic must mount. Accordingly in 1975 the Anglican Church in Canada voted that women could be ordained as priests.

In the same year the General Synod of the Church of England, under a new archbishop, Coggan, who believed without reserve that women should rightly be admitted to the priesthood, passed a resolution that there was no objection. That did not mean that the synod legislated to permit it to happen. Three years later it rejected a practical plan to that end.

Inside the Church of Rome the pressure mounted likewise. At the Rome synod of 1971 Cardinal Flahiff of Winnipeg said that when this was first raised twenty years ago it was argued that (1) Christ was a man, (2) He chose twelve men as apostles, (3) St Paul says women must keep silence in church, and (4) the primitive Church had women ministers but they were not ordained. All are agreed, said the cardinal, that these arguments are not now valid. The Church had said that it wished to end discrimination against women and he did not believe there to be any valid doctrinal argument against their ordination. The Church had seen the success of women in pastoral and apostolic work in modern times.

This speech did not win applause at the Rome synod. The vast majority of the synod was against the idea.

Since Rome and Canterbury were friendly, Pope and archbishop exchanged important letters. Coggan said why it was right, the Pope said why it was wrong, to ordain women as priests. In January 1977 the Congregation of the Faith, which was the former Holy Office of the Inquisition, ruled in the decree *Inter Insigniores* that the ordination of women to the priesthood was not possible. Eleven years after that an opinion poll in the United States showed that half the American Catholic priests thought that women should be able to be priests. But half, though a lot of people, was no compelling percentage to persuade Rome towards such a change, especially when the Pope was convinced that the idea was mistaken.

Meanwhile the (Anglican) Episcopal Church in the United States started to ordain women as priests. This led to some losses of Anglican priests to the Roman Catholic Church and a schism within the Episcopal Church, because a continuing group, or two continuing groups, wanted to go on being Anglican while they refused women priests as unCatholic. In 1988 an American Episcopal diocese elected Barbara Harris as the first woman to be a bishop. She was at first not a full diocesan but a suffragan. In the following year the Anglican Church in New Zealand elected the first Anglican diocesan bishop who was a woman.

But despite all the pressure in America, despite the far gentler pressure in Holland and France and Germany, despite the needs of so many countries in their shortage of priests, despite the ability of the Roman Catholic Church to allow women to run parishes so that they did all the work of priests except to consecrate the host and the wine in the sacrament and to give the absolution at confession – in Chile and Bolivia when nuns celebrated the holy communion for the Catholics the people often talked about the nuns 'saying mass' – Pope John Paul II (1978–) was like his predecessor in believing the ordination of women to be wrong because unapostolic.

The Eastern Orthodox Church was even firmer: it was wrong because it was contrary to holy tradition. This difference over women affected the trust between the older Churches and drew them apart at a time when otherwise they were growing together.

RETIREMENT FOR AGE

At one time in the Church it was supposed that no one should retire from the ministry, because when someone was made a minister his order was indelible and his commitment was for life. Ever since the age of the Reformation or before it was recognized that age or ill health might make it needful to shift a minister in older age from a work which demanded energy to something gentler. But no one could force him to retire, and always he should be found a place where his ministry would be fulfilled so long as that was possible physically. There was the practical point that if someone needed to retire no one could see how to pay him unless he remained in a job, for in those days all pay had duties attached. The problem was not so urgent as it would have been if the same conditions prevailed in the twentieth century, because the average length of life was shorter so the number of clergy whose life extended into the age of weakness was lower.

During the nineteenth century the English Church made provision in various half-adequate ways for voluntary retirement – until the end of the century by deducting part of the pay which went with the last post which the minister held, and so for his lifetime making his successor poorer. During the twentieth century all the advanced countries devised financial schemes which provided for occupational pensions and eventually for a minimum form of State pension. This was not before time for the Church. In several countries it eased the difficulty. The Church could run its own scheme for an occupational pension by deducting for that purpose from the annual stipend, and where the State pension existed it made it less financially burdensome to provide an adequate pension for ministers.

In the hard-time days of Marxist rule of Eastern Europe, some governments for a time refused priests or pastors the right to receive the State pension because they were ministers. That complicated the care of the older clergy in those countries.

Yet there was something odd about what was happening. The number of clergy and ministers in all Churches was declining because there were fewer ordinands. Medicine was ensuring that many more of the clergy lived longer, because many more of the human race lived longer, and this was not just living into ineffectiveness (though that happened) but meant that older men and women could be effective into their seventies. Yet the Churches, faced with declining numbers, were also faced with a clergy which now had a right to a State pension, who were tired like others, or more tired than others after long years of service, and wanted the retreat of a quiet old age without responsibility.

Since clergy retired anyway on the State pension if they wished, Churches were influenced by the habits in the State to make such provision for their own clergy and therefore compelled them to retire whether they wished to retire or not. It did not bother the Churches that in the Catholic Churches and the more Catholic Protestant Churches this ran up against the fundamental doctrine that a minister is called, and vows, to serve God at the altar or holy table until death.

In 1975 the Church of England decided to compel all its clergy to retire from their offices at the age of seventy.

Pope Paul VI ordered that bishops should retire at seventy-five. He was also plagued by ancient cardinals. The life of a cardinal was expected to be long. When Paul VI was elected, his Secretary of State was over eighty. For centuries the Vatican had the reputation of being a government by old men. The average age of the heads of the dicasteries (or departments) in 1967 was seventy-nine and a half, with one cardinal in office at ninety and ten of them over eighty. Paul VI managed to bring the average age down, for ten years later it was about sixty-nine.

But the 'revolutionary' act was to say that cardinals aged eighty should henceforth have no right to elect a new Pope. Since the right to elect a Pope was the essence of being a cardinal, it turned the cardinal's office into a mere honour. Some cardinals, and some canon lawyers, believed that even a Pope had no power to do such a thing to the constitution of the Church. Cardinal Tisserant, a tough and learned old Frenchman who thus saw his right taken away, protested on television. Cardinal Ottaviani, leader of the Curial conservatives, said that the decision was 'extraordinary, hasty, and even revolutionary, done with a contempt for a centuries-old tradition'.

It was now the rule that bishops must retire at seventy-five. But the Pope is a bishop. Must he retire? Paul VI did not retire at seventy-five. In 1977 as he approached eighty, when cardinals were ordered to give up their work, there was discussion whether Paul VI must retire. He had once and solemnly visited the prison of Celestine V (Pope in 1294-6), the only classical precedent for a Pope who retired. The one thing that he did was to set up a little committee of three intimates who should tell him if he was no longer capable.

A Greek government passed a law that bishops must retire at eighty. Four bishops over eighty went to court to get the law declared invalid; they lost. After the colonels took power in Greece by a coup in 1967, they forced through, with the aid of 'their' Archbishop of Athens, a law which made the Greek bishops retire at the age of seventy. The act was unusual in that the aim was to be rid of bishops who opposed the colonels. This did not last.

10

Monks and Nuns

The changes in attitudes to sex and the unmarried state affected the monastic life. We have seen too how some of the Marxist governments made monks and nuns illegal, and even if they allowed them they usually took away their houses and almost always removed their chances of doing good in education or welfare. The general unsettlement in the Christian Churches, which was part of an unsettlement in society, had the same effect on recruitment for monks and nuns as it had on the recruitment of priests.

Notice the change in Spain, where monks and nuns were numerous: in 1972 there were 31,000 monks and 97,000 nuns; in 1981 there were 19,000 monks and 100,000 nuns.

By 1979 no country in the world, not even Poland or Ireland, was producing enough nuns to maintain their nunneries in the strength, and therefore in the work, to which they were accustomed. Because recruitment was not adequate the orders aged, and the care of the old and sick became a more burdensome problem for some houses. Yet in Spain, even as late as 1981, almost half of the mentally sick patients were being cared for by nuns and monks.

The historic orders of men diminished every year from 1965 to 1975. The greatest order of men was still the Franciscans (23,337 of them in 1972). The Capuchins, a form of Franciscan, had 15,710 in 1965 and 11,497 in 1984; but since they were a religious order important to Eastern Europe it is probable that they were more hurt than some orders by Marxist nationalizations (for comparison they had 34,029 in 1761 and only 7,628 in 1888 – that being followed by revival). In 1974 there were 29,436 Jesuits, many more than when they dominated the religious life of Catholic Europe just before their suppression during the eighteenth century. Nearly 12,000 were in Europe and nearly 12,000 in the Americas.

But they were shrinking every year – the worst year was 1971-2, with a loss of 906.

The Reformed Cistercians, commonly called Trappists, had a total of 3,179 male members in eighty-four houses, plus their convents of nuns. Paradoxically, one modern Trappist became the most famous of modern monks. Thomas Merton (1915–68) dabbled in literature and in Communism and then was moved by the silence and the penitence which he found when he visited the Trappist house at Gethsemane in Kentucky. He remained there, at least nominally, from 1941 for the rest of his life. He began to write about the life of the spirit. He first published a book in 1948, *The Seven Storey Mountain*, as an account of his own spiritual life. He wrote attractively, and could explain the nature of spirituality to the laity. He represented the monastic vocation as a humane life amid industrial and technological society. His notion of the life of spirit was contemplative. But during the fifties he grew conscious that society also had its needs and he started to write about social injustice and world peace. Part of his fame was that at first he was the only Catholic to be an acrid critic of American policy in Vietnam. He had assailants who doubted whether the quest for publicity, and the social gospel, were suited to the Trappist vocation. In 1964 he began to practise the hermit life at his monastery and grew more interested in Buddhist contemplation, especially in Zen. He was electrocuted accidentally at Bangkok when he attended a meeting of different religions on the theme of contemplation.

The Carmelites were almost destroyed in the wars of the French Revolution but revived during the nineteenth century, and after the Second World War they were the great contemplative order of nuns (14,000 nuns in 710 houses). About a third of all the world's houses of contemplative nuns were in Spain. The Carmelites revered their most famous nun of the twentieth century, the Jewish philosopher Edith Stein who was murdered at Auschwitz, and it did them no harm when Pope Paul VI made their saint Teresa of Avila into a doctor of the Church.

Because of Edith Stein, the Carmelites felt that they were the order which should set up a house of prayer at Auschwitz which would by its prayers make reparation for all the murders of Jews and others which were perpetrated on that site during the Second

World War. In 1984 they got leave to set it up outside the camp, in a building built before the First World War – 'the old theatre' – since 1914 used as a store and then as a storage for gas. Late in 1984 they started their prayers on the site.

They had not reckoned with the Jewish people, for whom Auschwitz had become a shrine special to their religion. Even though others besides Jews were murdered at Auschwitz, some Jews felt it an insult to them that a group of Christian nuns should undertake the work of reparation on that place. There were many protests. A New York rabbi and a band of followers climbed into the nunnery as a demonstration and were set upon with violence by Polish workers. It was clear that the reverent plan had gone astray and the nuns must be withdrawn. By the time of writing the argument was not yet settled because the nuns had nowhere else to go, but almost everyone agreed that they must go.

France in historic times and again in modern times was a country of many nuns, in education, in nursing and in contemplation. In the age of anticlericalism at the end of the nineteenth century and the beginning of the twentieth, they suffered many losses and many were driven abroad to preserve their community life. By the 1960s all that strife was long in past history.

In 1973 there were still 100,700 nuns in France and 8,500 abroad. Nine-tenths of them worked in the active life, most in schools or hospitals. Fewer than one in ten were contemplatives.

Social changes were observed. The average age when women sought entry to a nunnery rose steadily. It was in the middle twenties for the active nuns, and nearly thirty for the contemplatives. The standard of education and of social origin of the applicants rose. Fewer novices came from country villages and more of them came from the big cities, and more of them had a normal middle-class education, with more people from families where a parent or parents was in a profession. Far fewer novices came as the result of a parent's decision: the element of personal choice was almost universal.

The age of reform produced a general desire to get away from the rigid patterns of the past. The most dramatic result was the decision of many religious to throw off the religious habit, at least when they were at work outside their nunnery or monastery. Even if they did not wear clothes like the laity's, they wore clothes which separated them less obviously from the laity. They did not diminish their prayer life – that was one of the reasons why people entered religious houses – but they had a new affection for little groups: little colonies of monks or nuns away from the bigger house and therefore more intimate with each other.

In the East of Europe where they were driven out of their houses, some superiors solved the problem by dividing them up into little groups each with its own premises and prior. Even then they were often at risk. But the West had the same desire for a totally different reason. Perhaps the monks had occupied some vast and historic monastic house, or an inherited chateau, and they felt inappropriate in the modern world. They wanted to move into lodgings more suitable for their way of life, more like the lodgings of those who did similar jobs in the secular world. Since the cry after the Second Vatican Council was participation, some communities wanted to diminish the power of an absolute superior and live as 'fraternities'; and part of the reason for moving into a smaller place was the chance of a brotherly family.

Church leaders half-welcomed and half-doubted what was happening. Sometimes big communities were needed. You could hardly have scholarship without a good library, and you cannot get a good library except in a big community. It is more difficult to arrange for the care of the old if the group is small. If the work of the community is the conducting of retreats or missions or the education of future priests, it must have adequate numbers or it will be overstretched. And the family group was a little more fragile as a group. It had difficulty in maintaining the regular life of prayer. It was likely to be less withdrawn from the world, and the influence of the world might be hardly compatible with the religious life. The authorities noticed cases where they thought the little group to be more inward-looking. The general of the Jesuits (Arrupe), seeing the desire for little groups, welcomed it and saw its strengths – in fraternity, in prayer, in everyone sharing in every decision, in simplicity. But – it needed anchoring. Therefore it was best if the little group was near to and attached to a big and stable community, with its library and its ease of regular worship, and enough people to step in at a crisis.

In Eastern Europe the endowments of monks and nuns were confiscated even if their community still managed to exist, and in Western Europe and the Americas their endowments were diminished by inflation. In Western states many of them were engaged in teaching or in nursing. But there were other ways of earning money. In the Eastern Churches the manufacture and sale of candles was necessary to their welfare. The French religious houses taught (and some were scholars) and nursed; but also they earned money by making and selling vestments, or curtains, or ceramics, or food like honey or chocolate or cheese or biscuits, or drink like liqueurs. In the technological age some of them developed printing, and those with a musical tradition were helped by recordings.

Scattered across Europe were a few houses among the most radical in the Church. They were exempt from the control of the bishops. Such communities were drawn towards radical policies, even to extremism, about the structure of the Church, or its authority, or the nature of the religious life. One example: the French Cistercian house of Boquen was in trouble (in 1965 and for many years[1]) because it gave the sacrament to the unbaptized and to people who were divorced and in other ways behaved not according to discipline, as well as being on the extreme left in politics.

Most of the historic houses had their history broken by dissolution or revolution or war. The Grande Chartreuse, Cîteaux, Montserrat, Mont Saint-Michel and such had been repurchased and reopened during the nineteenth and twentieth centuries after years of closure. But occasionally could be found a historic site with a continuous history, or almost continuous, which, because it was a place of pilgrimage, profited from the enormous increase of pilgrims by modern transport after the Second World War. Such a house was Einsiedeln in Switzerland. It was sacked by a French revolutionary army and fifty years after was troubled by the Swiss civil war of religion. But it remained, with buildings from the eighteenth century, and a historic library. In 1975 the community contained 153 monks and served sixteen parishes and

---

1. Boquen founded 1137; ended by the French Revolution; refounded 1936. In 1965, when the refounder died there, eight monks and two brothers. Eight years later the Cistercian order withdrew its recognition. By then the abbey consisted of one monk, five young laymen, a mason, a chauffeur and three girls. A year later the abbey decided to install a community of contemplative nuns.

received 150,000 pilgrims a year. It was the most continuously untroubled of the historic Benedictine houses. This was due less to the wisdom of its abbots than to its siting within the country of Europe which suffered the least political trouble of the modern age.

One or two of the very modern orders captured the imagination of the world. We have already seen what happened to Mother Teresa's sisters. A new male order of this kind was that of the Little Brothers of Jesus, after the example of Charles de Foucauld. He was a French hermit in Algeria, from a background of Trappist experience, and was murdered by tribesmen in 1916 when he was living solitary on the edge of the Sahara desert. At first, no one took much notice, but in 1933 five brothers adopted a rule based upon his writings. In the Second World War they were all called up for the army, which gave them experience of the world, but they went back after the war and then their way of life began to spread in little fraternities who lived in ordinary clothes and did ordinary jobs.

MOUNT ATHOS

The twentieth century was not a prosperous time for Mount Athos, the high peninsula in northern Greece sacred to monks and at the heart of Greek devotional life, where no women (but one queen of Serbia) were allowed since the tenth century. Before the Russian Revolution in 1917 more than half the monks were Russians, and many endowments lay in Russia, so the First World War was a disaster for the prosperity of the mountain. Then the monks lost many Greek endowments, because these were needed to help Greek refugees from Turkey after 1923. But even in the 1930s there were still 6,000 monks in the houses on the range. One or two houses found it hard to survive – in 1968 the ancient house of Stavronikita had only four monks, in cavernous buildings, and could give hospitality to no one. In 1972 there were 1,146 monks on the mountain; there are now more than 1,500.

The Greek government long refused to allow foreign monks to

settle on Mount Athos and still insisted that if they did they took Greek citizenship. But then the Russian and Greek governments agreed that five Russian monks might go to the old Russian house at Panteleimon and four Bulgarian monks to the old Bulgarian house at Zografon and a few Serbian monks to the old Serbian house at Chilandar. But the monks, though fewer, were not all old. Young men still grouped themselves round spiritual leaders on the mountain. The mountain also drew from monasteries inside Greece which were in decline, partly because their silence on the mainland was interrupted by tourists and they preferred a retreat inaccessible to buses.

When during the sixties the Ecumenical Patriarch Athenagoras was suspect to the monks because of his openness to Western Catholicism and to the Protestants, some of the houses on Mount Athos refused to pray for him. A number of monks left Mount Athos because they were not willing to be part of such irreverence. In 1990 the patriarch was again able to visit the holy mountain.

In 1963 the twenty monasteries on the mountain celebrated the thousandth year since the foundation.

When Greece entered the European Community, a clause provided for the free right of Community citizens to settle anywhere in the Community. A special clause that this did not apply to Mount Athos had to be inserted into the treaty.

During the summer of 1990, terrible forest fires burnt a third of the trees on the mountain, and timber makes the largest contribution to the endowment. None of the monasteries was destroyed.

OTHER GREEK MONASTERIES AND NUNNERIES

Certain monasteries outside Mount Athos were prosperous and influential. Patmos, on the island in the Dodecanese where St John wrote the Apocalypse, was a historic house which helped the fight for Greek independence against the Turks. Under Italian rule till 1944, it gathered monks and refugees from Asia Minor when the Turks drove out the Greeks in 1922. It had a famous school and a good library. The tourists came in crowds, but the monks kept their life apart and did not let themselves be turned only into the guardians of a historic building.

The isle of Paros had another monastery with well-educated monks. Megaspilaeon, high in the mountain overlooking the Gulf of Corinth, was a little too near the bus routes for comfort but kept its own way. The once great monastery on the Meteora rocks in Thessaly stood high on a great natural fortress and never fully recovered from its use as a strongpoint by the armies of the Second World War and in the civil war afterwards. The Greek government started to pay for the restoration of frescoes and refectories, but this was because it was a goal of tourists and it lost spiritual drawing-power because so many visitors wanted to see it. Monks who wanted quiet sought a home on Mount Athos or elsewhere. There were houses – Hosios Loukas near Delphi, and on Corfu – where it was almost impossible for the monks to be anything but guides to visitors.

High on Mount Sinai the most historic of all the Greek monasteries, St Catharine, was troubled by the Israeli–Egyptian wars fought across its mountains and had to be more rigorous with tourists than was compatible with the traditional rules of hospitality in the monastic ideal. It kept its way of life and still attracted young monks, but in 1987–9 the Egyptian government, in need of tourist money, created an air-strip nearby and designed hotels in the neighbourhood. It was not certain that the historic shrine could be a retreat much longer.

With the nuns there was an innovation in their way. Always they were contemplative, women of prayer. The cause of the change was a need which they inherited from Western Catholicism. Under Italian rule of the Dodecanese islands, Italian nuns ran an orphanage for 200 children at Rhodes. When, after the Second World War, Rhodes became Greek, the Italians went away. Who should care for the orphans? The superior of the house at Patmos found some Greek contemplative nuns and turned them into nurses for the orphans. From this model other nuns took up similar charitable work, and at Athens was founded an order of Orthodox deaconesses. Some of the theorists of historic Greek ideals objected. One or two of the leaders on Mount Athos said that this pushing of nuns into active charity was a corruption of their true way. But it met a need; the need grew; the number of 'active' Orthodox nuns grew. They attracted novices. In a village ruined by the war a Cretan bishop, Timothy, created a group of institutes for the care of the old and the very young and for education, and they were run by nuns of the new sort. Whatever the contemplatives of Mount Athos said, this was now an established way; and in 1978 Timothy became the primate of Crete.

Meanwhile the State cast envious eyes upon the monastic lands, the forests and the pastoral hills and the agricultural fields. In October 1985 the Greek government put forward a bill to nationalize the monastic lands. The bill said that the lands belong to the State and ought to be given over to farmers for agriculture. Some people thought this bill was a right way of using the lands of Greece more productively; some people thought that its secret desire was to get more control of the Church by the State. The Holy Synod considered the proposal in long debates behind closed doors. There was talk of the Church ceding four-fifths of the forests and a proportion of the olive groves and vineyards, while it still kept enough to maintain the endowment of the monasteries. They reached a reluctant agreement in 1988.

The devotional centre of the people's religion was the shrine on the island of Tinos, where a portrait of the Virgin painted by St Luke was believed to have been discovered during the Greek War of Independence against the Turks. Because the shrine was associated with Greek freedom, it had a national quality as well as a religious fervour for the cult of the Blessed Virgin; and, because Tinos lay on the main sea route across the Aegean, it had many visitors and was able to make substantial grants to help the university of Athens.

PROTESTANT MONKS AND NUNS

The Reformation abolished monks and nuns in the West. It thought most of the houses small and corrupt, regarded them even when they were not corrupt as useless mouths, and needed their vast lands to help the economy and build a modern state.

During the 1830s Anglicans found a need for bodies of men and women who would dedicate themselves to the pastoral care of the inner cities and to education and nursing. At the same time they recovered a sense of a continuity between the best of Protestantism and the best of Catholicism and were willing to countenance again the Catholic ideal of a monk and nun without thinking that they would betray their Protestant heritage.

Orders then and later sprang up in England – especially among males the Cowley Fathers, the Mirfield Fathers, the Society of St Francis and the Benedictines now of Sheen, and among females various small communities with different vocations. As the conditions of society changed – more male babies surviving the first few years, males not being killed in war and therefore not leaving too many unmarried females, women being taken into every sort of job and therefore having far more opportunity for service – the Anglican religious orders experienced the same vicissitudes as the Roman Catholic orders during the third quarter of the twentieth century. But the need was still there and the monastic houses had established themselves as a permanent feature within Protestantism to which no one any longer objected.

A few communities were created within German Lutheranism, though rather later than in England. They always remained, like the English ones, fairly small. In Lutheran Sweden there were communities in close touch with the English, but a little more suspect to the people than in England. Among the French Protestants there were quiet communities such as Pomeyrol near Avignon; in French Reformed Switzerland there was founded Grandchamp, near Neuchâtel, which after 1952 became the female order allied to Taizé. At Darmstadt in West Germany were the Ecumenical Sisters of Mary, whose vocation of prayer and reparation was formed during one night in September 1944, when Allied bombers destroyed the city's life totally.

Certainly by 1960 the monastic life was at home in the Protestant Church, and not only among the High Church Anglicans or Lutherans. It was no longer one of the differences which divided Catholic from Protestant.

TAIZÉ

Roger Schutz was the son of a Swiss Reformed pastor. When France fell to the Germans in the summer of 1940, he was a student at the university of Lausanne. He determined to help the refugees and bicycled into France. Near the historic monastic site of Cluny he found at Taizé old farm buildings suited to his purpose, for they lay two kilometres from the frontier between German-occupied and unoccupied France. There he sheltered refugees of every kind, including Jews. When in the autumn of 1942 the Germans occupied all France, he disappeared into Switzerland until better days and with Max Thurian and two others started to keep a monastic rule at Geneva. At the liberation of France in 1944 the four moved back to Taizé, where at first they had a very difficult time – hostility from the local people, shortage of food and money. They could only exist as a monastic order. In 1949 for the first time at Taizé seven brothers, four Swiss and three French, took the monastic vows.

The vocation of the house began to change. From being designed for refugees, it began to be a centre for Christian unity; for every kind of denomination was attracted to join in the work and the worship. The brothers got leave from the Catholic bishop to use the disused little church, but soon it was too small and a team of young German volunteers built them a much larger church, called the Church of the Reconciliation, for this was now the motif and theme of Schutz's life. By 1960 Taizé was famous throughout the European Churches, and pilgrims, mostly young, gathered there to say their prayers, or to engage in discussions, or to offer their labour for the farm or for building or for the shepherding of visitors. The visitors started to overwhelm the community, rather as tourists started to overwhelm some of the Greek communities, and the brothers seriously debated whether they must move away in order to preserve their integrity. The brothers now were not only Protestant in origin, but this was originally a French-speaking Protestant monastery within France, and therefore the French Protestants were most concerned and some of them were suspicious at so extraordinary a departure from their historic attitude to the monastic way.

11

Ethics

DIVORCE

As the social situation of men and women changed, the rate of divorce rose. All States had to make provision for it, or better provision. All Churches disliked it. They stood for the union of the family and the interests of the children. But there was a difference between Protestants and Eastern Orthodox on one side and the Roman Catholics on the other.

Since the Reformation, the Protestant Churches had behaved more flexibly over the pastoral situations which arose in unhappy marriages. For a long time this flexibility favoured only the rich, because a divorce needed lawyers and the lawyers needed pay. Nevertheless the principle was conceded: that the circumstances of humanity and even at times the interests of the children must mean that, in what it was hoped were exceptional cases, divorce must be allowed by the State.

The Orthodox were also flexible, on the basis of what they called 'economy' – that is, pastoral expediency. Jackie Kennedy, the Roman Catholic widow of the American president, married Aristotle Onassis, a divorced Greek shipowner. The Greek Church had recognized the divorce as valid and regarded him as free to marry. The marriage was conducted by the Orthodox priest in the little chapel of the Ionian island of Skorpios, among the jasmine and bougainvillaea. The Vatican said that it was a degradation and the spouses were public sinners. The representative of the Patriarch of Constantinople said that this marriage was rightly blessed by the Church.

These divorce laws depended upon proving some offence against the marriage – adultery chiefly, because that was mentioned in the New Testament, but soon other offences like the cruelty of one party to the other. Up to the Second World War all laws which provided for divorce used this idea of the offence against marriage. Someone must prove something done by the other. Someone was the guilty party in the break-up of the marriage. This was a natural way for lawyers to go. But it produced lawsuits of nastiness – for proving adultery or proving brutality from a witness-box was not likely to edify the world. In 1926, the British, nauseated by press reporting, passed a law against the disclosure of the detail of such cases. But it remained inside the lawcourt and pained everyone who heard it.

During the 1960s and 1970s Germany – both Germanies – and Britain decided that the idea of matrimonial offence should be dropped, and any attempt to say which was the guilty party should be abandoned. The sole criterion now was to be whether the marriage had broken down irretrievably. If the marriage was no longer a real marriage and never would be, there was no point in the State saying it must keep two people bound in law together because neither has proved anything against the other except that they cannot live together. This new doctrine of irretrievable breakdown was not opposed by the Protestant Churches in either Britain or Germany. Indeed, in Britain it was first put forward by a commission of the Church of England under the chairmanship of a conservative bishop, R. C. Mortimer of Exeter. It was accepted as the basis of law in the East German divorce law of 1965, the British divorce law of 1969, the West German divorce law of 1977 and the Austrian divorce law of 1978.

In certain largely Catholic states, for example, the republics of Ireland and Italy and Spain, there was still no law of divorce. Yet a modern state could hardly do without such a law. The difficulty in Ireland was less because persons wanting a divorce could go to England or Northern Ireland. But it was a source of strife in Italy. In 1970 the Italian government passed a law of divorce. The Pope and the Italian Church were against the new provision and forced upon the republic a referendum to see whether public opinion was behind the law. The referendum (in 1974) proved that, though a large majority of the citizens professed themselves Catholics, the Italian government had the majority of citizens on its side. In Spain the government proposed a law of divorce against the protest of the bishops, who said that they could not admit it to be one of the human rights to demand a divorce. The bill passed (1981) and so legalized Spanish divorce for the first time since 1939. In Ireland a referendum in 1986 went the way of the Church and by then left

Ireland and Malta the only states in Europe without a provision for divorce.

A consequence of the doctrine of irretrievable separation must be what was called unilateral divorce – that is, a husband obtaining a divorce after a certain period though divorce was contrary to the wishes of the wife; or vice versa. Germany had such a law under the Nazis from 1938 – dissolution after three years' separation if one partner wanted it and the marriage was irretrievably ended – but this had been abolished in West Germany in 1961.

Churches hated unilateral divorce because it would encourage the idea of a light attitude to the marriage commitment, and also on grounds of justice – marriage was a contract between two people which could only be ended by two people. In West Germany, Parliament proposed a new divorce law of 1975 – that is, the revival in substance of the Nazi law – which would allow unilateral divorce after three years' separation. The strongest protest came from the German Catholic bishops, and the new law was abandoned. In the following year the same quarrel touched Greece: Parliament proposed a law allowing unilateral divorce after separation and the Holy Synod of the Church rejected it. Three years later the Synod protested furiously over another such proposal – 'anti-evangelical, anticanonical, and antisocial'. In such cases the press was normally in favour of the State and against the Church.

By 1970–90 what was clear was the helplessness of the teaching of the Churches in the face of the social developments of the age in Europe. Protestants and Catholics were agreed that remarriage to another person while a previous spouse was still alive could only be justified as an exception; and most of Europe, at least in feeling and sympathy, was either Protestant or Catholic. Yet in some places one in four marriages, in others even one in three, were ending in divorce. The idea of an exception needed to be stretched. The Churches had to console themselves – and it was not a little consolation – that a considerable majority of marriages were successes – or at least survived until death parted the pair who had committed themselves to each other till death did them part.

CONTRACEPTION

Here was an ethical divide not between Catholics and Protestants, who mostly agreed, but between the Popes and the Protestants who were silently supported by a majority of Catholics. The Popes condemned the use of contraceptive methods as a frustration of the divinely ordained purpose of marriage. The Protestants all accepted the rightness of the use of contraceptive methods to plan a family, or to fulfil marriage affections, or to allow women more liberty in the use of their lives.

The most important condemnation by a Pope was the encyclical *Humanae Vitae* by Pope Paul VI (1968). This was in accordance with Catholic tradition. Marriage is for the creation of human life. That is God's law. Purposeful hindering of the fruition of the sexual act is essentially dishonourable, *intrinsece inhonestum*, and not open to Catholics – though they may avail themselves of the periods when the woman is infertile.

The force of the decree was weakened because its origin was strange and the strangeness was known to or guessed at by the world. John XXIII had started a commission to enquire into the moral doctrine. In this commission those in favour of permitting contraception said that the traditional ruling was not obeyed and could not in modern circumstances be obeyed. Those against said that a decision to change could shatter the unity of the Church. A reviewing committee accepted the opinion of the majority, and therefore the advice given to the Pope Paul VI was for moral liberty according to the individual conscience.

Paul VI went into silence for two years. He was convinced that the negative view was right but must be put in such a way as to be caring pastorally. He specially consulted the Polish cardinal Wojtyla, who was known to be an expert in this area of morality. And so the bull came out in its final form less rigid than some of his tougher advisers wanted but too rigid for a majority of the Catholic laity in Europe and North America. Never before in the history of the papacy was a bull drafted in such odd circumstances.

This encyclical was received with vehement reactions, from

gratitude to disgust. A majority of European Catholics disregarded what the Popes said on this subject. Nothing did more to weaken papal authority during this age. The Popes insisted; the Popes' people were deaf. They did not believe what was said. Therefore the argument threw into question two things of high import in modern Catholicism. First, an actual dogma: the definition by the first Vatican Council of 1870 that the Pope is infallible when he speaks formally in a matter of ethics. Some said, since the Pope is obviously wrong on a matter of such moral urgency, he cannot be infallible. Second, a constitution: whether, if Popes did not adequately represent the moral feelings of their people, the constitution of Church government, which in modern times had done so much to increase the sovereignty of a single see, was an adequate constitution for the modern age; and whether authority, or infallibility if that existed, did not lie with a wider group of apostolic men and women – perhaps with the bishops as a body, even though those bishops must be presided over by the Pope.

Hans Küng, a Roman Catholic professor of divinity at the university of Tübingen in south-west Germany, wrote a book to prove that the Pope is not infallible. The Catholic bishops of Germany condemned his doctrine, though in modern language. Rome tried to get him to recant. He refused. After some years he was forced out of his chair of divinity and his university kept him as a professor of philosophy. But he was not excommunicated. Evidently the opinion, however disreputable in the eyes of Rome, was not impossible for someone who still remained a Roman Catholic.

ABORTION

The Churches long agreed that an abortion was warranted if that was the only way to save the mother's life (though of course the intention must be not to kill the embryo and there was always a chance that its future life could be saved). Since methods of contraception were more effective and more universal, it was expected that fewer unwanted babies would start to come. This expectation proved to be wrong. The growth of cities and the development of ethics meant that more people went round sleeping with more people, and more and more girls needed or thought that they needed abortions. Most States had to legislate to allow abortion under medical safeguards.

In the Churches this was regarded either as totally wrong or else as a sad necessity of the human condition. If human life is sacred (which the Churches believed, though they were slow to make the inference about the wrongness of capital punishment) then it was safest to treat the foetus as though it had the rights of a human being from the earliest moment that it could be perceived. And if that were done then some argued that every abortion was the murder of a child. Pope Pius XII and his successors treated abortion as though it was the same as the killing of an infant.

But if there was no law of abortion there would be a lot more babies whom their mothers resented, some babies left on other people's doorsteps, and illegal abortions as desperate girls hired criminal surgeons to do what they needed so passionately, with greater danger to the girls' lives.

If abortion was freely available to any girl who asked for it, that seemed to the Churches equal to making human life disposable at the whim of a young person, in an emotional state, not able to see the full context of what she demanded. But the women's movement sometimes contended that every woman who became pregnant had the right to decide whether or not she would bear the baby. In 1971 a Swedish government commission proposed that women should be free to decide. The Churches protested against the proposal. Was any woman to be given a free choice in deciding whether to end a human life? Three years later there was a political quarrel in Austria when it was found that abortions were being performed in Catholic hospitals at the expense of the taxpayers. A year after that the French government made a new law of abortion. In West Germany a law for abortion was found by the Supreme Court to be unconstitutional; but, until another bill was to be proposed, the judges allowed abortion in the case of danger of the life *or health* of the mother. In 1977 even the Italian government adopted a law liberalizing abortion (in force from 1978); this law allowed medical people to plead that they had a conscience not to partake in the operation. In Switzerland a proposal that abortion within three months of pregnancy be no longer a criminal offence went to a referendum; the proposal only just lost, and it was observed that the Protestant cantons on the whole voted in favour while the Catholic cantons voted almost solidly against. In 1981 Pope John Paul II reiterated the old doctrine that abortion is the murder of an innocent creature. In Norway the Lutheran bishop Per Lönning resigned his see because the State promoted an abortion law which disregarded the opinion of the Lutheran Church. When East and West Germany reunited during 1990, one of the legal problems was that East German law allowed abortion on demand up to the twelfth week of pregnancy whereas West Germany had only an exceptional clause allowing abortion after examination by a panel of doctors. The two parts of the new Germany agreed for the moment to differ about this, but the situation could not last. By 1993 East German practice had affected West Germany.

By now Belgium and Ireland were the only countries which banned abortion altogether. It was easy for women of both countries to go to a neighbouring state. In March 1990 the Belgian Parliament passed a strict law of abortion (during only the first twelve weeks) and the Belgian bishops protested. King Bauduin refused to sign the law and so came a constitutional crisis. But the king accepted a device by which he abdicated for two days while the bill became law and was then restored to his throne. This was a curious way of conscience-saving. The Belgian act left Ireland solitary.

TORTURE

It was an extraordinary feature of the 1970s that for the first time the moral theory of torture should need to be argued. That could only be because in some countries, usually in Latin America, some policemen came to their pastors with moral problems about the commands which they were being asked to carry out. But not only in Latin America – there were problems of police actions by the

French police in the Algerian war and by some policemen behind the Iron Curtain.

The pastors were confronted with the fact that some Christians accepted torture as a necessity of a modern State in trouble. The early Christian Church was unanimous in condemning it. But during the later Middle Ages, under the influence of Roman law, the possibility of a right torture began to be imagined by lawyers. If one Pope anathematized it, four Popes gave it a limited sanction and the Inquisition used these permissions. It was finally proscribed in about 1800, and its abolition passed into various declarations of human rights and modern international law.

Yet it was still used, and not only by Nazis and Stalinists. And it was defended. A State is a supreme good because without it the citizen has no liberty or justice. In conditions of near civil war it is necessary to gain information for the sheer preservation of the State, and that can sometimes only be done by physical force. The Church, it was argued, cannot condemn this because it does not condemn capital punishment and torture is a lesser use of force than that. Experience in Brazil and Uruguay, said the defenders, showed that it is useful if not indispensable to the maintenance of the State. It may be unjust to an individual, but in a threat to the State the common good must take precedence over the individual good. Even some Frenchmen were not prepared to condemn it outright in the conditions of the Algerian civil war.

All Churches like all liberals were unanimous against it as immoral. The disapproval that mattered was the Catholic, because the defenders of torture were usually to be found in Latin America.

12

Church and State in Western Europe

In Eastern Europe outside Albania, where the Church was alleged not to exist, the relations of Church and State followed a common principle, even in Poland until 1988–9. The Church governed itself with a variety of interference from the State – massive interventions in Russia and Czechoslovakia, less everywhere else, and with most elbow-room in East Germany and Yugoslavia. The implementation of the State's policy varied according to the country and according to whether the prevailing religion was Catholic or Orthodox or Protestant.

In the West there was an equal variety. It varied by the prevailing religion and the history of the country and the nature of its constitution. At one extreme were old-fashioned prince-bishoprics, descended from the Middle Ages, where the bishop was the government (as in the Vatican City and Andorra, but there the bishop shared rule with the President of France). At the other extreme France was supposed to be since 1905 a wholly secular State with a total separation of Church and State, but the theoretical separation was modified by the practice of the French government. The West European states accepted religious freedom as a human right, and this usually led to some forms of State support for religion.

The one-time practices of Christian states had meant five main links. Firstly, the State declared in its constitution that it was officially a Catholic, or a Protestant, or an Orthodox State. Secondly, it felt a duty that all the population should contribute by tax to the maintenance of the Church approved by the State. Thirdly, only members of the approved Church could hold certain high offices in the State. Fourthly, the State felt a duty to bring up its young people in a Christian way and therefore helped the expense of Christian schools (and sometimes universities). Fifthly, since the heads of the Church had influence on public opinion, the State should rightly have a say in their choice. This last was the one place where some Western European states agreed with almost all the Marxist states of Eastern Europe.

None of these old habits still worked in Western Europe. But none of them was wholly without influence even in the second half of the twentieth century.

CONSTITUTIONS

Certain states declared in their constitutions that they were Catholic. These were Spain (till 1976–9), Portugal (till 1974), Italy (till 1984–5), the Republic of Ireland (after 1937 Catholicism held a special place as the religion of the majority of the Irish people – and this was true, because the 1981 census showed that Roman Catholicism was the religion of over 90 per cent of the people of the Irish Republic), and Vatican City.

In Italy after the Second World War the Lateran Treaty of 1929, which created the Vatican State and gave the Church many privileges, was challenged because it was the doing of Mussolini. But it was quickly accepted as valid law. In the 1970s a movement arose not to abolish it but to change some of its conditions. In February 1989 the Vatican signed the revised version with the Italian Prime Minister, Craxi.

Even when Italy altered its profession that it was a Catholic state, it substituted a similar sort of general clause: 'The Italian Republic, recognizing the value of religious culture and taking account of the fact that the principles of Catholicism make part of the historic inheritance of the Italian people', declared that it would continue to provide religious education in the schools, with a right of parents to withdraw. An added protocol agreed that the teachers of religion should have the approval of the ecclesiastical authority – which should also have a right of approval over the syllabus and the books used. Over this last clause there was controversy. In 1986 seven 'intellectuals' appealed against it to the United Nations, on the ground that children have the right to be protected from religious discrimination.

The constitution of Greece (1968) declared that it was 'dominantly' an Orthodox state (and it was, the 1961 census made the Orthodox 97.8 per cent) and that its president (for lately the Greeks had thrown out their king) must be Orthodox.

The Republic of Iceland (Lutherans 91 per cent of the people) declared that it was Protestant.

Wherever a state religion appeared in a constitution, it was invariably agreed that all citizens of the state should have the free right to practise their religion even if it was not a religion favoured by the State – unless that religion was a threat to morality or public order.

This declaration in constitutions had small effect. It would not be easy to set up a Protestant chapel inside the borders of Vatican City, and in Spain the Protestant chapels could not have prominent notices on the streets saying what they were. In Ireland the constitutional declaration was seen by the Protestant Northern Irish as a threat, which it was not. But otherwise the constitutional provision was far less important than the mood of general society.

TAXES

Only certain States still taxed the people directly for the benefit of the Churches. In West Germany and the Scandinavian countries the citizens could contract out, and they could direct their tax to the Church which they wished. In Iceland the congregations could themselves levy a local tax, but the State kept its level down to a small amount and the Church governments could not increase it without the leave of government.

In many more states there was an indirect tax, in that the State helped Christian education with grants of money to schools or universities or both, and in that the State appointed chaplains, of various denominations, to the armed forces or to hospitals or to prisons.

In several states the State paid the pastors, and a very few maintained the parsonages. But this was not taxpayers' money: it was derived from State confiscation or management of former

Church endowments. In this way it was parallel to the inadequate stipends or grants paid to clergy in some of the Communist countries.

THE HEAD OF THE STATE

In West Germany the heads of the State could be of any denomination or none. Actually they were all Christians. This was a common phenomenon which occurred elsewhere. Even if the constitution did not lay it down that the head of State should be Catholic or Protestant, it was impossible in certain states for anyone but a Catholic or a Protestant to be chosen; in the same way that it was impossible for the head of the secular state of India, or the head of the secular state of Turkey, to be a Christian.

Monarchy was supposed to have vanished from the world. Italy got rid of its king in 1946, Greece in 1966. But Spain got back a king in 1975, and several more of the West European states were under constitutional monarchies than were republics. In all cases (except Luxemburg perhaps) the sovereign was either legally bound or expected to be a member of the historic religion of the state. Britain laid it down that he or she should be a Protestant. In all the Scandinavian states except Finland (which was a republic) the sovereign was expected to be a Lutheran because he or she was head of the State Church. In Spain the sovereign could hardly be other than a Catholic.

MOVEMENTS TO SEPARATE CHURCH AND STATE

In all the states where the State still had rights in the Church, this was challenged by some members of the Church. This came to a constitutional conflict in Sweden. The liberal State aimed at entire neutrality in religion and the removal of all forms of favour for an established Church but was not willing to concede in return a total liberty for the Lutheran Church to govern itself. Some members of the Church were strong for disestablishment; others wanted the link between Church and State to remain. The result was the Swedish Church Act of 1982 which gave the General Synod a relatively wide power to make laws on doctrine and worship, but which ended in a general control of the Church by the State which made it even more of a State Church than before. Naturally this was welcome to many members of the Church.

In most states of Western Europe the State conceded something to the liberties of the Church – meaning allowing more power to the clergy and representative Christian laity instead of Parliament or the executive government. In Britain in 1974 the State handed over substantial powers over worship and doctrine to the General Synod of the Church of England. Three years later the choice of Anglican bishops, which had lately lain with the Queen on the advice of the Prime Minister, who was advised by the two archbishops, was in effect handed over to a committee of the General Synod, though the State also was represented on the committee.

The Second Vatican Council resolved that governments ought to give up their powers over the choice of bishops. In most cases these powers were enshrined in a concordat which could not be changed without a treaty and then legal change. The negotiations for the redrafting of a concordat were difficult and long. In several Roman Catholic states where the government gave up the power to nominate bishops or to retain a veto on the choice of bishops, it was still provided that Rome must tell the government the name of the candidate for a see before the appointment was made and that the State had the power to make objections on political grounds.

In 1976 the King of Spain surrendered the right, on which General Franco had insisted so tenaciously, to choose bishops. He retained the right to object on political grounds to bishops whom the Vatican chose.

The most remarkable of the survivals was in Haiti. There, by an agreement of 1966, the President was given power to nominate bishops, though Rome must agree. Thus Pope Paul VI in one case accepted the old world's system even though the Council had asked that it should not survive. No one could say that the nomination of bishops by the State was an unCatholic system.

Nevertheless in some respects the movement in the relationship between Church and State in Western Europe was in the opposite direction, away from separation. When the French separated Church and State they thought it right to drive the Churches out of public life, laicize the schools, have no State-paid chaplains in prisons or the army or the hospitals, and abolish State-paid theological faculties. In the other democracies the movement towards separation of Church and State was not expected by churchmen to have any of these consequences. And even in France, where old-fashioned anticlericalism was now a survival among grandfathers, the Churches began little by little to take more part in public life, especially in education. The French government was not now disturbed at help to denominational schools.

SPAIN

After the Second World War there remained in the West two dictators – Salazar in Portugal and Franco in Spain. Of these two, Franco was much the more disreputable in the eyes of the world because once he had been an ally of Hitler and Mussolini.

Both Franco and Salazar rested their authority on (1) having saved the nation from civil calamity and (2) the conservative forces within the Catholic Church, but Franco did so much the more openly because he claimed the civil war which he won had been a crusade against atheist murder and anarchy. After 1945, his isolation from the rest of the world except Portugal and Pope Pius XII made him want almost a theocratic state. The State helped the Church with numerous grants of money for stipends, buildings and colleges; the Church gave the State the legitimacy which it did not derive from a general election, and it exercised a rather puritan effect on the press and the theatre, and a limiting effect on the trade unions. Freemasonry and Communism were made illegal. Protestants could exist, but there must be no public sign of a non-Catholic place of worship. Universities and schools must teach in accordance with the Catholic faith. It was a confessional State. Both Franco and the bishops encouraged ardently conservative organizations like Catholic Action and Opus Dei.

In 1953 Franco agreed a concordat with Pius XII, a treaty very favourable to the Church and its rights. The world regarded this concordat with disfavour, as making Franco legitimate. But because he thought the Church important to Spain and its national revival and to his political power (which it probably was), Franco insisted on his right to choose the bishops. He promoted clergymen who agreed with him, and put some of them into Parliament.

Amid the harmony of Spanish Church and State, discords began to sound. In a world of new industry and tourism and young Spaniards who knew nothing of the horrors of civil war, Francoism was felt to be an anachronism. In the Basque country people started to throw bombs against the centralized State. And then came the Second Vatican Council and changed the Church – it voted for religious liberty, and was against a State choosing bishops, and it was not wholly uncompromising about Communism. Younger Spanish churchmen after 1965 were very different from their archbishops who survived from the civil war. The political right accused the new young of bringing Marxist ideas into the Church. By 1971 there was a practical block on the choice of new bishops. It was strange that at one end of Europe, in Slovakia, the Pope could not appoint bishops because the State thought them not Marxist enough, and at the other end, in Spain, the Pope could not appoint bishops because the State thought them too near to Marxism. In Slovakia there were occupations of bishops' palaces and of seminaries by the Communist State. In Spain there were occupations of bishops' palaces and seminaries by radical Catholics, with priests among them.

General Franco died at last in 1975 and was succeeded by Juan Carlos as a constitutional king, and Spain was changed. An agreement of 1976 accepted religious liberty as a fundamental right, but recognized that a majority of the Spanish people preferred the Catholic faith.

GREECE

In Greece, successive governments interfered, sometimes outrageously (from the point of view of the bishops), in the life of the Orthodox Church. From 1969 to 1975 the Holy Synod was given power to legislate without the need of State consent (compare the General Synod in England in 1974), but this was afterwards modified. There were little movements for disestablishment, to secure freedom for the Church. These protests were weak. The union between Church and State was so historic as to be part of the Greek way of life and of national consciousness. When almost all the people were Orthodox, archbishops had power. No government could afford not to interfere sometimes. The Greek people accepted this. It was archbishops who minded.

The link between the Greek Church and politics was startlingly illustrated in Cyprus. Makarios, the archbishop, was also the President of that country. In April 1973, three Cypriot bishops pronounced his deposition from the see, part of their reason being that the office of primate is not compatible with the office of head of State, and a real part being that the three bishops supported Grivas, who was the leader of bombs and murder for the union of Cyprus with Greece. The Greek Church on the mainland thought the deposition illegal. Makarios called a synod in the same year and reduced the three to lay status.

GERMANY

In 1933 Hitler made a concordat with the Pope. This treaty, which he had no intention of observing, was very favourable to the Church. After the war the lawyers treated it as still valid, and therefore in West Germany it was now observed for the first time and greatly benefited the Church. Objectors resented such favourable provisions (for example in State help for Catholic education) and went to court to argue that what Hitler had done was now invalid. In 1957 the Federal Constitutional Court of West Germany held that the concordat of 1933 was still the law of the land.

In West Germany only about 15 per cent of the people contracted out of paying church tax. The West German Churches were the richest in Christendom. It was easy for them to finance new buildings and to create theological instruction.

Since the West German figures for church tax are government statistics, they give a clue to the state of religion in the country. In the year before the Second World War, under Nazi pressure, the number of persons who left the Church reached a record 378,000. In 1945 in the postwar religious revival it achieved another record, of being only 9,493, a number much exceeded by the number of those who joined. Then, in the age of the student rebellion and the Vietnam war and general unsettlement especially among teenagers, there was a dramatic upswing in defection – 60,000 in 1967; 202,000 in 1970. A small majority of those who left were between sixteen and thirty-two years old, and a small majority were male.

West Germany still had a lot of churchgoers, whether Catholic or Protestant. An opinion poll of 1970 showed that 30 per cent still attended services regularly, though it was 20 per cent in cities. That was higher than in France or Britain. But doctrine was vaguer in both Churches. An opinion poll of 1970 showed that 52 per cent of Germans did not believe in life after death. That was. vast encouragement to the Christians – that nearly half the people had a Christian hope of death as no final end. But it proved what was proved in several other contexts: that to go to church was not the same thing as professing the historic articles of the Christian creed.

In East Germany, where the concordat was abolished, where no one could raise a church tax, where religious people could not hold high office in civil society, the government believed that during the 1970s fewer than half the population belonged to a Church. This was not the opinion of the East German Churches, which claimed, though with doubt, that over half the people still thought of themselves as members.

But who was a member? In the old Germany this was an easy

question, because if you were a member you paid church tax. After church tax was abolished, baptism was the classical way to decide whether someone belonged. The percentage of children baptized began to be low by the seventies: approximately 20 per cent in the East German population as a whole, but down to 10 per cent in cities. But by the 1970s this traditional way of testing allegiance began to be doubted. Some young parents did not have their children baptized because they were afraid it might later hurt them in schooling or the quest for a job. Many unbaptized young men and women took part in Church life without formally professing themselves as Church members. They cared about the casuses that young people anywhere cared about in the later twentieth century – peace, and disarmament, and the conservation of the environment; but also the cultural activities possible in the Church community, and the care of the growing adolescent. Therefore it was likely that the number of 'real' members of the East German Churches was greater than the number of 'formal' members, instead of the other way around which was the historic situation in Churches.

Yet by the mid-1970s the educated class in East Germany either doubted or disbelieved Christianity; and Church people were older in average age, not only because the average age of everyone was older; and it became socially noticeable that Christians were not among the leading members or classes in the State. It made a difference whether a religion was encouraged or discouraged by the State.

But the contrast was not so dramatic as statistics suggested. The effect of State hostility to religion was smaller than it looked. The number of persons going to church or using the sacraments fell in West Germany in much the same way as it fell in the East. Weddings in church fell fast, baptisms fell faster, only funerals remained almost universally a church rite. The loyalty to a Church shown by the payment of church tax might have nothing to do with Christian belief and little enough to do with trying to live a Christian life. It might be a sign that the Church was valued because it was part of German tradition and the German way of life and so it helped to make society more stable, with other people being left to go along to say their prayers if they wished.

This contrast or similarity between East and West Germany

suggests that the main reason for the decline of religious practice in the East was not likely to be the hostility of the State (though that was at least a subordinate reason), for the same thing happened in the West where the State was friendly.

Still, the Church in the West carried more weight in general society. If a bishop, whether evangelical or Catholic, said something important, it would have more influence than in the East, where it would have no influence at all. In the East it would not be reported in the newspapers, whereas in the West the bishop could have the media at his disposal. A Western bishop was eminent enough, and respected enough because of his office in society, to be listened to. The situation of the Churches in the West – not as drawing the young people to go to church or say some prayers or marry each other, but as institutions which affected general society – was easier.

SWITZERLAND

Switzerland made an exception in the relationships of Church and State in Western Europe. And yet it showed various faces which help the understanding of other countries in the West.

Each canton had power to decide between Church and State. The Federal Constitution (1874) started with 'In the Name of Almighty God' and then guaranteed religious liberty. But it had strange provisions. The Jesuits were excluded from Switzerland, and no religious orders might be there and no new convents opened. Federal leave was also needed to set up a new bishopric. The exclusions were so illiberal that they were abolished: the ban on new sees in 1972 and the bans on Jesuits and convents by referendum in 1973. But it was a sign both of the history of Switzerland and of the depth of the Catholic–Protestant antagonism in Western Europe, even in an ecumenical age, that the vote had a huge minority – 648,659 to the majority of 790,799 – which wanted to keep the Jesuits out by law. It was proved that some Catholics voted for the minority.

In the cantons, Geneva and Neuchâtel separated Church and

State early in the twentieth century but allowed exceptions. Otherwise all cantons recognized both Catholic and Reformed Churches as a sort of State Church; except the city of Basle, which only recognized the Reformed, and the Italian-speaking canton of Ticino, which only recognized the Catholic. Valais had a Catholic State Church till this was abolished by referendum in 1974. In St Gallen there remained a right to church tax. Zurich experienced loud cries for the separation of Church and State during the 1960s. But a majority of citizens preferred to keep the link and a revised form of it was agreed in 1967 and made the law of the canton. It kept the right to a tax, and the State retained the supreme oversight of the Church, and must sanction holidays, and clergy leave, and new parishes.

Thus Switzerland followed a general West European pattern which during the 1970s could be seen in Britain, Spain, Portugal, Italy and Sweden: continuing the process of religious liberty, which in some cases meant a form of partial disestablishment, but usually retaining most of the old forms and interpreting them in such a way that the Church authorities had less interference from the State.

13

Perestroika

In all elections there is a reaction against the last incumbent. The electors may value what the last person did but now they want someone who has different qualities. Paul VI was a man of the Curia. Therefore at the election of 1978 the chances of any Curial cardinal being chosen were diminished; not because the electors disliked Paul VI – many of them revered him – but because they must have someone different.

But to be elected, someone must be known. The heart of the Church was in Rome. That was where the cardinals visited and came to know each other. Therefore an Italian – if not of the Curia – had more chance than any other cardinal because the more eminent Italians were widely known outside Italy as well as inside. The Popes elected in the twentieth century (before September 1978) included three men of the Curia, one librarian (who was of the Curia but not in the normal sense) and three Patriarchs of Venice. That is a lot of patriarchs of one see. This was not because all the world visits Venice and therefore the cardinals knew its patriarch – most of the electors of 1978 hardly knew Luciani of Venice by sight – but if they were to find an Italian not of the Curia there were only four or five archbishops from whom it was possible to choose.

So Albano Luciani, the Patriarch of Venice, was elected in August 1978, with the right qualifications: not a man of the Curia, which he hardly understood; a pastor; outgoing, and not such an agonizer as his predecessor. His main opponent was the conservative Siri, who disliked the Second Vatican Council and wanted to reverse its programme. The new Pope surprised everyone by choosing the first double name in the history of the papacy. He took John because of John XXIII and Paul because of Paul VI. It was a double assertion of continuity with the programme of the Vatican Council. He surprised also by adding the First on the end – monarchs are not usually known as 'the First' until there is a Second.

He was the first member of the industrial 'proletariat' to be elected Pope. The two previous Popes born of simple families since the industrial revolution were of peasant, country origin. His father was a glassworker at Murano by Venice. Luciani had been a very good diocesan bishop.

He did not have time to show what kind of a Pope he would be, except that he had no pomp and was good at audiences and friendly. He had time to refuse to be crowned, thereby abandoning at last the papal ritual of a secular sovereign. Thirty days after the election he was found dead in bed in the early morning of 29 September 1978. This was not the shortest tenure of the office, because Urban VII (1590) caught malaria the night after his election and served twelve days.

The Curia was content with the doctor's death certificate and held no post-mortem. This gave the chance for all kinds of rumour. Within a few days it was being put about that the Pope must have been murdered. Who might have a motive? Did the Curia think he would reverse the policy of Paul VI, or enquire into the Vatican Bank, which at that moment was in bad trouble by association with two financiers whose empire had collapsed? The failure by the Secretary of State, the Frenchman Villot, to see a proper autopsy and inquest unjustly damaged the Church and damaged the repute of the prevailing bureaucracy. In 1984 David Yallop published a book, *In God's Name*, which systematically charged the Curia or its associate financiers with murder and which, despite the wildness of its claims, or because of them, had a world circulation.[1] It was a strange fate for a good, kind, unpretentious, religious north-Italian glassworker's son.

1. Further English consideration in J. Cornwell, *A Thief in the Night*, 1989. Cardinal Villot, who was the responsible person in the vital hour after the death, committed the two errors of (1) putting out a communiqué that said that the chaplain Magee found the Pope dead when in fact the nun Sister Vincenza found the body and fetched Magee, (2) allowing embalmment to go ahead that afternoon after accepting the doctor's quick verdict of a heart attack and without the autopsy and inquest which would be needed under Italian law – but they were not in Italy. (Motive? – they had to make the body quickly available for a lying-in-state of four days and so the body must not be allowed to deteriorate.) Afterwards Villot seems to have blamed himself for the death of the Pope because he put on

THE ELECTION OF POPE JOHN PAUL II IN 1978

In August the cardinals had found an Italian who was not of the Curia. Now they must look again, and they had ruled out the other Italian archbishops already.

The Pole Wojtyla of Cracow had been thought too young to be elected – he was fifty-eight. But the death of Luciani suddenly made it desirable, for once, to look for someone with health and energy and years of working life ahead. Wojtyla had all these. He was good at languages, attended international conferences when Poland interested the bishops of the West and America, and therefore was not an unknown or remote Easterner. He attracted the Western bishops because at the Second Vatican Council he spoke out for religious freedom as a human right and therefore helped the Council to a crucial change in Roman Catholic doctrine. Yet he was also known as a conservative on the ethical issues. He was known to think Paul VI right about contraception and abortion. The ethical liberals did not want him, nor did most of the Italians, for they were also electing a Bishop of Rome and a primate of Italy. But they had no candidate to measure against him.

Though the election of John Paul II (for Cardinal Wojtyla took the names of his too brief predecessor) was not welcome to many of the Italians, it was clear that such a Pope would be welcome to many Catholics in the Western world as a sign that the papacy and therefore Christianity was truly international and not ruled by a single nation. It was still clearer that Slav Europe was ecstatic in its welcome. But there were two queries about the new Pope.

He came from a country where the religion of the people was warm, emotional, unsophisticated and on occasion superstitious. He was known to be against things which some Western Catholics

---

to a new Pope, inexperienced in that sort of business, such masses of paper – the more voluminous because in Paul VI's last days it was difficult to do business and therefore many decisions waited. John Paul I had a record of poor health before he was elected, but not of such poor health as to make the cardinals foolish to elect him.

wanted – like a changed ruling on birth control, or on the ordination of married priests, and even more against the ordination of women. By the encyclical *Humanae Vitae*, Paul VI had caused a crisis of authority in Western Catholicism and this crisis was still with the Church. John Paul II inherited as much prestige in his office as Paul VI inherited fifteen years before but far less obedience among Catholics. How would this conservative cope with the fierce pressure from Catholic liberals – many of them from the United States, which was important in the material sense, for it helped the Vatican State to balance its budget, which was in the red, and sent aid to the hard-pressed Catholic Churches of Eastern Europe? He inherited a more divided Church than any Pope for a century.

Secondly, what would be the effect in Eastern Europe of a Pope from Eastern Europe? No one knew whether it would help the Marxist-ruled Churches or make their plight worse; though the expert on Eastern Europe among the cardinals, König of Vienna, was sure that it would help and had wanted Wojtyla while in the conclave.

What was certain was that the new papacy would be international, in a sense which it had never quite attained before in its history. This was not an Italian: he came from a country where the Church was under pressure and had not long before been under persecution and the hopes of which lay in help from other nations. No Pope for more than a century and a half had experience in earlier life of trying to help the Church under a non-Christian government. And he was a Slav. His election was like a symbol that all Eastern Europe was in the centre instead of at the fringe of the European idea. This was the first Pope since 1522 for whom Italy, the base of the papal existence, was but one country among a lot of countries; though Rome was not one town among other towns because it was the apostolic city and the seat of the vicar of Christ.

Paul VI had travelled in his earlier years as Pope. The new Pope now made travelling his greatest work. He became an evangelist of the world, wherever the world would invite him, whether the country which invited him was Catholic or not, Christian or not. His personality – outgoing, stable, unpompous, caring and spiritual – was equal to this extraordinary new conception of the papal office. He could sway the crowds and be unperturbed by the handful of mockers, and master the walkabout, and take care to greet personally the crippled and the incurable. Chairbound old women who had not come out of their hospice for years were taken to be blessed by him and came back with ecstasy in their memory. He always kissed the ground when he entered a country on coming down the steps of the aircraft, and vast crowds gathered to attend his celebrations of the mass in stadiums or parks, and his words to them fitted the occasion, and he could communicate himself even to a huge arena. No ruler ever understood pageantry better. He took whatever happened serenely. In most places he was the centre of a vast enthusiasm. In Turkey the government received him reluctantly and the people greeted him icily.

The public Pope was at risk. Paul VI had been attacked by a man with a knife in Manila. On 13 May 1981 John Paul II went out into St Peter's Square to greet the crowd by standing in a jeep and was shot in the stomach by a Turk, Mehmet Ali Agca. He was for a time in danger and endured severe cutting and took five months to convalesce. The attempted assassination did not alter the Pope's openness to the world nor his travelling, though everywhere the police took care over bulletproof glass windows.

He quickly made his views known: that priesthood is narrowly bound to the celibate life; that abortion is murder and children have a right to be born; that nuns ought to wear habits; that children should make their confession before first communion; that individual confession is necessary and general confession inadequate; that marriage is indissoluble; that violence is no solution to political and economic problems (he said this last emphatically in Ireland); that priests are not freedom-fighters or chaplains to terrorists; that materialism is selfish whether it is in individuals or in advanced industrial countries – and that *religious liberty is a fundamental right*. He was secure in himself, rounded as a personality, with a philosophy and doctrine which fitted his mission.

His piety was obvious. On Good Friday 1980 and 1981 he heard confessions in St Peter's, and he was able to hear them in Hungarian and Italian and Spanish and German. He said that the rosary was his favourite form of prayer. His personal devotion to the Blessed Virgin was manifest. He made pilgrimages to say prayers at the holy shroud of Turin, and at the shrines across the world – of Knock in Ireland, and at Guadaloupe in Mexico, and at Santiago de Compostela in Spain, and at Fatima in Portugal. He showed that he loved the now unfashionable cult of the Sacred Heart when he prayed at the tomb of its founder, Alacoque, and went to Paray-le-Monial. The personality gave that sense of quiet and of leisure amid business which comes to the men of prayer.

In some ways he was the most popular Pope there had ever been, certainly the best-known Pope through the world. But this world conception of his office had three problems. As the peoples got used to his visits, they became occasions when demonstrators could assure themselves the maximum publicity before the television cameras.

In 1987 he went to Chile and criticized General Pinochet's government as dictatorial. On a visit to the general he called for democracy. But as he said mass in a large park scores of anti-government protesters were beaten back with water-cannon and tear-gas and there were many injuries.

And though he was so popular with the crowds, there were places where he was the most unpopular of Popes. Some American and Canadian Catholics would hear not a word in his praise, because of his ethical attitudes and his antifeminism. At San Francisco on 17 September 1987 100,000 people demonstrated against the Pope – not noisily nor with violence, but the antipathy to his moral doctrines was made plain. The old custom of the Catholic Church was to blame the Curia for any of the Pope's actions that were unpopular, thus exempting the Pope himself from blame; now, instead, the Pope was blamed for the obstructiveness of the Curia. The more venomous abused him as a star of show business, or called him a new Torquemada trying to force the Church into the model of conservative Poland. He was blamed for encouraging the organization Opus Dei, which was paraded in the press as an instrument for reaction. But for more of the world what mattered was the fulfilment of the new attitudes of the papacy on religious freedom, the value of democracy and human rights. And the bishops who wanted a change in the ethical rulings were content to make their points quietly, sure that in the end they or their successors would get their way.

The ecumenical movement was another place where the Pope was not acclaimed. People said that in 1970 the ecumenical movement was making rapid advances and in 1985 it was stationary or moving backwards. Yet his relations with the Ecumenical Patriarch of Constantinople, Demetrius, were friendly, and he came to pray with Archbishop Runcie in Canterbury cathedral – the first Pope ever to attend an Anglican way of worship. He went to the synagogue in Rome – the first Pope ever to attend the Jewish way of prayer. When he visited India (in 1986) he said prayers at Gandhi's tomb and called Gandhi 'a hero of humanity'. He received the Dalai Lama at the Delhi nunciature. At an interfaith meeting in Calcutta he quoted the Upanishads and praised their religious sense and said that the Roman Catholic Church recognized the truth in the religious tradition of the Indians. At Madras, where he talked to a million people, he spoke warmly of the religious tradition of India and extolled its interior spirituality. On 27 October 1986 he presided at a great meeting in Assisi of representatives of all the faiths, a unique moment of worship in the history of faith and the faiths: forty non-Christians, mostly from India and Japan; fifty non-Catholics, Archbishop Runcie of Canterbury and the Duke of Edinburgh; and some thirty Roman Catholic cardinals and bishops. So, if the ecumenical movement was not prospering, this was not because that Pope was narrow-minded about the relationship between religious people.

In June 1979 he was able to secure from the Polish government freedom to visit Poland. The government was nervous of having him. It had enough difficulties in the relation of Church and State on its chessboard without allowing the invasion of a new Queen upon the side of Black. But it could hardly refuse to have him as the Russians or the Czechs could refuse. The visit was very successful and caused no conflict. He addressed 3.5 million Poles at the shrine of Czestochowa. But this provided impetus for the trade-union movement of Solidarity and the relation between the Polish workers and the Catholic Church.

The election of John Paul II had results among the Slav peoples which were impossible to test but which were far-reaching, especially among the Catholic Slavs – Poles above all, but also Slovaks, Slovenes, Croats, Lithuanians, and to a lesser extent among Czechs – but also among Hungarians, and even among Protestant Czechs or Poles or Hungarians. From that moment the Slavs, who mostly lived under anti-religious rule, were now in the

religious leadership of humanity. They stirred, they began to think
and say things that they would hardly have dared to say only a
decade or two before. The ideal of religious liberty was what they
took from the Pope, and they knew at once that religious liberty
was not possible without much more political and social liberty
than they possessed. Freedom was indivisible.

GORBACHEV

During 1988–90 it became visible to the world that the Soviet
Empire could not go on as it was: that its economy was near
collapse, its peoples resurgent and its failure confessed. The Soviet
President Gorbachev's liberalizing policy transformed what was
possible in Eastern Europe and the rigidities of the Cold War and
hence the situation of the Christian Churches.

In all Russia, congregations found it easier to get licences to
exist legally. It did not happen at once: Moscow could say that
licences should be given but that did not mean that local authorities did not continue to find excuses not to give licences. But it
was easier to get back closed churches, easier to get permission
and materials to build a new church. In Lvov in the Ukraine the
director of the museum of atheism threw out his propaganda
materials, saying that he was an atheist but one must respect other
people's opinions, and turned it into a proper museum of the
history of religion.

In the Soviet Union there were still three times more churches
open when Stalin died than in 1988. There were more students in
seminaries, but still there were only three seminaries. Some prisoners were freed, among them the rebel priest Gleb Yakunin.
Fairer laws were promised. Gorbachev (mis)quoted the Bible in
Pravda. Billy Graham preached in St Vladimir's cathedral, Kiev,
but the streets were barricaded by the police to avoid a crowd.
The Lithuanian bishop Steponavičius was at last allowed to be
again the bishop. The Protestant cathedral in Latvia was returned
to the Church. Three months later the Catholic cathedral in
Vilnius, for thirty-eight years an art gallery, was returned to the

Church and the first mass was celebrated there on 5 February 1989 by Bishop Steponavičius, returned from twenty-eight years of exile. There was a link between the revival of the Church and Lithuanian nationalism. In 1989 the State conceded that Christmas Day should be a holiday in the Baltic states.

There was a new and much more liberal Commissar for Religious Affairs, Konstantin Kharchev. He publicly estimated the number of believers at 70 million, which was larger than any previous admission. Orthodox and Catholics and Baptists all began to be encouraged. Kharchev said that they could not expect the sudden end of an ideology that saw the priest as an alien and the Church's faith as an outlook hostile to society and the believer as a third-rate human being, but the citizens must be relieved of their sense of injury and shown how the cultural heritage of the fatherland was valued. A democratic State, he said, ought to be totally neutral between religion and atheism – let the self-financing organizations engage in atheist propaganda but not the State. There was no reason to ban voluntary religious education. And the churches needed protection from the high-handedness of local power. At the moment a local authority could decide to run a road through the churchyard or to knock down a cupola.

All this was too much for some members of the Party, and Kharchev was removed from office. But his successor did not change the way things went.

The most successful of all the atheist journals, the Russian *Nauka i Religiya* (Science and Religion) published in January 1989 an article on the atheist campaign. It was authoritative, by the director of the Institute of Scientific Atheism, V. Garadzha. The change of policy was startling in its frankness. It may be briefly summarized as follows.

In a socialist society, religion still exists. Our philosophy of setting up 'good' atheists against 'bad' believers alienated groups of people and undermined social unity in the struggle for a better society. It is ludicrous to suggest that religion is the greatest hindrance to the development of socialist society. There were clergy against Communism and clergy against imperialists; they have been active for nuclear disarmament, and for a greener treatment of the environment. Do we say such activity is harmful because it has a religious motivation? We must face it that religion sometime helps our struggle for a better society. 'We should not deny the necessity for unity between believers and atheists in the struggle for the renewal of socialism.' Let us not present atheism as a new creed alternative to religion. Religion will die out with the establishment of socialism, as Marx foresaw that the need for the State would die out. But meanwhile we need it as a fellow-traveller along the road, and must recognize that this will be for a long time to come. 'Atheism in its present state is like a boat caught in a force-9 gale, tossed about in the waves.'[2]

In December 1989 Gorbachev was in Rome to visit the Pope. He told the Pope that a law on religious freedom would soon be enacted. The atmosphere was friendly.

One by one, all the satellite states (Albania, no longer a satellite, was last to do it) got rid of their Stalinist government where that still existed. In 1989 a Solidarity government, based upon a very Catholic party with particular strength among the working men but also among the liberal intellectuals, came into power in Poland. Where the Church had made much headway towards its freedoms already, as in Poland or Yugoslavia or East Germany, the coming of the freer governments did not make so much difference: it made action in public affairs more possible, but it took away the power that came from the loyalty given to any body that stood against an unpopular Communist government.

But where the Church was still rigorously controlled by the State, as in Czechoslovakia or Romania or Bulgaria or the Soviet Union, the coming of perestroika made a vast difference.

The Catholic Church in Czechoslovakia had been run by the Catholic cooperators, Pacem in Terris. These were at once out of office – not dismissed from priesthood, but transferred to less important work – and the bishops working in factories came out and resumed their ministry. The Patriarch of Romania, Teoctist, was forced to resign in January 1990 because he had been so sycophantic to Ceaușescu. Two days after a December 1989 mass-acre by police in the square in front of the Orthodox cathedral at Timișoara, Teoctist had sent Ceaușescu a telegram congratulating him on his wisdom and bold guidance. As soon as Ceaușescu fell in the revolution, the patriarch called him the modern Herod and

2. Translated in *Religion in Communist Lands* 18:1 (1990), 72ff.

summoned a synod to revive religious education and to lift the excommunications which the synod had been forced by the State to inflict. He was driven to retire to the monastery of Sinaia; but then he pleaded that such sycophancy was a necessary ritual in a Communist state and three months later he was restored to office, not without some protests.

But the trouble between bishops compromised by subservience to a regime and former radical clergy once treated badly and now freed would in none of the States be settled easily or quickly. Two Reformed Church leaders in Romania were also forced to resign. The Patriarch of Armenia was nominated to run as a candidate for the Soviet Parliament, the first leader for whom so strange a fate was even possible. Then the Patriarch of Moscow and two of his bishops joined the Parliament.

The worst problem was, who owned the buildings? The Hungarian State had dissolved all the monasteries. It now ordered that the buildings should be handed back where possible. This was a cause of much argument about ownership. A Salesian house near Esztergom with a seminary and a hostel for pilgrims had been turned into a collective farm. Learning that changes were afoot, the farm put the buildings up for sale – and the Salesians could not buy them because technically the Salesians were still illegal. They had applied for legality, but bureaucrats worked no faster because of perestroika. Hungary abolished the State Church Office because it stood for an unacceptable control of the Churches by the State, but it still needed an office very like it if it was to sort out the problems of the new day. But the State no longer exercised a veto on appointments, and no longer restricted the number who entered seminaries.

In Czechoslovakia the new government also abolished the State Office for Church Affairs (in December 1989), and the religious orders made a statement that they did not intend to claim back property which was not part of their direct vocation – like land, or forests. All thirteen Catholic dioceses in the country had real bishops again. In April 1990 Pope John Paul II visited Prague. It felt extraordinary to both Czechs and Slovaks.

In Poland, who owned the property? Some of the old property – churches, vicarages, some nunneries, some bishops' offices – was still being used by the Churches as tenants of the State. The Polish law of 1989 said that whatever a Church was using was now the property of the Church. But there was a large area for dispute. Some of the property had been put to what the State regarded as better use, like a school or a hospital, and would not return to the Church. But what of a hospital formerly run by nuns in their habits, nationalized but afterwards still staffed partly by nuns not in their habits? Was that a Church-used institution which became the property of the Church? To settle this large area of dispute, a commission was created with equal numbers from government and the Church. Claims had to be made in two years. But it looked certain that the Church would recover a lot of religious houses and hospitals and schools. What about works of art – chalices or statues or pictures or reredoses, seized from churches by Stalinist governments and now in museums? Some of them were much better kept in museums: was it sacrilegious of a Church to let them stay there if it could get them out? The Polish commission decided (in principle) that where the object was needed for worship it should go back, but where it was not it should remain in the museum.

The worst problem over property happened over the Uniats. In the Ukraine and in Romania they were now again legal. In the Ukraine they moved back into their old churches. But the Orthodox had been using many of those churches for forty years. There was a little local violence and very little agreement on the right legal answer, and a fundamental difference of view between a former Uniat underground Church and an Orthodox Church which thought this whole Uniat business an unnecessary schism quite out of keeping with modern ideals of Christian unity.

In Romania the Vatican suddenly made five new Uniat bishops (in March 1990). But the new Romanian government protested that this was an illegal act because it still needed legislation. The Greek Orthodox Church protested fiercely against the new bishops. The Romanian Orthodox Church seemed less perturbed by the new legality of the Uniats, though it thought the new bishops to be a mistake, but it was worried about the old questions of property – to whom did the former Uniat churches and vicarages now belong? It made an offer: to agree a commission to settle the just ownership according to the numbers of adherents. It was not likely that the commission would be harmonious.

With all this happening everywhere but in Albania, the world looked at Albania. It was alleged that by the end of April 1990 some of the younger technocrats were becoming 'supporters of religion'. There was a campaign, successful at last, to get rid of the power of that militant atheist the widow of the late dictator Hoxha. At Easter 1990 in a very few villages an old priest celebrated the Easter liturgy. A French diplomat had evidence of an old Orthodox priest, three of whose fingers were cut off in the 1950s, celebrating the liturgy in a village near Elbasan. On 9 May 1990 the Albanian prime minister, struggling for a shred of international respectability, announced that persons who propagated religion would no longer be persecuted but that the State would continue to propagate atheism. In November 1990 Catholics in Shkodër (Scutari) began to rebuild a church and Muslims there began to build a mosque. Early in 1991 the Catholic bishop of Shkodër was released and allowed to visit the Vatican. But the Albanian regime was under the illusion that it had brought Albania into the modern world by abolishing religion and at first shrank from releasing the forces which, in the special circumstances of that country, might follow a toleration of religion.

Throughout Eastern Europe the difficulties were fourfold. Firstly, change of government was no automatic recipe for prosperity. Communism as a system failed the people by its heavy hand of bureaucracy. But if Communist leaders disappeared the people were still poor.

Secondly, to survive and be effective, to keep sacraments among their people and churches in being, Christian leaders from Moscow to Prague and Belgrade had played along with their dictatorial politburos. They had not all gone so far in adulation as the patriarchs Justin and Teoctist of Romania, who had had to endure a dictator with megalomania, but they had had to say things and do things of which it was not easy afterwards to be proud. When the Communists fell, everyone who had worked with them was in trouble. There was a potential source of conflict, even of schism, between the legitimate Church authorities and their clergy and people, some of whom thought that their superiors had lost all credibility. This was not true of a few – Cardinal Tomašek in Prague, because he went on so long without being corrupted, and most of the Church leaders in Poland and Yugoslavia.

Thirdly, for forty-five years the schoolchildren of Eastern Europe had been taught scientific materialism at school. We have seen that nevertheless a majority of undergraduates in Slovenia went to church. And everyone is agreed that children do not listen to what they are taught in school. Nevertheless this long process of education which was an impracticable form of miseducation must have consequences which no one can yet foresee. If Churches were going to be important again in the States because nationalism was again a force and they were a shrine of the history of the nation – if Churches were going to be important in the State because the people wanted freedom and for forty years Churches were identified with the ideals of freedom and human rights – then the Churches were going to need to be adaptable in the face of a population which had been schooled in Marxism even when it had not listened. And they were bound to continue to meet the contemptuous dismissal of faith, which was less common in the West where those who dismissed religion as obsolete usually did so with respect for it and sometimes with regret.

This dismissal of religion was likely to be especially flat in countries where previous experience led some of the people to an anticlerical or antireligious outlook – East Germany, which was Nazi for twelve years before the Communists; Bohemia, with its tradition of anti-Habsburg atheism; Kosovo in southern Yugoslavia, where there looked to be little future in Islam and yet all the Christian peoples seemed to be enemies; and above all Russia, because of its fading reverence for Lenin – Marx was sick, but Lenin lived on.

Fourthly, though persecution strengthens Church people in their fervour, it also makes them more conservative as they cling to what they have inherited which is now under attack. That had made dialogue difficult in the Communist states. After 1990 dialogue was possible. But, so far as the dialogue meant Christians opening their minds to their critics, it must at first be more difficult because of the immediate past of repression.

To what extent was the persistence of Christianity responsible for the toppling of the regimes in most of Eastern Europe during 1989–90?

This varied. All the East European states had had Communist governments forced upon them. The people would put up with them only so long as they brought work and good wages or, if they failed in that duty, so long as force was backed by the threat of Russian tanks. When Communism failed to achieve what it intended and was little but a heavy-handed bureaucracy, and when the Soviet economy ran into such trouble that the menace of invasion receded, the satellite states need no longer be satellites. Not all the revolutions needed the Churches.

And yet the East German revolution began in Leipzig, where demonstrators met in churches and then went out to the squares to confront armed police. The Romanian revolution began when the Hungarian Reformed pastor Tökes at Timişoara refused to be evicted and was backed by his congregation and then by the people. In Poland the party which attained power to overthrow the Communists was a Catholic party: the elections were often organized by the local priest, and the committee met in his church hall. In Latvia the Lutheran pastor Modris Plate, whose group had overthrown a complaisant archbishop, was one of the leaders of the party for the independence of Latvia, the Latvian Popular Front. In Slovakia the Catholic Church, or rather its 'dissenting' elements who refused to toe an official prelatical line, was the focus of opposition to the government in Prague.

To account for these, and other incidents like them, this much can be said:

(1) Christianity was the only 'official' opposition which the Marxist states allowed. They deplored religion but recognized that it existed and tried to neutralize it by keeping it inside church walls and by controlling its leaders. For a while they largely succeeded. But still, it was an opposition in being. And as such it started to draw in others, who were not particularly religious but cared passionately about freedom and human rights.

Western Europe knew several world-views. Because it was permitted no other, Eastern Europe knew only two outlooks on the world, the Marxist and the religious, and the first despised the second and the second regretted the first. The clash had social theory in it because Christians contradicted axioms in the philosophy and world-view of Marxism. But the urgent conflict was about morality. Do ethical values ultimately rise from the community and its temporary needs or do they also come from outside and above the community? This juxtaposition of only two world-views made the Christians into the quiet and unofficial critics in the realm of ideas. To those who rejected Marxism, they were the only home that beckoned.

(2) None of the Communist governments was 'legitimate': without exception they had been installed by coup. Former Western leaders of coups from King Pepin to Napoleon and Hitler and Mussolini, and even contemporary Western leaders of coups like General Franco and the Greek colonels, had tried to gain the legitimacy which they lacked with the aid of religion, by coronations or by bestowing privileges upon the Churches. This option was not usually open to the Marxist governments. In Romania the dictator Ceauşescu succeeded with Patriarch Justin, who (as near as made no difference) crowned him, but this hardly had any effect upon the people. Only in East Germany, with its tradition of Christian Social-ism among the Lutherans and the high Lutheran doctrine of the State, could religion be a help to a relatively less inhuman Marxist government.

Therefore the governments' doctrinaire attitude to their religions had in the long run to be a weakness in their claims upon the loyalty of their peoples.

(3) Churches were part of the history of the nations. They helped to frame the language, and raised the most historic buildings, and shared in all the great events of the centuries. The Communists said that the unity of mankind was a unity by class – workers or not – and not a unity by tribe or clan, which was obsolete and could lead to war between the peoples. But since the heart of humanity was its family and, wider, its clan and, wider, its nation, Communism pretended that what was inherent need not exist. The peoples needed their past. But there was a danger: that nationality, barely tolerated, would take its revenge in nationalism, and that the East European Churches might find themselves caught again, as already in Kosovo and the Ukraine and Yugoslavia, in a strife

where they were expected to be assistants in a struggle between rival nationalisms.

The Churches of Eastern Europe emerged from their forty years or more of trouble with varying moods. It felt a miracle to find devout Christians being elected leaders of States; especially in December 1990, when Lech Wałęsa was chosen president of Poland in a landslide victory backed by the Catholic Church. It felt a marvel to find the States passing laws guaranteeing freedom for religion, and to find governments easily and without much pressure making State schools available for voluntary instruction on religion at request, as with Poland in August 1990; but this did not always please everyone, for in a largely Catholic State like Poland Protestant or atheist families feared that the instruction in schools would be too Catholic for their liking and preferred the old separation of Church and State. All the Churches were grateful when several new governments put the theological faculties back into universities from which the Stalinists had ejected them and (as in Bucharest) allowed the study of theology, like the study of any other subject, to be supported by State taxes. In Prague the Catholic faculty of theology had been used as a training college for the police. In Debrecen in Hungary the Reformed theological faculty was again made part of the university in the summer of 1991.

Most heart-warming of all was the renewed ability of Churches to undertake social work – to start again hospices for the old or for orphans, to create centres for drug-addiction, to set up counselling services. They had hardly any money to achieve these good ends and, at first, few people capable of giving a lead, but the sensation that now nothing stopped them from such ways of helping their neighbour was important to them. And at first they felt the moral lift when Europe destroyed the immoral barriers which were the legacy of world war – especially the coming down of the Iron Curtain and the union of the two Germanies (3 October 1990).

They suddenly found far greater fairness or lack of prejudice on the part even of the scholars. The Russian Ozhegov dictionary defined Christianity as a religion based on a cult of Jesus Christ who was mythical. The 1990 edition removed the idea of the mythical. It was inspiring to them to find serious enquirers treating Christian ethical values with sympathy in public, and asking whether the Christian tradition had not contributed to the better qualities in their nation, and putting forward compassion as a virtue instead of a weakness.

And there was a deep gratitude that faith proved itself so real, and spirituality so deep, by the ability to survive the most systematic attack on Christianity mounted since the end of the third century AD.

One of the difficulties was the shortage of priests; because inadequate numbers had been allowed to be ordained under Communist governments (except in Poland). In all East European countries except Poland the average age of priests in post at the fall of Communism was high, nearer to 70 than 60. The age of leaders was sometimes high: Tomašek in Prague was 91; Lubachivsky, the new head of the Ukrainian Uniats, was nearly 80; Mstyslav, the head of the Autocephalous Ukrainian Orthodox Church, was 94. They had been isolated from their fellow Churches. The books in their libraries were almost all old. They knew little of what had been happening in the West. The Eastern Catholic Churches, for example, were often ignorant of the radical changes which the Second Vatican Council made in the customs and polity of the Church and when they met them were not sure that they liked them. In extreme cases it was hard to find new leaders. When Albania at last reopened to religion, the Ecumenical Patriarch Bartholomew could not find an Albanian to make the new Orthodox bishop in Tirana and risked the extreme step of appointing a Greek, Yannoulatos, who was a professor at the university of Athens, and so provoked a little schism in Albania.

Another difficulty was the immediate past. Wise chief pastors wanted to draw their Churches together and not run witch-hunts against those who were on the other side in the past. The opening of the archives could be formidable – how many people had cooperated, willingly or under duress, with the secret police in any of the States, but especially Russia, Germany, Bulgaria, Romania, Czechoslovakia? The new Catholic Archbishop of Prague, Vlk, was enthroned in June 1991; he was formerly a priest in country parishes who was stopped and became a window-cleaner in Prague but went on secretly as a priest and after the fall of the Communists became Bishop of Budweis, a see which had been vacant for eighteen years, and then succeeded Cardinal Tomašek. He was much against the publishing of the names of the people who had thus compromised themselves. So was his president, Vaclav Havel. In Moscow Pimen's successor, the new Patriarch Alexei II, also asked that names should not be made public. Where they were published it could have a devastating effect – the opening of the Moscow police archives showed that Patriarch Filaret of Kiev had cooperated with the KGB, and this was one reason why Patriarch Alexei II of Moscow had the strength to depose him, though another reason was Filaret's desire to separate the Church in the Ukraine from Moscow. In Bulgaria the opening of the archives gave a handle to everyone who was against Patriarch Maxim and caused a small schism.

Another problem was the underground. In stiff Communist States like Czechoslovakia or Lithuania, where there were many Catholics or other Christians but a systematic attempt to prevent an effective ministry to them, there were priests and pastors who were banned by government and then took lowly work but still continued to minister secretly until they were caught again. Under such conditions all the rules could not be observed and some of these ministries were irregular; especially in Czechoslovakia there were secret bishops, and several hundred secret priests, including fifty or sixty married men and perhaps two or three women. Bishop Felix Davidek (see page 89) had died in 1988, but his work remained. Now that the Churches were again above ground and 'proper' order could be restored, what was to happen to these clandestine clergy? For some they were heroes who had served God and the Christians at great risk, and every form of recognition and gratitude was due to them. To others they were now a nuisance because the authority for their work was doubtful, especially if they were Catholic priests and married. The most vocal bishop among them was Fridolin Zahradnik; he was a tiler repairing old buildings, and this was wonderful cover because he could easily move across the country. He had been made a secret bishop in 1968, spent six years in prison, had eight grandchildren and certainly had suffered for his work for the Church; he asked for recognition but did not get it. Rome did, however, recognize one of the bishops consecrated secretly by Bishop Davidek. Rome tried to persuade the married priests to move to join the Uniats of Prešov in Eastern Czechoslovakia, where Uniat clergy were married, but it was not a popular idea, and a lot of Czechoslovaks could not see why, when these clergy had kept the Church going under ground, they could not be allowed to keep it going above ground.

A further problem was whether to accept old privileges which the Communists had abolished. Enthusiastic Parliaments voted the Church its old rights without considering the consequences. The Serbian Parliament (April 1991) voted to give the Church back the land and the monasteries which the Communists had confiscated. No one in government could see how to carry out the resolution. The monastery of Tronosa had five monks and 30 hectares; if it got back its old land, it would get 1,226 hectares, which was more than was needed for five monks and would deprive other valuable objects of their funds; so the still Communist ruler Milošević vetoed the bill. The Czechoslovak Assembly passed a law giving church weddings a legal status equal to that of civil weddings (May 1992). The Hungarian Parliament in February 1992 voted £15 million a year to aid the Churches, to be distributed in accordance with the number of members. But the Hungarian president Goncz said that if Churches insisted on getting their property back, higher education could be in serious trouble for want of funds. In 1992 the German Parliament, which had church tax in West Germany – a tax which the Communists had abolished in East Germany – introduced it into East Germany, an unpopular measure.

The historic monarchies had been part of the old Church establishments, though by now hardly anyone could remember them. The murder of the Tsar and his family at Ekaterinburg in 1918 was unforgettable as a stain on Communist history, yet no one had been able to make a reparation, so a requiem liturgy was celebrated in Ekaterinburg on the seventy-fourth anniversary of the murders, and less wise folk had a plan that the Orthodox Church ought to canonize the Tsar as a martyr. In June 1991 the citizens of Leningrad voted to change the name of the city back to St Petersburg, a name associated with Tsars and the Orthodox Church. But Christian motives were not specially present: 40 per cent of the people voted to keep Leningrad not because they loved Lenin but because the name stood for heroic Russian defence against a terrible siege, and one motive of the city council was to encourage Western tourists. Mindszenty was a stout monarchist and it would have pleased him vastly that the person who organized the removal of his corpse from its grave at Mariazell in Austria to its final resting place in Esztergom in Hungary was Rudolf of Habsburg, descendant of a long line of Austrian emperors.

There was at first a chance of politicization of the Churches towards the more conservative wing in the new democracies; not to the extreme right, for they disliked Fascism as much as Communism, but in the swing of the pendulum away from the left towards the centre right.

A similar feeling bred the desire to rehabilitate those who had been badly treated – Mindszenty, for example; and there was a Croat plan to declare Cardinal Stepinac innocent and unjustly condemned. In February 1992 the Croat Parliament issued a declaration condemning the political trial and sentence passed on Stepinac – and many other political trials of priests and monks and others under the Communist regime. In Slovakia there was much talk on the question of rehabilitating Tiso, but that was more controversial.

The question was whether the socialist content in all the Communist regimes had nothing of which Christians might approve. Several Christian leaders saw the danger that was coming, in that the recreation of freedom, and therefore of 'market forces', might, in the climate of repudiating the immediate past, foster the naked capitalism in which poor people are expendable; and Communism as a way of coping with the problem had been such a failure that in Eastern Europe there were many poor people. In the encyclical Centesimus Annus of 1 May 1991 Pope John Paul II asked whether the collapse of Communism meant that capitalism is what Christians now ought to encourage. He answered his own question: if that means accepting freedom which includes freedom to trade and private property and the use of markets, yes; if it means a freedom in industry and finance and profits not placed within a framework of law which puts it at the service of freedom for everyone, no. If it means that the consumer society is the goal of humanity, that is a materialism as bad as Communism. These limitations on the freedom of money are for the Church bound up with the rights of the poor and the need to give them a preference in social arrangements.

Were all the innovations of Communism bad? In East Germany it was expected that youth dedication, the replacement for confirmation which was *Jugendweihe*, would vanish instantly. But some parents still wanted it. They asked whether it was not more real for their son or daughter to affirm their duty to be a good citizen of the State rather than to be confirmed when they were not likely to remain regular churchgoers.

The new freedom of association produced complexities between Churches in eastern Europe. For example, at the extreme West of Russia lay Byelorussia, with its capital at Minsk, where the people in former centuries had been partly Polish and therefore where Roman Catholics were more likely to be found anywhere in Russia outside the Baltic States and the Uniats of the Ukraine. In the town of Harodnia, near Minsk, was a former Basilian monastery which had been turned into an anti-God museum. In the autumn of 1991 the town authorities released this museum building to a Uniat congregation for its worship. But the Orthodox in Harodnia were not pleased at this sudden appearance of a 'rival' congregation, and for a time it needed police protection. The most striking moment of this difficulty was a meeting at Istanbul called by the Ecumenical Patriarch Bartholomew (aged only 49) who succeeded in October 1991 after the death of Patriarch Demetrius. The meeting was attended by all the chief Orthodox prelates – Alexei II of Moscow, Pavle of Yugoslavia, Teoctist of Romania, Maxim of Bulgaria, Ilya of Georgia, Seraphim of Athens and the patriarchs of the ancient historic sees of Antioch and Jerusalem. The meeting solemnly protested against the intrusions of the Uniats in all the eastern States of Europe and the Middle East, as well as the dangers produced by the efforts of new Protestant evangelists who could divide their peoples.

Another difficulty was the moral law. In the Communist States abortion and divorce were easy to get. Abortion now became a political issue in united Germany because of the difference in the laws of East and West, in Slovenia because it was nearly half a Catholic country and in Poland because the Catholic Church was now so powerful and because Pope John Paul II, who regarded abortion as murder, was a Pole.

The worst problem of all was the tension produced by the splitting of the States. The dictator of Romania, Ceauşescu, was killed in December 1989 when the Protestant pastor Tökes was a hero of the revolution. But once the dictatorship was removed the old tension between Hungarians in Romania and Romanians rose again to the surface. Many Hungarians were Protestants, and the name of Tökes, who was now a bishop, was vilified by the Romanian press and people as someone who made for the disunity of the State.

Of various States from the end of the First World War in 1918, some were affected: the three Baltic States (which Stalin absorbed into the Soviet Union at the end of the Second World War) and Czechoslovakia and Yugoslavia. Lithuania declared its independence from the USSR in March 1990, and the other two Baltic States followed. In Czechoslovakia and Yugoslavia the question was whether their constituent parts could stay together.

Bohemia and Moravia, in the Czech part of the State, wanted to stay with Slovakia, and their Church leaders approved prayers to that end. Slovakia was the largely Catholic part of the State. Their Church leaders, but certainly not all their Slovak members, preferred to keep the union with the Czechs; though the Christian Democratic party opposed a split, the Slovaks declared their sovereignty in July 1992, and all the Slovakian bishops welcomed the claim to be a sovereign State; barely an hour later Vaclav Havel resigned the presidency of the united State of Czechoslovakia.

In 1918 the interested parties made a state out of all the southern Slavs except Bulgaria, a state from the remains of the Serbian State and the relics of Ottoman and Austro-Hungarian empires. Thus Yugoslavia had no long history to give it roots and was held together over its short life of seventy years by dictatorships. The first survived till 1941, despite internal tension and the assassination of a king. Then Hitler came into Yugoslavia and divided it. We have seen (p. 63) that then murder was done: hundreds of thousands of lives were lost by tyranny or civil war, and such deaths, unforgettable in the folk memory, must mean that the tensions which existed in 1939 were far worse after Tito's death in 1980. In the long run the unity of the State was now impossible. It was only a question of time before the constituent parts pulled apart. The tragedy that happened after 1990 was a result of the mingling of two processes; getting rid of Communism, and more difficult still, getting rid of the settlement of the First World War.

For if the State split up into its constituent parts and peoples, the different peoples did not all live in their named provinces. When Slovenia declared its independence the Serbian attack was half-hearted and brief because its only motive was to preserve the old Yugoslavia which soon was past preserving. But when Croatia and Bosnia-Hercegovina declared their independence, the Serbian motive to fight was far stronger – for the Serbs in those provinces rose in revolt. In such conditions, where there is no government and guns lie about, criminals are out of control and murder, robbery, rape and cruelty are perpetrated. Christian Serbs who were Orthodox and Christian Croats who were Catholics and Muslims in Bosnia used to live in peace and friendship, and now it became impossible.

The Roman Catholic archbishop of Zagreb, Kuharic, and the Orthodox Patriarch in Belgrade, first German (but he faded and died) and then Pavle (a gentle, ascetic monk aged 76, not at first the sort of person likely to be a politician), did what they could to show Christian charity across the divide; but it had little effect, especially as Kuharic could not help being a symbol of Croat national feeling and the Patriarch a symbol of Serbian national feeling. In December 1990 Milošević won a landslide victory in the Serbian election although he was a Communist; part of the landslide was due to Serbian nationalism and part was due to his freeing of the Church from the old Communist restrictions.

In July 1991 the Patriarch and his bishops wrote to the United Nations mediator Lord Carrington that the Serbian people faced genocide again, that it was no longer possible for Serbs and Croats to live together, that Serbia must try to protect the Serbs who lived in other parts of Yugoslavia and that all we could do was to strive for justice and peace and to help refugees wherever we could. Meanwhile the Serbian clergy in Croatian and Bosnian Dalmatia reported that the persecution from non-Serbs was most severe against the Orthodox clergy and their families, and similar reports came from the other side about Catholic clergy. Another couple of bishops in Dalmatia, the Orthodox and the Roman Catholic, appealed to the Serbs in northern Dalmatia to live in harmony with the Croat people but such appeals no longer bore much relation to the political facts which surrounded them. In Banja Luka 1992 the Croat Roman Catholic bishop and the Serbian Orthodox bishop did everything they could to persuade the mixed people to behave to each other in a Christian and honourable manner, and yet they felt continuously powerless. On 15 June 1992 Patriarch Pavle led a public procession in the streets of Belgrade to protest against the war. But the old State had fallen apart, and the Churches were entangled in its fall.

In August 1991 a group of conservative Communists in Moscow attempted to overthrow Gorbachev in a military coup and held him prisoner in the Crimea. In the parliament house in Moscow Boris Yeltsin led the resistance to the coup. He appealed to all Russia not to condone this illegality and made a special appeal to Patriarch Alexei and the Churches of Russia to use their authority among all religions and believers to persuade them not to be bystanders or the Church could again experience the burden of tyranny and lawlessness. From the balcony of the parliament house, during the tension over whether the tanks would overthrow this resistance, the once-rebel priest Gleb Yakunin was among the famous who appealed to the crowds. In a long night the army refused to overthrow Yeltsin, and so the coup failed. Gorbachev was restored to his position but the power now lay with Yeltsin. This meant that the centrifugal forces within the Soviet Union, with all its different nationalities, began to pull apart; and sooner or later Gorbachev, as the last representative of the old Soviet Union, must fall. He fell in December 1991. That meant the almost immediate dissolution of the Soviet Union into its constituent parts, with unforeseen consequences and with the threat of a measure of violence such as had already hit Yugoslavia as minorities strove to be protected – Armenians in Azerbaijan, Azeris in Armenia, Russians in

Moldavia, Russians in the Ukraine, Ukrainians in Russia, Russians in Latvia and Estonia, Abkhazians and Ossetians in Georgia, Poles in Lithuania, the Polish community in Kazakhstan.

In this dissolution the Churches were the one link which spread across all the borders and could contribute to a peaceable way forward, and simultaneously the differing peoples expressed their feeling of freedom partly through their religion, so that the argument between Orthodox and Catholic and Moslem must become entangled with the political argument. In the new atmosphere some people pitched their expectations too high and expected the Churches to achieve politically what no Church was ever constructed to achieve.

The future of Europe was unknown. It was at a turning-point. The Churches found it difficult enough to cope with a free Western world: how would they manage with a newly free Eastern world, if it was yet free? It remained to be seen how the two big differences between Eastern Europe and Western Europe over forty-five years would react on each other: in the one, nearly all the children taught religion, though often badly; in the other, all the children taught irreligion, though often badly; in the one, the easy sense that freedom and human rights are independent of religions; in the other, the painfully gained experience that the religious conscience is an ultimate safeguard of human freedom.

Suggestions for Further Reading

This is kept where possible to books in English. The place of publication is London unless stated otherwise.

GENERAL BACKGROUND

K. S. Latourette, *Christianity in a Revolutionary Age*, vol. iv: *The Twentieth Century in Europe: the Roman Catholic, Protestant and Eastern Churches*, 1962.

GENERAL STUDIES

K. Aland, *A History of Christianity*, vol. 2, Eng. trans. Philadelphia 1986. Roger Aubert et al., *The Church in a Secularized Society* (The Christian Centuries vol. 5), 1978.

G. Adrianyi et al., *The Church in the Modern Age* (vol. 10 of Hubert Jedin and John Dolan, eds., *History of the Church*), Eng. trans. 1981.

EASTERN EUROPE

The fundamental guides are in the periodicals, of which the indispensable guide is Keston College's *Religion in Communist Lands* – continually valuable journal not only because it is in English but because it provides a lot of information not accessible in other languages. For Protestantism in the East it is the only general guide in the English language. Those who wish to go further will need especially the periodicals *Tablet, Ostkirchliche Studien, Kirche im Osten, La Documentation Catholique, Chrétiens de l'Est, Irénikon, Istina* and *Eastern Churches Review*.

There are two general books of much help: Trevor Beeson,

Discretion and Valour. Religious conditions in Russia and Eastern Europe, rev. ed. 1982, which is the best general survey, and B. R. Bociurkiw and J. W. Strong, eds., *Religion and Atheism in Eastern Europe*, 1975, a fundamental book. See also J. F. Starr, *The Communist Regimes in East Europe*, 2nd rev. ed., Stanford, California, 1971, and P. Walters, ed., *World Christians: Eastern Europe*, Eastbourne 1988.

Albania

P. R. Prifti, *Socialist Albania since 1944*, Cambridge, Mass., 1978.

B. Tönnes, 'Religious Persecution in Albania' in *Religion in Communist Lands* 10:3 (1982), 242ff.

Pauline Hodges, 'Albania after Hoxha's death' in *Religion in Communist Lands* 14:3 (1986), 286 ff.

Bulgaria

James F. Brown, *Bulgaria under Communist Rule*, 1970.

Czechoslovakia

V. V. Kusin, *From Dubček to Charter 77*, Edinburgh 1978.

L. Nemec, *Church and State in Czechoslovakia*, New York 1955.

F. Nemec, *The Soviet Seizure of Sub-Carpathian Russia*, Toronto 1955.

M. Simecka, *The Restoration of Order*, 1984.

For Tiso etc. there are two histories of modern Slovakia from opposite viewpoints: J. A. Mikus, *Slovakia: a political history*, Eng. trans., rev. ed., Milwaukee 1963, and J. Lettrich, *History of Modern Slovakia*, 1956.

For the Ruthenian Uniats, M. Derrick, *Eastern Catholics under Soviet Rule*, 1946.

East Germany

David Childs, *The GDR: Moscow's German Ally*, 1983.

David Childs, *Honecker's Germany*, 1985.

R. W. Solberg, *God and Caesar in East Germany* (with foreword by Otto Dibelius), New York 1961.

Hungary

J. Közi-Horváth, *Cardinal Mindszenty*, Eng. trans. 1979.

J. Mindszenty, *Memoirs*, Eng. trans. 1974. (Numerous useful documents in the appendix.)

F. Hainbuch, *Kirche und Staat in Ungarn nach dem zweiten Weltkrieg*, Munich, 1982. (Valuable.)

Lithuania

Michael Bourdeaux, *Land of Crosses*, Chulmleigh 1979.

Poland

There are two valuable studies:
R. F. Leslie, ed., *The History of Poland since 1863*, Cambridge 1980.
Norman Davies, *God's Playground: a History of Poland*, 2 vols., 1981. (The Polish translation, Kraków 1990, has revisions.)

Russia

Christel Lane, *Christian Religion in the Soviet Union*, 1978.
Michael Bourdeaux, *Patriarch and Prophets*, 1969. (Useful collection of samizdat documents.)
D. Pospielovsky, *The Russian Church under the Soviet Regime 1917–1982*, 2 vols., New York 1984.
W. C. Fletcher, *The Russian Orthodox Church Underground 1917–1970*, Oxford 1971.
Jane Ellis, *The Russian Orthodox Church: a Contemporary History*, 1986. (Though all the above accounts of Russian events are valuable, this one is especially so.)
H. J. Stehle, *Eastern Politics of the Vatican 1917–1979*, Eng. trans., Athens, Ohio, 1981.
S. Durasoff, *The Russian Protestants 1944–1964*, Cranbury, New Jersey, 1969.
Michael Bourdeaux, *Religious Minorities in the Soviet Union*, 4th ed. 1984.
Michael Bourdeaux, *Religious Ferment in Russia: Protestant Opposition to Soviet Religious Policy*, 1968.

Yugoslavia

Stella Alexander, *Church and State in Yugoslavia since 1945*, Cambridge 1979. (A fundamental work.)
S. K. Pavlowitch, four articles in *Eastern Churches Review* 1967–9, including (1967, 374) an article on the breaking away of Macedonia.
For Stepinac, see A. H. O'Brien, *Archbishop Stepinac: the man and*

his case, Dublin 1947, R. Pattee, *The Case of Cardinal Aloysius Stepinac*, Milwaukee 1953, and Stella Alexander, *The Triple Myth*, New York 1987.

For Medjugorje, Mary Craig, *Spark from Heaven*, 1988.

The Secular Rites

Christel Lane, *The Rites of Rulers*, Cambridge 1981. (A fundamental book for Russia.)

C. M. Hann, 'Socialism and King Stephen's Right Hand', *Religion in Communist Lands*, 18:1 (1990), 4ff. (Includes useful references.)

Christopher Binns, 'Soviet Secular Ritual: Atheist Propaganda or Spiritual Consumerism?', *Religion in Communist Lands*, 10:3 (1982), 298. (A fine article on naming ceremonies.)

The Christian Cooperators

Lucjan Blit, *The Eastern Pretender*, 1965. (A life of the Polish cooperator B. Piasecki.)

J. L. Hromádka, *Thoughts of a Czech Pastor*, Eng. trans. 1970.

J. L. Hromádka, *A Gospel for Atheists*, Eng. trans. 1965.

J. M. Lochman, *Church in a Marxist Society*, 1970. (On the Czechoslovak Christian–Marxist dialogue.)

WESTERN EUROPE

The Vatican

W. A. Purdy, *The Church on the Move*, 1966.

Carlo Falconi, *The Popes in the Twentieth Century*, Eng. trans. 1967.

Oscar Halecki, *Pius XII*, 1954.

E. E. Y. Hales, *Pope John and his Revolution*, 1965.

P. Hebblethwaite, *John XXIII*, 1984.

E. O. Hanson, *The Catholic Church in World Politics*, Princeton 1987.

G. Poggi, *Catholic Action in Italy*, Stanford, California, 1967.

P. Hebblethwaite, *The Christian-Marxist Dialogue*, 1977.

P. Hebblethwaite, *The Runaway Church*, rev. ed., 1978.

The Second Vatican Council

The Documents of Vatican II, 1966.

H. Vorgrimler, ed., *Commentary on the Documents of Vatican II*, 5 vols. Eng. trans. 1967.

J. C. Murray, ed., *Religious Liberty*, New York 1966.

A. Muller and N. Greinacher, *The Church and the Rights of Man*, New York 1979.

For intelligent description by an observer, Xavier Rynne (pseudonym), *Letters from Vatican City. Vatican Council II, 1st session: background and debates*, 1963; *The Second Session: the debates and decrees of Vatican Council II, Sept. 29–Dec. 4 1963*, 1964; *The Third Session: the debates and decrees of Vatican Council II, Sept. 14–Nov. 21 1964, 1965; The Fourth Session: the debates and decrees of Vatican Council II, Sept. 14–Dec. 8 1965*, 1966. Cf. *Vatican II: by those who were there*, 1986.

For a modern radical Catholic thinker, see John Bowden, *Edward Schillebeeckx*, New York 1983. Cf. P. Hebblethwaite, *The New Inquisition?* 1980.

For Lefebvre, M. Lefebvre, *A Bishop Speaks*, Edinburgh 1979.

France

A. Dansette, *A Religious History of Modern France*, Eng. trans. (partly abridged) Edinburgh 1961. French rev. ed. 1965, but for the purposes of this period superseded by the indispensable G. Cholvy and Y. M. Hilaire, *Histoire religieuse de la France contemporaine*, vol. 3 (1930–1988), Toulouse 1988.

West Germany

David Childs, *West Germany: Politics and Society*, 1981.

F. Spotts, *The Churches and Politics in Germany*, Middletown, Conn., 1977.

P. Weymar, *Konrad Adenauer*, Eng. trans. 1957.

James Bentley, *Martin Niemöller*, Oxford 1984.

Eberhard Busch, *Karl Barth*, Eng. trans. rev. ed. 1976.

Otto Dibelius, *In the Service of the Lord*, Eng. trans. 1965.

Monks and nuns

M. Muggeridge, *Mother Teresa of Calcutta*, 1971.

Mary Craig, *Mother Teresa*, 1983.

For non-Roman Catholic monks and nuns, including Taizé: A. Perchenet, *The Revival of the Religious Life and Christian Unity*, Eng. trans. 1969.

G. Moorhouse, *Against All Reason*, 1969.

For the Greek Orthodox tradition of monks and nuns:

D. M. Nicol, *Meteora*, rev. ed., 1975.

P. Sherrard, *Athos*, 1960.

T. Ware, *The Orthodox Church*, Harmondsworth 1963.

For the Greek Orthodox Church generally, a useful essay by F. Heyer, 'Kirchen und Religionsgemeinschaften' in *Griechenland*, ed. K.-D. Grothusen. (Südosteuropa Handbuch vol. 3), Göttingen, 1980.

The ecumenical movement

The journal *Ecumenical Review* is useful.

H. E. Fey, *The Ecumenical Advance 1848–1968*, 1969.

N. Goodall, *Ecumenical Progress: a Decade of Changes in the Ecumenical Movement 1961–71*, 1972.

W. A. Visser t'Hooft, *Memories*, Eng. trans. 1973.

J. M. McDonnell, *The World Council of Churches and the Catholic Church*, Toronto 1985.

Marc Boegner, *The Long Road to Unity*, Eng. trans. 1970.

B. and M. Pawley, *Rome and Canterbury through Four Centuries*, rev. ed. 1981.

S. A. Quitslund, *Beauduin*, New York 1973.

For the Old Catholics, G. Huelin, ed., *Old Catholics and Anglicans 1931–1981*, Oxford 1983.

Pentecostalists

J. V. Thurman, *New Wineskins*, Frankfurt am Main, 1982.

W. J. Hollenweger, *The Pentecostals*, 1976.

J. L. Sandidge, *Roman Catholic/Pentecostal Dialogue, 1977–1982*, 2 vols, New York 1987. (Wider interest than the title sounds.)

Church and State in Western Europe

David Barrett, *World Christian Encyclopedia*, Oxford 1982.

The general histories of each country are the best guides to begin with.

On Scandinavia, apart from Barrett, there is little in English of recent date, but the Uppsala Journal of Church history, *Kyrkohistorisk årsskrift*, usually adds English summaries at the end of its articles.

For England: Adrian Hastings, *A History of English Christianity*, 2nd ed. 1987 and P. A. Welsby, *A History of the Church of England 1845–1980*, Oxford 1984.

For Church and State in Scotland, see A. R. Vidler, *The Church in an Age of Revolution* (Penguin History of the Church vol. 5), new ed. 1990.

For Ireland, J. H. Whyte, *Church and State in Modern Ireland 1923–1979*, new ed. Dublin 1980.

Perestroika

Michael Bourdeaux, *Gorbachev, Glasnost and the Gospel*, 1990; rev. ed. entitled *The Gospel's Triumph over Communism*, Minneapolis 1991.

J. Forest, *Free at Last? The Impact of Perestroika on the Religious Life in the Soviet Union*, 1990.

Paul Johnson, *John Paul II and the Catholic Restoration*, 1982.

Index

abortion, 177–9, 195, 197, 214–15
Adenauer, Konrad, 10
Agca, Mehmet Ali, 197
aggiornamento, 116, 151
Alacoque, Marguerite Marie, 198
Albania, 14, 21n, 24, 46–51, 58, 60, 84, 101, 181, 202, 205
Alexei (Sergei Simansky: Patriarch of Moscow 1945–70): allowed by Stalin to reconstruct Orthodox Church, 93; forced to forbid tonsure of young monks, 31; man of stature, 52, 94; welcomes Uniats of Ukraine to Orthodoxy, 52, 58, 94; and Vatican, 93; goes to millennium of St John of Rila, 84; willing for some compromise with the State, 64, 94; revolution in parish life, 95–9; death (1970), 78
Alfrink, B. I. (Archbishop of Utrecht 1955–75, cardinal 1960), 122, 148, 149
Algerian war, 180
Alia, Ramiz, of Albania, 49
Alternative Service Book, new Anglican liturgy, 124
Andorra, 181
Andrewes, Lancelot, 144
Angelico, Fra, 130
Anglicans: calendar, 144–5; ordination of women, 156–8; monks and nuns, 170
anti-God museum, 23–4, 200
anti-Semitism, 12
Apocrypha, 125n
Aquinas, St Thomas, 111
Armenia, Catholicos of, 203
Arrupe, Pedro (Spanish Jesuit general 1965–83), 164
Asmussen, Hans, 11n
Assisi, 129, 199

Assumption, doctrine of the, 16
atheist clubs, 23, 24
Athenagoras (Spirou: Patriarch of Constantinople 1949–72), 89, 118, 167, 173
Athos, Mount, 166–7, 168, 169
Auschwitz, Carmelites at, 143, 162–3
see also Kolbe, Maximilien; Stein, Edith
Austro–Hungarian Empire, and Uniats, 51

Baker, Bishop, of Hong Kong, 156
Baltic states: Christmas Day, 201; pass back under Russian rule (1939), 5, 30; pressure against voluntary RE, secular rites, 27–8
see also Estonia; Latvia; Lithuania
Bánovce, 61
Banská Bystrica, 39, 61
baptism: adult, 135; declining importance in Christendom, 26, 81, 82, 190
Baptist Churches: in Byelorussia, 82; in Estonia, 26; *Initsiativniki*, 92–3; affect Pentecostalists, 135; are affected by Pentecostalists, 137; illegal printing-press, 87; growing of numbers in Russia, 92, 201
Barth, Karl, 40
basis-groups, 91–2
Basle, 192
Bauduin, King of Belgium, 179
Bavarian Lutheran Church, 125
Bea, Cardinal, 117
Belgium: abortion, 179; Catholics and democracy, 119; charismatic movement, 136; abbey at Maredsous, 150; priests at Tournai, 133
Benedictines, 142, 150; Anglican, 170
Beran, Joseph (Archbishop of Prague and cardinal), 41, 120

Beresztocy, Canon, 38
Berggrav, Eivind (Bishop of Oslo 1937–
51), 6, 7; and resistance to govern-
ment, 8
Berlin Wall, 4, 11, 45, 86, 146
Bernadette, St, 139, 140
Bessarabia, 5, 30
Blaj, Romania, 57
Bohemia, 21n, 61, 62, 206
Bohemian Brethren, 40
Bolshevik Revolution, 30, 92; and
schism in Russian Orthodox Church,
88
Bonhoeffer, Dietrich: and conspiracy
against Hitler, 8, 9, 145; religionless
Christianity, 43
Boquen, Cistercian house, 165
Boresivičius, Vincentas (Bishop of Trel-
siau, Lithuania, 1944–6; shot 1947),
106
Bosnia-Hercegovina, 75, 102
Bourdeaux, Michael, 212, 216; Keston
College, 210
Bratislava (Pressburg), 61
Brest-Litovsk, Union of, 51, 54
Brno, 81
broadcasting, 44
Brothers of Mercy, 72
Budějovice, 39
Bukovina, 5
Bulgaria, 14, 21n, 24, 29, 32, 52, 58,
81–2, 84, 89, 115, 167, 202
Bulgarian Academy of Sciences, 81, 89
Bunyan, John, 144
Bursche, Julius (Lutheran Bishop of
Warsaw, died 1942), 106n

Calciu, George (Romanian Orthodox
priest), 98–9
Calcutta, 199
calendars of saints, 144–6
Calvin, John, 145
Canada, Anglican church in, 156
capital punishment, 178, 180
Capuchins, 161
cardinals *see* Vatican
Carević (Bishop of Dubrovnik), 63
Carmelites, 136, 143, 162–3
Casaroli, Cardinal Agostino, 71

Castro, Fidel, 114
catechism, 21, 49, 104, 107
Catherine of Siena, St, 155
Catholic Action, 114, 186
Catholic Democratic People's Party
(Hungary), 37
Ceaușescu, Nicolai 98, 99, 202–3, 208
Cecilia, St, 145
Celestine V (Pope 1294–6), 160
celibacy, and Catholic priests, 90, 147–
50, 151, 152, 197
charismatics, 135–7
Chenu, M. D. (French Dominican),
111, 112, 114
Chervenkov, Wulko (general Secretary
of the Comintern in Moscow 1935–
44, dictator of Bulgaria 1948–61), 84,
89
Chiang Kai-shek (President of China),
4
Chilandar 167
Chile, Pope John Paul II visits, 198
China, and Cultural Revolution, 47
Christian Democratic Union (CDU),
10
Christian Peace Conference, 41
Christian Socialism, 36, 41, 43, 208
Christof (Orthodox Archbishop in
Albania), 47
Chub, Mikhail (Bishop of Smolensk
1955, then of six sees in quick suc-
cession, Archbishop of Tambo 1974),
94–5
Church of England, 113, 124, 144, 154,
157, 174, 185
Church of the Reconciliation, 171
church tax, 189, 190
Cistercians, 165
Cîteaux, 165
clerical dress, 92, 130, 132; 163–4, 197
Cluj, Romania, 57, 99
Coggan, Donald (Archbishop of Can-
terbury 1974–80), 157
Cold War: use of term, 3; and religious
liberty, 119
collegiality, 177
Communism: acts of aggression, 75–9;
officially atheist, 3; Catholic attitude
to, 14–16; class war, 14; dialogues

with Christians, 35–6, 40–42; in Eastern Europe, *passim*; Marxist attitude to religion, 19; papal decree against, 103; private property not a justified freedom, 14; religion bad for society, 14, 19
concelebration, 133
Confédération Générale du Travail, 112
Confessing Church, 6, 11n
confession, John Paul II's views on, 197
Congar, Yves (Dominican), 152
confirmation, 27, 80, 108
Congregation of the Faith (previously Holy Office of the Inquisition), 157
Constantinople: see of, 89; and Turin shroud, 140
constitutions, 182–3
contraception, condemnation of by Paul VI, 176–7, 195
Corfu, 168
Cornwell, J., 194n
Counter-Reformation, and liturgy, 126
Cowley Fathers, 170
Cranmer, Thomas (Archbishop of Canterbury), 123
Craxi, Bettino, 182
Croatia, 34, 63, 64, 82, 101
Cultural Revolution, 47
Cushing, Cardinal Richard (Archbishop of Boston 1944–70), 120
Cyprus, 188
Cyril, St, apostle of the Slavs, 86
Czechoslovakia: choice of bishops, 33–4, 39–40; and Christian Socialism, 36; Church and State, 181, 202; cooperating priests, 38–40, 202; guidelines on materialist education, 22; Hussite Church and women, 155; Kralitzer Bible, 125n; against monks and nuns, 29, 30; opinion poll, 81; perestroika in, 202; visit of Pope, 203; Prague Spring, 21n, 39, 41, 55, 98; Prague University, 40; under Russian dominion, 3; secular rites, 28; Slovakia, largely Catholic, 14, choice of Catholic bishops, 34, of Protestant bishops, 33, RE, 21n; Tiso trial, 60–62; Uniats in, 51, 52, 55–6

Czestochowa, shrine, 104, 199

Dalai Lama, 129, 199
Damian (last Orthodox primate of Albania), 47, 48
dancing in the liturgy, 130–31
Daniélou, Cardinal Jean, 152n
Danilov monastery, Moscow, 86
Darmstadt, 170
Davidek, Felix (bishop in Czechoslovakia), 89–90, 211–12
De Smedt, E. J. M. (Bishop of Bruges), 119
Declaration on Religious Liberty (1965), 121, 187
Demetrius (or Dimitrius, Papadopoulos: auxiliary to Athenagoras 1965, Archbishop of Imbros 1965, Patriarch of Constantinople 1972), 146, 199
democracy and religion, 1, 119–20, 198, 206
Denmark, Lutheran Church, 153
Dezséry, Laszlo (Intruded Lutheran bishop in Hungary 1950–56), 90
diakonia, theology of, 90n
Dibelius, Otto (Prussian aristocrat, General Superintendent of Kurmark, later Bishop of Berlin-Brandenburg), 6; record of courage under Hitler, 7; signs Stuttgart Declaration, 11n; anti-Communist, 7, 28, 91; autobiography, 214
Dimitrius (Ecumenical Patriarch) *see* Demetrius
Dimitrov, Georgi, 84
divorce, 173–5
Dominicans, 144
Dresden, 44
Du Roy, Olivier (Benedictine), 150
Dubček, Alexander, 41, 55, 56, 98
Dudko, father Dimitri, 76–8, 91
Durazzo (Durrës), 46, 47–8
Dutch Reformed Church, 36

East Prussia, 5
Eastern Orthodox Church, 59
Ecône, 128, 129

ecumenical movement, and Pope John Paul II, 198–9
Ecumenical Patriarch, 35, 46, 118
see also Athenagoras, Demetrius
Ecumenical Sisters of Mary, 170
ecumenical spirit of age, 144, 158, 171–2, 198–9
Edinburgh, Prince Philip, Duke of, 199
education in materialism, 21–3, 206
Edward the Confessor, King, 142
Einsiedeln (Benedictine monastery), 165–6
Elizabeth of Thuringia, 51
Ellis, Jane, 97n
emigrants and loss or preservation of faith, 5
Enrique y Tarancón *see* Tarancón, Cardinal Enrique y
Episcopal Church, 157
Ermland, 106n
Estonia, 26, 27, 31, 33, 69, 86
see also Baltic states
Esztergom (Gran), 38, 67, 71, 72

Fatima, 17, 117, 138, 198
Feltin, Cardinal, 113
films, experimental use of, 131
Finland, 184
Flahiff, Cardinal George (of Winnipeg), 157
Foucauld, Charles de, 166
France: decline of anticlericalism, 151, 163, 186; and celibacy, 151, 152; Church and State, 21, 181; government and the bishops (1944–5), 6, 115; support for Lefebvre in, 128; Lourdes importance for French Catholics, 139; and married priests, 150, 151; nuns, 163; shortage of priests, 148; Protestants, 114–15, 170; student revolution, 113–14; and women pastoral workers, 151
Francis de Sales, St, 144
Francis of Assisi, St 51, 129
Franciscans, 29, 63–4, 76, 161; Society of St Francis, 170
Franco, General Francisco (dictator of Spain), 4, 186; Concordat with

Rome (1953), 17; friendly to Church, 208; bishops' gratitude to 121; insists on choice of bishops, 185, 187
Frank, Hans (Nazi governor of Poland), 4
Frings, Josef (Archbishop of Cologne 1942–69, cardinal 1946), 10
Fulda declaration, 11
funerals, 25, 27, 81, 82, 190

gaiters, 132
Gandhi, Mahatma, 199
Garadzha, V., 201
Gaudium et Spes (pastoral constitution), 121
Gaulle, General Charles de, 6, 151
Gedda, Luigi (lay leader of Catholic Action in Italy), 15
Geneva, 171, 191
George, St (patron saint of England), 145
Georgia, troubled Church in, 97n
German (Patriarch of Serbia 1958–90): refuses to recognize Macedonian Church independence, 89; presides over revival, 100–102
Germany: Lutherans redraft prayer-books, 124; *Federal Republic (West Germany)*: and abortion, 178, 179; Catholic areas of, 10; and charismatic experience, 135; Christian socialism in, 36; Church in quarrel between East and West, 11; divorce, 174, 175; East Prussia under Russian rule (1945), 5; expulsion of Germans from East Prussia, 5; head of State, 184; and Hitler's Concordat with Pope, 188–9; prisons of war in Russia, 5; state of religion, 189; taxation, 183; *German Democratic Republic (East Germany)*: 21n, 43–5, 206, 207, 208; abortion, 179; Berlin Wall comes down, 45; Church and State, 181, 202; church members, 189–90; Communist attack on Churches in, 7; *Jugendweihe* rite, 28; *Kirchentag* 11; and Luther anniversaries, 86; respects Lutheran constitution, 33;

monks and nuns, 29; Pentecostalists in, 137; revolution begins, 207

Gienke, Horst (Bishop of Greifswald), 44, 45

Gijsen, J. B. (Bishop of Roermond), 150

Glemp, Józef (Archbishop of Warsaw 1981, cardinal 1983), 91

Goebbels, Joseph, 61

Gojdic (Uniat Bishop of Prešov), 55

Gomulka, Wladyslaw (First Secretary of Polish Communist Party 1956–70), 104

Good News Bible, 125n

Gorbachev, Mikhail, 200 202, 217

Gorky (USSR), 24

Graham, Billy, 200

Grandchamp, Switzerland, 70

Grande Chartreuse, 165

Greece: bishops' retirement age, 160; Church and State, 182–3, 188; civil war in, 3; clerical dress, 132; outside Iron Curtain, 4; marriage after ordination, 151; and monarchy, 184; monastic lands, 169; monks and nuns, 166–9

Greek Orthodox Church: protests over new Uniat bishops in Romania, 204

Greifswald, 44, 45

Grivas, George, 188

Grönlund, Eric (Swedish translator of Bible), 125n

Guadalupe, shrine, 198

Haiti, 185

Harris, Barbara (assistant bishop), 157

heads of State, 184

Heinemann, Gustav, 11n, 155

Hemer, West Germany, 9

Herbert, George, 144

Herder Bible, 125n

hermits, 98, 166

history: and Churches, 84–7, 95, 206, 208; and saints, 142, 144–6

Hitler, Adolf, 3, 11n, 32, 43; *Mein Kampf*, 9; makes Concordat with Pope, 188–9, 208; causes schism in German Protestant Churches, 88; ally of Franco, 186; occupies Bohemia, 61; occupies Yugoslavia, 62; and Macedonia, 89; occupies Ukraine, 53; occupies Rome, 17; occupies Hungary, 68; bomb plot (1944), 8

Hnilica (Jesuit bishop), 121

Hochhuth, Rolf, 12–13

Holland, and marriage of priests, 147–50

Holocaust, Christianity and, 12–13

homosexuality, 118

Honecker, Erich, 44–5

Hong Kong, 156

Hooker, Richard, 144

Hopko (auxiliary Uniat Bishop of Prešov), 55

Horváth, Richard, excommunicated, 37–8

Hosios Loukas, near Delphi, 168

Hossu, Juliu (Uniat bishop in Romania, later cardinal *in petto*), 57

Hoxha, Enver (dictator of Albania), 46–9, 205; his widow, 205

Hradec Králové, 39

Hromádka, Josef, 40–41, 111

Hrushiv, 139

Huguenots, 36

human rights, 4; importance in Eastern Europe, 19, 78, 180, 198, 206, 208

Humanae Vitae (encyclical, 1968), 176–7, 196

Humani Generis (1950), 17

Hume, Cardinal Basil, 86

Hungarian Revolution, 43, 68, 104

Hungary, 67–72, 86, 104; basis-groups, 91; big Catholic population, 14; Karolyi Bible, 125n; choice of Lutheran bishop, 33–4; and Christian Socialism, 36; Lutherans and Reformed and women pastors, 154–5; millennium, 85; loyalty to Mindszenty, 90; monks and nuns, 30, 203; new religious order, 30; perestroika, 203; patriotic priests, 37; Protestant Christian Socialists, 114; statistics of religious practice, 79–81, 83; Uniats in, 52, 58; voluntary RE allowed, 21

Iceland: Church and State, 183; taxation, 183

Ilya II (Patriarch of Georgia), 97, 214

Initsiativniki, 92–3

Institute of Scientific Atheism, Brno, 81

Institute of Social Sciences, Belgrade, 82

Inter Insigniores decree, 157

Iov, Archbishop *see* Kresovich, Iov

Ireland: abortion, 179; Church and State, 182, 183; divorce, 174–5; religion and nationality, 208

Italy: and abortion, 178–9; Church and State, 182; and divorce, 174; and monarchy, 184

Jamieson, Penelope (Bishop of Dunedin [first Anglican woman diocesan]), 158

Jerusalem Bible, 125n

Jesuits, 37, 50, 121, 152, 155, 161–2, 191

Jews: helped by Marton in Transylvania, 99, by Mindszenty, 68, by Roncalli from Istanbul, 115, by Schutz in France, 171, by Stepinac in Zagreb, 64, 67; Holocaust, 12–13; Pope Pius XII and, 12–13; protected by Dibelius, 7, by Kiev nuns, 31, by Szeptycki in Ukraine, 53, said to be protected by Tiso in Slovakia, 61; Pope John Paul II attends prayers at Rome synagogue, 129, 199 *see also* Stein, Edith

John (Orthodox Metropolitan of Prague), 52

John XXIII (Angelo Roncalli, Pope 1958–63): career, 115; the name, 116, 193; attitude to Communism, 115, 117; tries to persuade Mindszenty to leave Hungary, 71; and worker priests, 113, encyclicals, 117, 155; creates Secretariat for Christian Unity, 117; summons Second Vatican Council, 116; starts enquiry into contraception, 176

John of Rila, St, millennium and Bulgaria, 84

John Paul I (Albano Luciani, Pope 1978); person, 193–4; first double name, 193–4; refuses to be crowned

King of the Papal State, 132, 194; no post-mortem, 194

John Paul II (Karol Wojtyla, Pope 1978–): Cardinal Archbishop of Cracow, 120; in favour of religious liberty, 122; election made possible by internationalization of cardinals' college, 116, 195; the traveller, 196–7; attempted murder, 197; attitude to the Reformation, 13; receives Albanians, 49; openness to Eastern Europe, 54; openness to other religions, 129; conservative in many respects, 129, 176, 179, 195–6; against women priests, 158; accepts change in Lateran Treaty, 182; affects age of perestroika, 199–200; makes Sladkevičius a cardinal, 201; visit of Gorbachev, 202; visits Czechoslovakia, 203, 213–15

Josif (Metropolitan of Alma-Ata), 96–7

Journet, Cardinal (Swiss–French theologian), 152n

Juan Carlos, King of Spain, 187

Jugendweihe, 28, 44, 214

just war, idea of, 117

Justin (Moisescu: Metropolitan of Jassy [Iasi], then Patriarch of Romania), 69, 98, 99, 205, 208

Justinian (Marina: Patriarch of Romania 1948–77), 151; Western education, 97; man of stature, 52; reforms monasteries, 29; welcome Uniats to Orthodoxy, 58; willing for some compromise with the State, 69; Christian Socialist by conviction, 98; and Ceauşescu, 98

Kaczmarek (Bishop of Kielce), 103

Kakol, Kasimir, 74

Káldy, Zoltan (Protestant bishop in Hungary), 90, 115

Kaunas, 106 *see also* Skvireckas, Juozapas

Keble, John, 144

Kennedy, Jacqueline, 173

Kerizinen, 138

Keston College, 210
KGB, 53, 78
Kharchev, Konstantin, 201
Khrushchev, Nikita, 74, 95, 104
Kiev, 31, 87
King James Version, 125n
Kirchentag: all Germany, 11; East Germany, 44
Kiril (Markov: Bishop of Plovdiv 1938–53, prison 1949, Patriarch of Bulgaria 1953–72), 69, 89
Knock, Ireland, 198
Kolbe, Maximilien, 143
Kominek, Cardinal Boleslaw (of Wroclaw), 35
Komsomol (Communist youth movement), 24
König (Archbishop of Vienna), 122, 196
Kosovo, 50, 101, 206, 208
Kostelnyk (Uniat priest), 53
Közi-Horvath, J., 71n
Kralitzer Bible, 125n
Kresovich, Iov (Archbishop of Kazan), 96n
Kuharic, Franjo (Archbishop of Zagreb 1970, cardinal 1983), 66–7, 216
Küng, Hans, 177

Las Casas, Bartolomé de (1474–1566), 144
Lateran Treaty (1929), 182
Latin America, 113, 179
Latin in the liturgy, 123, 126, 127, 128
Latvia, 27, 33, 69, 86, 92, 200, 207
see also Baltic states
Latvia Popular Front, 207
lecturers, anti-religion, 23, 24
Lefebvre, Archbishop Marcel, 125, 127–9
Leipzig, 207
Lékai, László (apostolic administrator of Esztergom 1974–6, archbishop 1976–86 and cardinal), 71, 91
Lenin, 23, 26, 27, 75, 206
Leningrad (St Petersburg), 23, 26, 27, 93, 94, 107, 212–13
Leo XIII (Pope 1878–1903): encyclical on socialism and workers' rights, 14

Li, Florence, 156
liberty, religious, 118–20
Lilje, Hanns (Bishop of Hanover 1947–71), 6, 7, 11n
Lithuania, 14, 27, 34, 106–7
see also Baltic states
Little Brothers of Jesus, 166
liturgy: dancing in, 130–31; 'interiorizing', 131–2; and Lefebvre, 127–9; reforms in, 123–7
Living Church (Russian Schism), 88
Ljubljana university, 83
Loew, Jacques (French Dominican), 112
Lönning, Per (Bishop of Borg, Norway 1969; resigned over abortion law 1975), 179
Lorraine, 134
Lourdes, 133, 136, 138–40
Lubac, Henri de (Jesuit), 152n
Lublin (Catholic university), 43, 74, 83, 102n, 103
Luther, Martin: translator of Bible, 125n; reputation, 13, 145; John Paul II and, 13; Vatican refuses to lift excommunication, 13; celebrations in East Europe, 85–6
Lutheranism, 5, 13; and confirmation, 27; Pentecostalists among, 135; Protestant religious communities, 170
see also Baltic states; Bursche, Julius; Denmark; Germany; Sweden
Luxemburg, 184
Lvov, 53, 200
Lydia of Philippi, 146

MacArthur, General Douglas, 3–4
Macedonia, 50, 62, 89
Madras, 199
Magee, Father John (later Bishop of Cloyne), 194n
Makarios (Archbishop of Cyprus), 188
Malta, 175
Mao Tse-tung, Chairman, 47, 114
Marahrens, August (Lutheran Bishop of Hanover 1925–47), 6
Maredsous (Benedictine abbey), 150
Marella (nuncio to France), 112
marriage: and contraception, 176; and

marriage – *contd*
  divorce, 173–5; and priests, 147–53;
  as a rite, 25, 26
Marseilles, 112
Marton, Aron (Latin Bishop of Cluj),
  99–100
Marx, Karl, 19, 27, 48, 202, 206
Marxism *see* Communism
Mary, The Virgin: Assumption, 16;
  Queen of Heaven, 17; devotion of
  John Paul II to, 197; revered by a
  Russian group, 92; shrines: Black
  Madonna at Czestochowa, 104, 199,
  Fatima, 16–17, 117, 138, 198, Guad-
  elupe, 198, Hrushiv, 139, icon of
  Kazan, 23, Kerizinen, 138, Knock,
  198, Lourdes, 133, 136, 138, 139,
  140, Marija Bistrica, 65, Medjugorje,
  75, Paray-le-Monial,136, iron of Peć,
  100, Tinos, 169; her virginity
  doubted by Catholic professor, 155n
Masaryk, Thomas, 40
mass, priests' obligatory celebration of,
  132–3
Masuria, 106n
Mater et Magistra (encyclical, 1961),
  117
Matulionis, Teofilius (bishop in Lithu-
  ania), 106–7
Medjugorje (Yugoslav shrine), 75–6,
  138, 213
Megaspilaeon, 168
Meiser, Hans (first Lutheran Bishop of
  Bavaria), 11n
Merton, Thomas, 162
Mesić, Yugoslavia, 102
Mesters, Erik (Lutheran archbishop in
  Latvia), 92
Meteora, 168
Methodius, St, 86
Mindszenty, József (Archbishop of Esz-
  tergom, 1945–74, cardinal 1946), 60,
  68–72, 90–92, 102, 211, 213
Mirfield Fathers, 170
Missionaries of Charity, 50–51
mitre, worn by a Lutheran bishop, 92;
  on statue, 106
Moldavia, 5
monarchy, 184

monks and nuns, 29–31; concelebration, 133; in East Germany, 44;
  historians, 42; historic orders, 161–
  6; in Poland, 103, 104; the religious
  habit, 163–4, 197; Protestant, 169–
  70; in Romania, 98; in Russia, 86–7;
  and sanctity, 143, 145; disturbed in
  sixties, 118, 161–2; in Yugoslavia,
  101–2
Mont Saint-Michel, 165
Montserrat, 165
Montenegro, 62, 83
More, Sir Thomas, 144
Mortimer, R. C. (Bishop of Exeter),
  174
Mostar (bishop's see in Hercegovina),
  75–6
Mount Athos, 166–9
Movement of Catholic Priests for
  Peace, 37
museums, anti-religious, 23–4, 200
music, experiments with, 131
Mussolini, Benito, 17, 182, 186, 208
mystics, 144

Napoleon I, 10, 23, 208
National Unity Front, 98
Nauka y Religiya (atheist journal), 24,
  201
Nazis, 13, 27, 60, 61; and calendar of
  saints, 145; and Confessing Church,
  6 (*see also* Niemöller); changes of
  cooperation with, 6, 20, 65, 66; and
  divorce, 175; and Jews, 12; and
  Poland, 4; and Reichstag fire, 84;
  conquer Yugoslavia, 62–3
  see also Hitler, Adolf
Neuchâtel, 191
New English Bible, 125n
Nicholas II, Tsar, 8, 77, 212
Nicholas of Myra, St (Santa Claus),
  145
Niemöller, Pastor Martin: in concentration camp, 3; regarded as hero,
  6; Stuttgart Declaration of guilt, 11;
  postwar bishop, 7
Nikanor (Bishop of Karlovac, later of
  Novi Sad), 101–2

Nikodim (Metropolitan of Leningrad), 69

Nikolai, Metropolitan of Krutitsky, 94

Ninety-Five Theses, 85

Norway: Church resistance to Nazis, 6; Pentecostalists in, 135; ordination of women, 154

nuns *see* monks and nuns

Odessa, 31

Ohrid (Macedonian see), 89

Olmütz, 39

Onassis, Aristotle, 173

opinion polls on religion, 79–83

Opus Dei, 186, 198

Ordass, Lajos (Lutheran Bishop of Budapest 1945–50, prison 1948, restored 1956, ousted 1958), 90

ordination of women, 153–8, 196

Ottaviani, Cardinal, 160

Pacem in Terris (Czech clergy group), 38–40, 202

Pacem in Terris (encyclical, 1963), 117, 155

Paisios, Bishop (primate in Albania), 47

Paltarokas, Kazimieras (Bishop in Lithuania), 107

Panteleimon, 167

Paray-la-Monial, 136, 198

Paros, 168

Pastoral Council (Dutch), 148–9

Patmos, 167–8

Patriotic Movement for the National Revival (PROM), 105–106

Paul, St 146, 157

Paul VI (Giovanni Montini, Pope 1963–78), 117–18, 196; product of Curia, 117, 193; personality, 118; as pilgrim, 117; attacked by knife in Manila, 197; turns Holy Office into Congregation of the Faith, 157; reduces age of cardinals in office and makes bishops retire, 159–60; makes cardinals retire as electors, 160; approves Mother Teresa's order, 50; canonizes Ugandan martyrs, 142; and Second Vatican Council, 118;

alters resolutions, 118; postpones vote on liberty, 120; withdraws subject of celibacy, 148; carries out decisions wholeheartedly, 127; helped thereto by the French, 151; chooses a French Secretary of State, 152; gives bishop's ring to Archbishop Ramsey, 118; kisses foot of emissary of Ecumenical Patriarch, 118; tries for reconciliation with East European states, 54; sends representatives to Patriarch Pimen in Moscow, 54; makes Hossu cardinal *in petto*, 57; gets Mindszenty out of Hungary and then removes him from see, 71–2; unpopularity with some for this action, 90; receives French anti-capitalist delegation, 114; encourages charismatics, 137; rejects discrimination against women, 155; makes two women doctors of the Church, 155; pain at nuns leaving orders, 118, at abandonment of clerical dress, 132; encyclical on celibacy, 148; disturbed at Dutch Church encouraging idea of married priests, 149; appoints conservative bishops in Holland, 150; demands referendum on Italian divorce law, 174; and Haiti, 185; against abortion and contraception, 176–7, 195; denounced by Lefebvre, 127–8; last days, 195n

Pavelić, Ante, 63–5

Pax, 42–3

Peć, 100, 101

Pentecostalists, 135–7

Pepin, King, 208

Perrin, Henri (Jesuit worker-priest), 111

Peter the Great, Tsar, 23

Philadelphia, 156

photographs, experimental use of, 131

Piasecki, Count Boleslaw, 42–3

pictures, experimental use of, 131

pilgrimages, 138–41

Pimen (Sergio Izvekov: Patriarch of Moscow 1971–88), 54, 77, 91, 97, 211

Pinochet, General Augusto (dictator of Chile), 198

Pittsburgh, 135

Pius IX (Pope 1846–78): and Syllabus of Errors (1864), 14; loss of Rome to Italians (1870), 16, 17, 117; big influence on Church, 117

Pius X (Pope 1903–14): canonized by Pius XII (1954), 17

Pius XI (Pope 1922–39): Vatican librarian, 193; Concordat with Hitler, 188

Pius XII (Pope 1939–58): and the idea of the prisoner in the Vatican, 16; man of prayer, 16, 18; reserved, 115; and Jews while Pope in Second World War, 12–13; blesses Father Tiso, 61; promotes Roncalli, 115; attitude to Communism, 14–17, 36, 103, 115; and Franco, 186–7; makes Mindszenty archbishop and then a cardinal, 68; condemns Mindszenty's trial, 70; makes Stepinac a cardinal, 66; makes Wysziński a cardinal, 102; makes Roncalli a cardinal, 115; condemns Russian suppression of Hungarian Revolution, 70; supresses worker priests, 112, 113; condemns abortion, 178; definition of the Assumption of the Virgin, 16; Mary as Queen of Heaven, 17; and the pilgrimage to Fatima, 17; canonizes Pope Pius X, 17; makes cardinals more international, 17; last years, 17, 151

Plate, Modris (Latvian pastor), 92, 207

Pochaev (Pochayev, USSR), 31

Pokutnyky (Penitents), 92

Poland: no anti-God museum, 24; choice of bishops, 32, 34, 103; the Carmelites at Auschwitz, 163; largely Catholic, 14; Catholic cooperators, 42–3; Church and State, 181, 202; Church property, 203–4; churchgoing, 83; election of a Pole as Pope, 105; Glemp/Solidarity friction, 91; millennium, 85; monks and nuns in, 29; under Nazis, 4; nunneries, 161; enough ordinands, 20, 104; Pax movement in 42–3; some Poles forced to move to western

Europe from 1945, 5; Polish liturgy, 127; Popiełuszko, 78–9; power of the Church, 73; Reformed Church, 154; no secular rites, 28; passes under Russian rule in 1939, 3, 5, 30; Solidarity government, 202; Uniats, 52, 58–9; pressure against voluntary RE, 21

Pomeyrol, 170

Popiełuszko, Father Jerzy, 78–9

Portugal, 186; Church and State, 182; duty to discourage error, 119; dictatorship, 4, 17

Prague, 39, 73, 86, 98, 111

Prague Spring, 21n, 39, 41, 55, 98

prayer-book, regular recitation of, 133

Prenushi (Archbishop of Durazzo [Durrës]), 46–7

Prešov, 52, 55–6

priesthood: celibacy, 90, 147–50, 151, 152, 197; daily celebration of mass, 132–3; decline in numbers, 73; ordination of women, 153–8, 196; question of married, 147–53, 196; regular recitation of prayer-book, 133; retirement, 158–60

priests' associations, 37

property, church, 203–4

Przemysł cathedral, 59

Pskov (USSR), 31

Quimper, Brittany, 138

Rahner, Karl (Jesuit), 155

Rákosi, Matyas (Hungarian dictator), 68–70

Ramsey, Michael (Archbishop of Canterbury 1961–74), 118, 132, 156

Ranke-Heinemann, Uta, 155

Rebirth and Renewal revival group, 92

Reformation: abolishes monks and nuns in the West, 169; and liturgy, 123, 124; and saints, 145

Reformed Cistercians *see* Trappists

religionless Christianity, 43

Remer, Major (later General), 9

Rennes, Brittany, 114

Rerum Novarum (encyclical, 1891), 14

retirement, 158–60

Rhodes, 168
Riga, 87
rites, secular, 25–8
Robin, Marthe (stigmatic), 136
Romania, 208; loss of Bessarabia, 30; Catholic minority, 14; choice of bishops, 32, 33; charismatics in, 137; Church and State, 202; Justinian, 97–100; painted monasteries, 84; accepts monks and nuns, 29–30, 203; voluntary RE allowed, 21; revolution (1989), 202–3, 207; Uniats in, 51, 52, 57–8, 204
Romanian Orthodox Church, 204
Rome synod (1971), 149, 157
Runcie, Robert (Archbishop of Canterbury 1980–91), 129, 199
Rusnack, Michael (Ruthenian titular bishop), 121
Russia: annexations, 5; keeps St Basil the Blessed, 84; Bibles imported, 87; choice of bishops, 32; Church and State, 181; control of Czechoslovakia, 3; suppresses Dubček, 41, 56, 98; recantation of Dudko, 76–8; ally of Communist partisans in Greece, 3; occupation of Hungary, 67; *Initsiativniki*, 92–3; journal of science and religion, 24, 201; Komsomol, 24; reverence for Lenin, 75, 206; millennium, 86–7; and monks and nuns, 29–31; Russians on Mount Athos, 166–7; Pentecostalists in, 137; control of Poland, 3; death of prisoners of war, 9; pressure against voluntary RE, 21, 23; gains of territory (1945), 51; weddings, 27
Russian Orthodox Church: and Bolshevik Revolution, 88; and Stalin, 93; and Uniats, 54, 94; and World Council of Churches, 95
Ruthenia/Ruthenians, 51–2, 55, 56

Sacerdotalis Caelibatus encyclical, 148
Sacré-Coeur cathedral, Paris, 114
St Basil the Blessed, Moscow, 84
St Catherine (Greek monastery on Sinai), 168
St Gallen, Switzerland, 192

St John of Rila monastery, Bulgaria, 84–5
Saint-Louis de Port-Lefebvrists church, 129
St Nicholas of the Transfiguration church, Moscow, 76–7
St Nicholas-du-Chardonnet church, Paris, 129
St Peter's Rome, 136–7
saints, making of, 141–6
Salazar, Antonio (dictator of Portugal), 186; Concordat with Rome (1940), 17
Salesians, 203
Samarkand, 94
samizdat literature, 76, 93
Santa Sophia, Istanbul, 84, 117
Santiago de Compostela, Spain, 198
Sarić (Archbishop of Sarajevo), 63
Saulchoir, 111
Sava, St, 100, 101
Savonarola, Girolamo, 144
Schjelderup, Kristian (Bishop of Hamar, Norway 1947–64), 154
Schönherr, Albrecht (Lutheran Bishop of [East] Berlin-Brandenburg 1972), 44, 69
Schuster, Cardinal, 15
Schutz, Roger, 171
Secretariat for Christian Unity, 117
secular rites, 25–8
seminaries: in Eastern Europe, 20, 44, 48, 94, 98, 100, 102, 187, 203; in Western Europe, 113, 128, 151, 197
Serbia/Serbs: Albanians in, 49, 50; and election of bishops, 32–3; and Orthodox Church, 100–101
Serédi, Cardinal Justinián (Archbishop of Esztergom), 68
Sergei (Starogodsky: Archbishop of Finland 1905, administrator of Moscow patriarchate 1925, Patriarch of Moscow 1943–4), 93
Shevardnadze, Eduard (Georgian, member of Politburo), 97n
Shkodër, 205
show trials, 20–21, 60–72
Sibiu, 98
Silesia, 105, 106n

Simonis, Adrien (Bishop of Rotterdam 1971, Archbishop of Utrecht 1983, cardinal 1985), 150

Sinai, Mount, 168

Sinaia (Romanian monastery), 203

Siri, Cardinal Giuseppe (Archbishop of Genoa), 193

Sisters of Loreto, 50

Skopje, 89

Skvireckas, Juozapas (administrator of diocese of Kaunas 1926–44, died in Austria 1959), 106

Sladkevičius (Bishop in Lithuania, later cardinal), 107–108

Slipyj, Josif (Uniat Metropolitan of Lvov, later cardinal), 53, 54, 117, 120, 149

Slovakia/Slovaks, 21n, 33, 34, 40, 56, 61, 62, 187, 207

Slovenia, 34, 62, 63, 102

Smiljanić, Milan, 37

Soares de Resende (Archbishop of Beira in Mozambique), 121

Social Democratic Party (SPD), 10–11

Society of St Francis, 170

Sofia, see of, 89

Solidarity (Polish trade union), 78, 91, 105, 106, 199, 202, 207

Soviet Union *see* Russia

Spain: Church and State, 182, 183; civil war, 41, 121; dictatorship, 4, 17, 186; divorce, 174; duty to discourage error, 119; head of State, 184; monks and nuns, 161; difficulty with Vatican on bishops, 187

Spellman, Cardinal Francis (Archbishop of New York 1939–67), 120

Stalin, Joseph, 3, 35, 47, 70, 93, 104, 111, 200

state: and Church in Western Europe, 181–91; control of the churches, 32–5

Stauffenberg, Claus Schenk von, 8, 9

Stavronikita, 166

Stefan (exarch [head] of Bulgarian Orthodox Church), 91

Stein, Edith, 143, 162

Stepanovičius, Julijonas (bishop in Lithuania, died 1991), 107, 200, 201

Stephen (king of Hungary), 85

Stepinac, Aloysius (Archbishop of Zagreb and cardinal), 60, 64–7, 75, 91, 102, 213

student revolution, 113–14

Stuttgart Declaration (1945), 11

Suciu (Uniat bishop in Romania), 57

Suenens, Léon-Joseph (Archbishop of Malines-Brussels 1961–79, cardinal 1962), 136–7

Sukhenko, Andrei (Archbishop of Chernigov), 96n

Sweden: abortion bill, 178; Bible, 125n; Church and State, 184–5; Pentecostalists, 135; Protestant religious communities, 170; ordination of women, 154

Swedish Church Act (1982), 185

Switzerland: and abortion, 179; Church and State, 191–2

Szepticky, Andrij (Uniat Metropolitan of Lvov), 53

Taizé, 170, 171–2

Tarancón, Cardinal Enrique y (Archbishop of Toledo 1969–71, of Madrid 1971–83), 149

Tashkent cathedral, 94

taxes, 183–4, 189

Trelsiau (Lithuania), 106
  see also Boresivičius

Teoctist (Patriarch of Romania), 202–3, 205, 214

Teresa, Mother, 50–51, 166

Teresa of Avila, St, 130, 155, 162

Thaci (Archbishop of Shkodër [Scutari]), 46

theft from churches, 134

Thirty Years War, 13

Thurian, Max, 171

Ticino, 192

Tildy, Zóltan, 68, 70

Timişoara, 202, 207

Timothy (bishop in Crete), 169

Tinos (Aegean shrine), 169

Tirana, 47

Tiso, Josef (President of Slovakia), 60–62, 213

Tisserant, Cardinal Eugène, 160

Tito (Josip Broz), 37, 47, 63, 66, 100, 102, 216

Togliatti (Italian Communist leader), 15

Tökes, Pastor, 207, 215

Tomašek, Cardinal (of Prague), 86, 205, 210, 211

tongues, speaking in, 135–6

torture, 179–80

Tournai, Belgium, 133

Trappists, 162, 166

Trent, Council of (1545–63), 126

trials, show, 20–21, 60–72

Truman, Harry S., 4

Tübingen university, 177

Turin shroud, 140–41, 197

tyrannicide, morality of, 8–9

Ukraine, 26, 27, 30, 31, 51–4, 58, 82, 90, 92, 117, 139, 149, 204, 208
see also Slipyj, Josif

Uniat Churches, 51–60, 90, 117, 147, 149; and perestroika, 204, 214

United Baptist Council, 92

United Church of the Bohemian Brethren, 40

United Nations, 19, 70, 117, 182

United Nations Charter 4

Urban VII, Pope, 194

USSR *see* Russia

ustasche (private Croat police), 63, 101

Valais, 192

Van Asten (White Father), 149, 150

Vatican, the: average age in, 160; cardinals made more international by Pius XII, 17; John XXIII alters rule of numbers, 116; Curia, 116, 152, 193, 194, 198; Holy Office, 16, 42, 72, 121; becomes the Congregation of the Faith, 157; claim to appoint bishops, 34; defence of French bishops (1944–5), 6, 115; excommunication of three Hungarian priests, 36; and Italian government, 15; against divorce, 173; and nuns in Hungary, 30; papal decree (1949), 15–16, 103, 121, 122; and Russian

persecution of Uniats, 54; makes Uniat bishops in Romania, 204

Vatican Bank, 194

Vatican City, 181, 182, 183

Vatican Council, the First (1869–70), 116, 177

Vatican Council, the Second (1962–5), 115–20, 121, 128, 155, 164, 195; bibliography, 213–14; wants State not to choose bishops, 185, 187; consents not to debate celibacy, 148; collegiality, 152; allows communion in both kinds, 130; and Communism, 121–2; allows concelebration, 133; Declaration on Religious Liberty, 121, 187; French opinion poll, 128–9; Siri dislikes, 193; allows vernacular liturgies, 126–7; on worker priests, 113

Velehrad, 39, 86

Venice, 115, 193

vestments at liturgies, 130

Veszprém (Hungarian see), 68

Villot, Cardinal Jean, 152, 194–5n

Vilnius, 106, 200–201

Vincent de Paul, St, 51

Vincenza, Sister, 194n

Visser t'Hooft, W. A., 215

Vladimir cathedral, 94

Voronaev (Pentecostalist in Russia), 137

Voronezh (USSR), 82

Vrána, Josef, 39, 40

Wałęsa, Lech, 105, 209

weddings, 25, 26–7, 81, 82, 190

Wesley, John, 144

White Fathers, 149, 150

Wittenberg, 10, 86

women in the church, 143, 145, 151; ordination, 153–8

women pastoral workers, 151

Workers' Catholic Action, 114

worker priests, 111–13

World Council of Churches, 7, 35; German as president, 100; joined by the Russian Orthodox, 95

Wurm, Theophil (Lutheran Bishop of Württemberg), 6, 7, 11n

Wysziński, Stefan (Archbishop of Warsaw 1948, and cardinal 1953): stature, 91; career, 102n; compromise with State, 103; arrest, 103; and Gomulka, 104; relations with Solidarity, 105, 106; death and statue, 106

Yakunin, Gleb (Russian Orthodox priest), 91, 200, 217
Yallop, David, 194
Young Rationalists, 104
youth-consecration, 28
Yugoslavia, 34, 73; big Catholic population, 14; Church and State, 181, 202; clergy associations, 37; Patriarch German, 100–102; Kosovo, 50, 101; Medjugorje, 75–6; and monks and nuns, 29, 167; Nazis conquer, 62–3; opinion polls, 82–3; voluntary RE allowed, 21; protocol with Rome, 75; Stepinac, 64–7; and Uniats, 58

Zagorsk, 30, 31, 87, 94–5
Zagreb, 64–6, 76, 82
Zahradnik, Fridolin, 211
Zografon, 167
Zurich, 192